Transnational Lives and the Media

Also by the editors

Olga G. Bailey
UNDERSTANDING ALTERNATIVE MEDIA *(co-author)*

Myria Georgiou
DIASPORIC MEDIA ACROSS EUROPE: Multicultural Societies and the Universalism–Particularism Continuum
DIASPORA, IDENTITY AND THE MEDIA: Diasporic Transnationalism and Mediated Spatialities
CITIES OF DIFFERENCE: Cultural Juxtapositions and Urban Politics of Representation

Ramaswami Harindranath
PERSPECTIVES ON GLOBAL CULTURES
THE CRASH CONTROVERSY
APPROACHES TO AUDIENCES

Transnational Lives and the Media

Re-Imagining Diaspora

Edited by

Olga G. Bailey
Nottingham Trent University

Myria Georgiou
Leeds University

Ramaswami Harindranath
The University of Melbourne

First published 2007 by
PALGRAVE MACMILLAN
Houndmills, Basingstoke, Hampshire RG21 6XS and
175 Fifth Avenue, New York, N.Y. 10010
Companies and representatives throughout the world

PALGRAVE MACMILLAN is the global academic imprint of the Palgrave Macmillan division of St. Martin's Press, LLC and of Palgrave Macmillan Ltd. Macmillan® is a registered trademark in the United States, United Kingdom and other countries. Palgrave is a registered trademark in the European Union and other countries.

ISBN 13: 978–0–230–01983–6   hardback
ISBN 10: 0–230–01983–8   hardback

This book is printed on paper suitable for recycling and made from fully managed and sustained forest sources.

A catalogue record for this book is available from the British Library.

Library of Congress Cataloging-in-Publication Data

Transnational lives and the media : re-imagining diaspora / editors: Olga G. Bailey, Myria Georgiou, R. Harindranath.
        p. cm.
    Includes bibliographical references and index.
    ISBN 10: 0-230-01983-8 (cloth)
    ISBN 13: 978–0–230–01983–6 (cloth)
        1. Transnationalism. 2. Ethnicity. 3. Mass media and minorities.
    4. Ethnic mass media. 5. Mass media and ethnic relations. 6. Mass media and culture. I. Bailey, Olga G., 1958 – II. Georgiou, Myria, 1971 –
    III. Harindranath, Ramaswami, 1959.

    JV6035.T73 2007
    304.8–dc22   2007060028

10   9   8   7   6   5   4   3   2   1
16 15 14 13 12 11 10 09 08 07

Transferred to Digital Printing in 2013

In the memory of Roger Silverstone

Contents

**Part 1V   Voices Across Cultural and Political Diasporic
Media Space**

List of Figures

Acknowledgements

As Sidney Tarrow has observed, 'like a social movement, a book is a collective action'. This collection is indeed the product of the collective action of many people who have supported it. From interviewees, colleagues, NGOs, students, to our families and friends who have supported us and lived with our absence, this book has resulted from the varied contributions of several individuals, too numerous to name here. We thank them all.

We are grateful to our contributors for their essays which are the soul of this book, for believing in our project, and for their patience through the editorial processes. We are very proud for the outcome – a rich collection of contributions from the academia and the non-governmental sector, which will hopefully serve as a point of reference in the academia and beyond. We hope that all contributors share our sense of excitement and satisfaction for the final product.

We would like to thank Nickyanne Moody at John Moores University for supporting the seminar 'Re-imagining Diasporas' in 2003, where this project started. Olga Bailey would like to thank Prof. Roger Bromley at Nottingham Trent University, for providing her a period of sabbatical leave to complete this and other projects. Ramaswami Harindranath expresses his gratitude to colleagues at the University of Melbourne for their support through a difficult time. Myria Georgiou is grateful to Roger Silverstone for his inspiring comments on many of the ideas behind her contribution in this book. He will always be remembered.

We would like to thank the editor of *New Perspectives on Turkey*, for permission to include copyright material.

O.B., M.G. and R.H.

Note on Contributors

Olga Guedes Bailey is a journalist, and Senior Lecturer in the Institute of Cultural Analysis, Nottingham Trent University, UK. She is a Visiting Professor at the Shanghai University of Finance and Economics, Humanities College, China. She has published essays on global audiences, environmentalism, journalistic practice, alternative media, race and representation, and politics of communication of ethnic minorities and diasporas . She is co-author of 'Understanding Alternative Media' (Olga.bailey@ntu.ac.uk).

Susan Bink graduated in Mass Communications in 1999 at the Radboud University Nijmegen, the Netherlands. She specialized in media & ethnic minorities. Since 2001 Susan has been working as a researcher at Mira Media in Utrecht. Mira Media aims to improve the representation of ethnic minorities in the media.

Reynald Blion has been working on international migration issues for over 15 years. In 1998, he became director of the International Migrations and Media programme at Panos Paris. In May 2000 he initiated a process of research and reflection on ethnic and minority media in Europe. In 2002 this led to the design of a wide-ranging European programme on ethnic and minority media, called Mediam'Rad, which was implemented mid-2004. He has often acted as consultant to the International Organization for Migration, the Council of Europe and the North-South Centre. His publications include 'From One Journey to Another' (2001) and 'Stories of Knowledge' (2004). He is the Programme Director of the INSTITUT PANOS PARIS – France, a non-governmental organization specialising in support for media pluralism.

Sandy Close is founder and Executive Editor of New America Media (newamericamedia.org).

Mohammed Colin is one of the founders of the Internet News magazine, *SaphirNews.com.* and is currently the magazine's editorial director. Already holding a Master's degree in Information and Communication Science, and having studied suburban knowledge at university level, in 2006 he completed a Master's thesis on European cities and new forms of governance, at the Institute for European Studies.

Sonja de Leeuw is Professor of Dutch Television Culture in an international Context at the University of Utrecht, The Netherlands. She is the author of *Television Drama: Stage for Identity: A Study on the Relationship Between Identity of Broadcasting Companies and Dutch Television Drama 1969–1988.* Recent publications include: (co-authored with N. Christopoulou), 'Children Making Media: Constructions of Home and Belonging', in Knörr, J. (ed.) (2005), *Childhood and Migration: From Experience to Agency.* Bielefeld, pp. 113–35, 'Migrant Children Mediating Family Relations', in Pisters, P. and Staat, W. (eds) (2005), *Shooting the Family. Transnational Media and Intercultural Values.* (Amsterdam) pp. 41–55. Her research areas include television culture, media and diasporas, and media and youth culture (sonja.deleeuw@let.uu.nl).

Susan J. Drucker (JD, 1982 St. John's University School of Law) is a Professor in School of communication, Department of Journalism/Mass Media Studies, Hofstra University, New York, USA. She is an attorney, editor of *Qualitative Research Reports in Communication,* and Series editor of *Communication and Law Series.* She is the author or co-editor of six books and over 85 articles and book chapters. Her work examines the relationship between media technology and human factors, particularly as viewed from a legal perspective.

Shehina Fazal is Senior Lecturer in Media and Communications in the Department of Applied Social Sciences at London Metropolitan University, UK. Her research interests are diaspora and media, and transnational communications. Her forthcoming co-authored book is Television in India (2007) and she has also written articles on media and the diaspora (s.fazal@londonmet.ac.uk).

Myria Georgiou teaches international communications at the Institute of Communications Studies, Leeds University, UK. Her area of expertise is transnationalism, diaspora, identity and media consumption. She has conducted ethnographic and cross-national research on diasporic media cultures and on cosmopolitan cities and politics of diversity. Her book *Diaspora, Identity and the Media: Diasporic Transnationalism and Mediated Spatialities* was published in 2006.

Gary Gumpert (PhD, 1963, Wayne State University) is Emeritus Professor of Communication at Queens College of the City University of New York, USA and co-founder of Communication Landscapers, a consulting firm. He is the author or co-editor of nine books. His primary research focuses on the nexus of communication technology and social relationships, particularly looking at urban and suburban development, the alteration of public space, and the changing nature of community.

Ramaswami Harindranath is Senior Lecturer in the media and Communication Program at the University of Melbourne, Australia. He co-authored *The 'Crash' Controversy* (2001) His most recent book is *Perspectives on Global Cultures* (2006).

Charles Husband is Professor of Social Analysis at the University of Bradford, UK, and a docent at the University of Helsinki. He has combined academic analysis with practical policy innovation. He is currently a Scientific Adviser to the UNESCO initiative; the European Coalition of Cities Against Racism. He has written extensively on ethnicity and the media; and his co-authored book with John Downing *Representing 'Race'* was published in 2005.

Kira Kosnick is Junior Professor in Cultural Anthropology and European Ethnology at the Johann Wolfgang Goethe University in Frankfurt, Germany. With a background in cultural anthropology and sociology, her work focuses on minority media practices, Turkish migration to Europe, and transnational cultural formations.

Lia Markelin was the research officer on the Sami Media Project carried out by the Ethnicity and Social Policy Research Unit at Bradford University. Since that time she has been actively involved with Sami colleagues in developing Sami media training and policy initiatives.

Aime Claude Ndongozi is Director of Refugee Focus, a Liverpool-based research, training and consultancy organisation specialising in asylum and migration. He previously worked as an Asylum Advice Caseworker and New Asylum Model Manager for a UK national refugee agency

Gary Needham is based in the College of Arts, Humanities and Education, Nottingham Trent University, UK. He is the co-editor of *Asian Cinemas: A Reader and Guide* (2006) and a co-editor of the forthcoming *Pleasures of the Tube: Television/Queerness/Politics*.

Maggie O'Neill is Senior Lecturer in Criminology and Social Policy at Loughborough University, UK. She has written extensively on prostitution, new arrivals/refugees/asylum seekers and renewed methodologies for conducting research with vulnerable and marginalized groups. Currently she is convening a regional network in the East Midlands funded by the AHRC www.makingtheconnections.info

Nikos Papastergiadis is Associate Professor and Reader in the School of Communication and Culture, University of Melbourne Australia and writes on contemporary art and migration. His recent book is *Spatial Aesthetics: Art Place and Everyday* (2006).

Bashy Quraishy is Chief Editor of *Media Watch*, Copenhagen, Denmark and President of the European Network Against Racism, Brussels, Belgium.

Sandip Roy is an editor with New America Media (newamericamedia.org), the first and largest national collaboration of ethnic news organizations in the United States. Founded by the non-profit Pacific News Service in 1996, NAM's headquarters is in California, and produces and aggregates content from ethnic media and conducts multilingual polls to bring voices of ethnic audiences into national focus. NAM's goal is to promote the editorial visibility and economic viability of this critical sector of American journalism. He is also host of UpFront, New America Media's award-winning radio show about ethnic communities and has written for various anthologies such as *Storywallah!, A Part Yet Apart – South Asians in Asian America*, etc.

Ingegerd Rydin is Professor in Media and Communication Studies at Halmstad University, Sweden. She has written extensively on media, children and young people, for example *Media Fascinations: Perspectives on Young People's Meaning Making* (ed.) (2003). Her research interests also cover issues related to media and citizenship, media, migration and globalization as well as media history.

Eugenia Siapera teaches in the Media and Communication Department of the University of Leicester, UK. Her work is concerned with the politics of multiculturalism and the new media, political and social theory and the internet, and inter-media relations. Recent work has appeared in the *European Journal of Cultural Studies* and the *Journal of Ethnic and Migration Studies*. Eugenia has co-edited (with Joss Hands) *At the Interface: Continuity and Transformation in Culture and Politics* and (with Lincoln Dahlberg) *The Internet and Radical Democracy* (Palgrave).

Introduction: Exploration of Diaspora in the Context of Media Culture

Olga Guedes Bailey, Myria Georgiou and Ramaswami Haridranath

This book is an attempt to understand recent changes in the grammars of diasporic politics and cultures, including the media. At its heart is the feeling that contemporary diasporas present us with profound transformation, with a shift from the traditional political formations and identities characterizing diasporic communities, to the ways we learn how to engage with the new 'Other', generating new grammars of experience and subjectivity. At stake are not only relationships between the transnational lives of those diasporic subjects, individual and collective, and their new 'home' or a shift in their access and uses of new technologies and media, but ways of being in a world dominated by contradictory and chaotic processes of globalization. The challenges those shifts pose to us compel us to rethink and re-imagine not only what we understand by contemporary diasporas but also what we understand by the role of culture and media in the experience of transnational diasporic lives. In the process, diasporas open new ways of thinking about nationalism, transnationalism, human mobility, urban communication, ethnicity, gender, identity, representation, multiculturalism, politics, and media. This allows us to move away from crystallized notions of what constitute diasporas in a global world marked by fear of the unknown, and to start to grasp diasporas in terms of their connections with new experiences and subjectivities and perhaps new ways of being and belonging. More than ever, we face the choice of either living in fear of the other in fortified borders or opening our mind and hearts to engage and exchange with the other. The choice is political. This book hopes to contribute to the way we make our choices regarding engagement with diasporas/migrants. It addresses academics and non academics – involved in experiencing, feeling, and thinking about diasporas in new ways.

1

The book comes together after three years of intense intellectual encounters, initiated during the symposium 'Re-imagining Diaspora' at John Moores University in Liverpool in 2003. It would not have been possible without the willingness of the contributors to share their transnational experiences, research, and critical thoughts, as well as their commitment to a political project of articulating ideas that break old ways of thinking about diaspora. The book does not merely celebrate diasporas. If we contribute to a better understanding of the ways we become subjects through our encounters with the other – migrants and diasporic communities, then that is more than enough.

Diaspora and media culture

The growing visibility of diasporas, as expressed in their numerical presence, but even more so in their cultural practices and the development of projects of cultural particularity and expression, challenge ideologies of cultural homogeneity and imaginings of ethnic and cultural hierarchies in national and transnational spaces. Diasporic media's visibility and influence (celebrated, or more often, feared) now surpasses diasporic contexts and attracts attention across wider audiences, politicians and policy makers. Diasporic media are not necessarily more inclusive and democratic than mainstream national and transnational media. Many of them are commercial corporations aiming at maximizing audience and profit. Others aim to play a community role. Diversity is immense, not only across different populations but also within diasporas. If there is an overarching point of significance for diasporic media that surpasses particularity, it is their growing cultural presence in cosmopolitan societies. Diasporic media's presence within western mediascapes destabilises the dominant hierarchies of control over cultural resources. The symbolic presence and real availability of different media open up new possibilities for expression and representation and thus of imagining the self and belonging within and across space. In this way, diasporic media cultures become strategic positions for self-expression and representation, even if the intentions of their producers are not political. Diasporic media are not set points of difference; their role and their significance to audiences and users are conditional and shaped within wider societal and communication processes. Rather than revealing some natural Otherness or a process by itself and for itself, diasporic mediated communication becomes a socially relevant cultural and political form of expression (Balibar, 1991).

Diasporic imagination and the media

Imagination, cultural life and mediation are closely interlinked. Media negotiate the content, as well as the context of imagination. They construct images, text and sounds that mediate relations within specific communities, but also mediate connections among fellow members of diasporas and communication between different cultural groups and individuals in local, national and transnational spaces. Though imagination is neither purely emancipatory nor entirely disciplined, it is a space of contestation (Appadurai, 1996). As numerous studies of media and diaspora have shown, in the media commonality is not only imagined, but also negotiated. The media participate in sustaining imagined commonality, but they also advance processes of critical and reflexive engagement with imagined communities – national and transnational ones. Imagination helps to make sense of the world – the intimate and the distant. Imagination, through mediation, turns abstractions and ideologies of identity and community into familiar, intimate and sensual references (Anderson, 1983). But imagination is also a product – it is a product of those repertoires that are circulated across networks and in transnational communities. Increasingly, imagination and mediation become tightly interlinked to processes of globalisation – especially the intense mobility of people, ideas, images and sounds. Transnational media become outlets and means for transporting and translating ideologies and cultural repertoires beyond bounded physical places.

Conceptual and methodological explorations

The chapters in the first section of the book explore a number of key epistemological, conceptual and methodological issues for the study of diaspora, transnationalism and mediated communication. They engage with the relation between media and diaspora, the consequences of intense mobility and mediation for transnational political and cultural formations, and with the politics of solidarity and action as they take shape in participatory methodologies and in the arts.

Georgiou presents three themes corresponding to an equal number of conceptual and methodological challenges emerging in the literature on media and diaspora. The first theme interrogates the key concepts and analytical categories used extensively in this field; the author argues that the meanings of the national *vis-à-vis* the transnational need to be reconceptualised in the context of cosmopolitanism. The second theme engages with the challenges that diasporic communication presents to the three-step media analysis that assumes a divide between production, text/representation, and consumption. The third theme discusses the methodological tradition of studies in media and diaspora and argues that reflexive, experiential and ethnographic methods are the most appropriate in processes of understanding diasporic cultures and politics on local, national and transnational level.

Fazal examines the concept of diaspora, and its intersections with transnationalism and multiculturalism. With reference to the case of the transnational Indian network Zee TV, Fazal discusses the dynamic relation between the national and the transnational, arguing that debates on multiculturalism need to learn from transnationalism analysis and the transnational media. She explains how commercial transnational media like Zee TV do not provide a space of empowerment, but a space for 'tuning out' of the concerns of everyday life. One of the key strengths of the transnational, she argues, is that it offers a tool for understanding both the cultural and the political economic role of transnational media. Transnationalism thus is useful in shaping multicultural politics which is more reflexive to national and international affairs.

Papastergiades argues that the contradictions and tensions in the deterritorialization of cultures and peoples demand new theories of flow and resistance and are compelling artists and intellectuals to rethink their methods. Cultural critics and curators are also in need of new conceptual frameworks, he adds. In his chapter, he focuses on a selection of cases in contemporary art that challenge the mainstream political discourse of sealed borders and cultural nationalism, explore the complexities of cultural difference, represent the hidden forms of violence in contemporary society, and propose ethical alternatives through interpretative strategies that emerge from collaborative practices in specific communities.

O'Neill's chapter builds upon renewed methodologies for conducting ethnographic research with asylum seekers and refugee groups in the UK and explores the political implications of 'ethno-mimesis' as critical theory in practice. The author's concept of 'ethno-mimesis' is defined in this chapter through a combination of participatory action research and participatory arts informed by the work of Adorno and Benjamin. 'Ethno-mimesis' draws upon 'feeling forms' such as photographic art, performance art and life story narratives, and engages dialectically with lived experience through critical interpretation, towards social change. 'Ethno-mimesis' as critical theory in praxis seeks to counter negative stereotypes in the public imagination and produce self-representations of refugees and asylum seekers that speak of the utter complexity of lived relations through 'feeling forms' as 'sensuous knowing.

Transnational and diasporic politics

The essays in this section focus on different aspects of the politics of diasporic and migrant experience, and how it impacts on and informs reconceptualisations of theories of diaspora and the media. Siapera's essay on the articulation of transnational Islamic identities raises issues that are particularly topical, given the current global context in which the Islamic 'other' is seen, in both some academic and media representations, as inimical to 'Western' values, including democratic and individual rights. Such representations clearly infuse government and public attitudes to Islamic communities living in Europe, North America, and Australia. Siapera's argument on the dialectic between transnational Islam as a socio-cultural imaginary and the local configuration of action and experience is pertinent in this political climate. Treating the existence of the Sami community across Norway, Finland, Sweden and Russia as their starting point, Markelin and Husband explore the politics inherent in indigenous identities and their deep historical connections with locality and territory. Their concern is with the complex ways in which the Sami media navigate the contradictions between territory and identity on the one hand, with national media and government policies on the other, and how this informs indigenous identity and the struggle for Sami rights across and within national borders.

Do refugee communities constitute the quintessential diasporic subaltern? Harindranath's examination of this question in relation to cultural identity focuses on the vexed issue of subalternity and representation, and its links to the notion of experience, which often informs subaltern political practice. He argues that the 'politics of recognition', intrinsic to which is representation, includes the acknowledgement of the unequal power relations intrinsic to the marginalisation of refugee communities in official and mainstream media discourse. This has significant implications for both the ethics of subaltern media practice as well as for the academic researcher. Kosnick's essay on the politics of communication of Turkish migrants in multicultural Germany shows the importance of transnational media produced by and for migrants. She discusses the problematic of representation of diasporic groups by diasporic media in terms of Spivak's question: 'Can the Subaltern Speak?' (1988) and questions the kind of political 'voice' that is reaching the media public space as representative of Turkish migrants 'speaking for themselves'.

Media, diaspora and everyday life

We live in a mediated world. Media scholars are almost unanimous in suggesting that the media exert a certain degree of influence in our daily lives be it by empowering individuals and social groups or by reproducing social evils such as racism, crime and sexism. Regarding media and diasporas in cross-cultural landscapes, the assumption is similar in that the daily, ordinary cultural and media practices of migrants and diasporic communities might help to forge feelings of 'belonging' and 'bridging', creating mediated, symbolic spaces for political expression, senses of inclusion or/and exclusion, and hybrid identity articulations which transcend the binary of 'homeland' and 'new land'. This section explores these assumptions through the work of De Leeuw and Rydin who argue that the media and communication technologies play an important role in the process of cultural identities, based on a ethnographic research with migrants families in Europe. The urban context in which most diasporas groups consume and use communication technologies are at the centre of Gumpert and Drucker discussion. They argue that the analysis of diasporic urban communication is an appropriate approach for the study of 'diasporic progression', i.e. the changes in the migrant experiences, particularly because the physical and social structures of the city are closely linked. In searching for patterns of cultural and media practices and identity negotiation, Bailey brings a personal account of her experience with Latin American women in England and their search for a meaning to the signifier of 'Latin American' in their experience of hybrid identities in the new home. She suggests that the media and social practices of Latin Americans have made it possible for them to question and articulate their identities according to the transformative experiences they are living as 'Latinas'.

Looking from the perspective of the text in the analysis of media and diasporic identity, Needham subverts the analysis of diasporic experience through the study of recent 'diasporic' films that challenge normative views of sexuality. For him, it is paramount to couple the use of 'diaspora' and 'queer' categories in order to go beyond its limitation in terms of ethnicity and normative sexuality to reach the complexities and experiences of diasporic queer subjects as diaspora pluralizes queer studies.

Voices of diaspora

This section is devoted to NGOs working with and from within diasporic communities, and being particularly active in the area of media and communication. The section includes a selection of diverse contribution from organisations from across the world (US, Britain, cross-European) addressing issues of self-representation, potentials for participation and inclusion in/exclusion from media cultures, good practice. Contributions from *Mira Media*, an independent Dutch media organisation devoted to empowering minorities, *SaphirNews*, a website dedicated to Muslim issues in France, *MediaWatch*, a US-based NGO, *New America Media*, *Refugee Focus*, and *Mediam'Rad*, a Europe-wide program set up by Institut Panos in Paris to facilitate and promote minority media, all make significant recommendations for addressing to the complex issues relating to ethnic minorities and the media. These include journalistic practice in terms of more balanced reporting, minority media advocacy, scrutiny of mainstream media representations of diasporic communities and recommendations for increasing the visibility of the concerns of minorities, the relations between mainstream and alternative media, and the priorities of diasporic media. By engaging with such aspects of minority media practice therefore, the contributors to this section provide a useful counterpoint to the more conceptual arguments presented in the preceding sections.

This collection thus attempts to cover a variety of topics concerning the transnational and national aspects of diasporic experience and its relations to the media, ranging from epistemological issues that animate intellectual discussions and academic research, to the politics of cultural expression and representation. Underlying all this is our concern with minority communities, their status in Western democracies, their presence in mainstream and diasporic media, and their perceptions of themselves, which informs their collective identities. We believe that in the current, post-9/11 climate of suspicion that characterises not only policies of immigration and multiculturalism, but also concerns regarding national security, the experience of migrant communities is fraught with new difficulties and challenges. We hope that this book is a timely intervention into the transnational lives of such communities, and that the chapters in it contribute to re-thinking the concept and experience of diaspora.

References

Anderson, B. (1983) *Imagined Communities: Reflections on the Origins and Spread of Nationalism* (London: Verso).

Appadurai, A. (1996) *Modernity at Large: Cultural Dimensions of Globalization* (Minneapolis and London: University of Minnesota Press).

Balibar, E. (1991) 'The Nation Form' in E. Balibar and I. Wallerstein (eds), *Race, Nation, Class* (London: Verso).

Spivak, G. Ch. (1988) 'Can the Subaltern Speak?' in L. Grossberg and C. Nelson (eds), *Marxism and the Interpretation of Culture* (Urbana: University of Illinois Press), pp. 271–313.

Part I

Conceptual and Epistemological Explorations

1

Transnational Crossroads for Media and Diaspora: Three Challenges for Research

Myria Georgiou

The extension of diasporic life across cultural and political spaces has challenged a number of key conceptual and methodological trends in social sciences. The diversification of cultural and political affairs within and across countries, next to the vast growth of more varied media production and consumption, have significantly altered the roles and meanings of the nation, citizenship and media culture. Consequently, the study of diaspora, culture and the media broke off the boundaries of a particular sub-field, attracting attention among media and communications scholars, sociologists of race, ethnicity and migration, historians and international relations' experts. When in the spring of 2006 Latinos took over the streets of American cities after mobilising action around community centres, minority media and blog calls for participation in a movement for recognition and citizenship, many American politicians and social scientists were taken by surprise. Before that, a much more sudden, widespread, and on-going interest in diaspora emerged in the post-9/11 political atmosphere of tension, conflict and blaming. Events such as the London 7/7 bombings and the revelation of a plot for attacks on a number of flights in the UK in summer 2006 gave a further push to public and academic debates about diversity and migration. In just a few years, *diaspora* has become a keyword used widely by academics, politicians and the media. Diasporic mobilisation and ability to network with consequences for representation and political action are now more than an affair for the actors directly involved in them.

In this intense context, the field of diaspora and media studies has found itself at a crossroad of recognition and growing up. Having already a considerable body of research conducted on media and diaspora and having attracted wide attention, the demand for reflexive evaluation of theory and practice is now as necessary as it is timely. After a decade of research, which includes focussed, ethnographic, and cross-national studies, we need to evaluate our categories, concepts and research practices. Some, which we might not have considered as significant ten years ago, have grown to be important, inviting, challenging. Broader societal and political changes – e.g. growing role of global markets, the so-called *war on terror* – but also more specifically relevant developments – e.g. intensification of border control; retreat of multicultural policies and the advance of new xenophobic politics; growing cosmopolitanization of cities; mobilisation of transnational movements; increased production of and access to diverse media and technologies – need to be seriously looked at.

This chapter hopes to make a contribution to the debate about the future of media and diaspora studies. It engages with a conceptual and epistemological discussion about where media and diaspora studies are going, while considering the achievements and origins of the field, and the explorations that take place at present among specialist scholars and scholars across social sciences. It addresses three specific themes that emerge as core for the future of the field in three distinct sections. The first theme interrogates the concepts and analytical categories often used in the study of media and diaspora. It argues that in the context of cosmopolitanism we need to look again at the meanings of the national *vis-à-vis* the transnational. Cosmopolitanism, especially as developed in recent explorations (cf. Beck 2000, 2002; Featherstone 2002), emphasises the imagined and real interconnection between places and people through systems of communications and transportation. Cosmopolitanism also implies growing challenges to the nation-state as a coherent category and invites us to think of participation and representation outside the formal (national and international) systems of political organisation. The second theme focuses on the media and explores the relevance of the established and assumed research divide between production, text/representation, consumption. It questions the extent to which this divide is relevant in contemporary – and very diverse – media cultures. It argues that diasporic media becomes an area where this three-step media process is particularly challenged, as often the boundaries between producers and consumers are blurred. The third theme relates to the methodological practice in the study of media and diaspora. It makes a claim for more complex and diverse methodologies that draw on transnational experience, everyday life and its nuances. While research focussing on (media) consumption and identities has been extensively ethnographic and experiential, studies of the politics of diaspora have largely ignored culture and everyday experience. However, practice of everyday life can reveal many elements of political action among migrants and diasporas, including alienation from processes of political participation. Additionally, research has reproduced the centrality of the nation-state as the key category for analysis undermining the key relevance of the transnational and the local. Most cross-national research has compared national cases; arguably the study of themes and transnational cases is often more useful. The key point made at this section is that methodology needs to be more complex and take more seriously into consideration – both in design and analysis; both in the study of diasporic cultures and politics – the transnational and the local (especially the urban), the experiential and everyday.

This discussion is a continuation and not a break from the existing studies on diaspora and the media. It aims at actively engaging with issues that are already emerging in literature and ongoing debates across the transnational community of younger and established scholars and signals concerns that are emerging and growing in times of intense political and intellectual interrogations.

'Where are you from?'

'Where are you from?' might be the most frequently asked question to diasporic subjects. Like for most of them, diaspora and media scholars have (or should have) a difficulty in giving a straightforward answer about (intellectual) origins and affiliation. This being a rather new field, it has attracted scholars from across the social sciences and the humanities who have brought with them theoretical and methodological traditions from across the range. Some of the core conceptual influences can be traced in the studies of diaspora, migration and post-colonial studies in the last twenty years.

Diaspora is a concept with more than 2500 years of history and originates in Greek *speiro* (to sow) and *dia* (over). Scholars of diaspora studies, such as Marienstras (1988), Safran (1991) and Cohen (1997) have reconceptualised diaspora in addressing the diverse experience of populations who have moved and settled across the globe throughout human history. Though for them diaspora is largely a historical category and remains closely linked to the original *homeland*, its diversification invites new enquiries. As Cohen puts it:

Nowadays, with the increased use of the term to describe many kinds of migrants from diverse ethnic backgrounds, a more relaxed definition [of diaspora] seems appropriate. Moreover, transnational bonds no longer have to be cemented by migration or by exclusive territorial claims. In the age of cyberspace, a diaspora can, to some degree, be held together or re-created through the mind, through cultural artefacts and through a shared imagination (1997: 26).

Cultural mobility, imagined or real, is recognised by Cohen as an element of growing relevance to diaspora, next to physical mobility and migration. Media, telephony and digital technologies have altered transnational communication practices in the last couple of decades to such an extent as to allow daily and vast transnational exchanges online, on the phone and on television screens. Thus, even scholars who engage with diaspora from a historical perspective (like Cohen above) admit that the significant role of the media and communication technologies cannot be ignored.

Intellectual meetings of postcolonial thought and diaspora studies – especially in the works of Bhabha (1996), Brah (1996), Gilroy (1991; 1993), Hall (1990), Spivak (1987), among others – have looked even deeper into the cultural significance of diasporic experience beyond the particular groups directly engaged with it. Postcolonial scholars have discussed the long and ongoing cultural exchanges across boundaries and between the west and the east and they demonstrated the impossibility for clarity and homogeneity in culture. Instead, they have argued that hybridity characterises all cultures as they always meet and mix. Diaspora is a key element in cultural exchange and reflects the mobility of ideas, artefacts and people in time and space. Also, diaspora, as scholars from within cultural studies further emphasised (cf. Boyarin and Boyarin, 1994; Durham Peters, 1999; Hall, 1990, 1992), are not stable formations defined by blood relations, but they are decentralised cultural formations that sustain real and imagined connections across spread populations and/or a country of origin.

Postcolonial thought and cultural studies have also further politicised diaspora as an analytical category. With influences from literature on racism and migration (cf. Anthias, 1992, 1998, 2001; Fanon, 1986; Goffman, 1959), postcolonial studies and cultural studies have emphasised that diasporic presence in diverse societies destabilises the project of national or ethnic clarity and reveals inequalities which are outcomes of colonial rule and racial discrimination. Diaspora thus has become more than a historical category; it is also a social category which, next to race (or racialised) politics, addresses socio-political inequalities and exclusions. Many of these works also hinted that it is important to think about such inequalities on a global scale and across or beyond the nation-state. Anthropological thought looked into the local – sometimes but not always in dialogue with the global – as the space of the realisation of diasporic cultural and political practice. Diaspora became an attractive category for anthropologists, especially in the 1990s. Anthropologists studied diasporic experience, memory and particular cultural practices, as they relate to mobility, transnationalism and deterritorialisation. They have unfolded the connection between cultural practices, identity and community construction, but also started problematising the significance of the local in its dialectic relation to the global (cf. Clifford, 1994, 1997; Miller, 1998; Miller and Slater, 2000).

The vast explosion of studies on globalisation, especially in the 1990s, has advanced further the recognition of diaspora as an important analytical category in understanding social conditions such as social cohesion, conflict, global culture and cultural globalisation. Though relatively peripherally, globalisation scholars explored the role of diaspora in the emergence of global networks, transnational affiliations and political loyalties across boundaries (cf. Appadurai, 1996; Bauman, 1996; Castells, 1996). From among the critics of globalisation literature and the celebratory discourse that characterised much of it in the 1990s, emerged the first wave of studies on transnationalism. Transnationalism scholars looked into the political role of diaspora in the countries of settlement and the countries of origin and started exploring their role as political and cultural networks across boundaries (cf. Portes, 1997, 2001; Schiller *et al.*, 1995).

Another significant influence in the study of media and diaspora comes from media and communication studies. This influence is twofold. The important – though brief – ethnographic tradition in audience and media consumption studies (cf. Ang, 1991, 1995; Morley and Silverstone, 1990; Nightingale, 1996; Seiter, 1999; Silverstone, 1994) has inspired a substantial amount of work on diasporic and migrant uses of media and communication technologies, especially in relation to questions of identity and belonging (cf. Aksoy and Robins, 2000; El-Nawawi and Iskandar, 2002; Georgiou, 2002, 2006; Gillespie, 1995; Kolar-Panov, 1996; Morley, 1999; Naficy, 1993; Ogan, 2001). On the other hand, research on new technologies – and the internet in particular – has inspired many of the studies on diaspora that explored the significance of networking across boundaries but also the role of new technologies, particularly in advancing (or restricting) participation in political and cultural affairs. In this area, a number of theoretical and empirical explorations of the emergence of public spheres and of transnational decentralised networks across the diaspora emerged (cf. Berker, 2005; Siapera, 2005, 2006; Tsaliki, 2002).

The rich intellectual origins, affiliations and influences on the study of media and diaspora have made this field inevitably and inescapably interdisciplinary and similarly exposed to critique from many different directions. The unease of this area of study to be positioned within one discipline has also turned into an advantage. This is a field, which is constantly open to new explorations, both in terms of theoretical orientation and empirical conduct. The conceptual and methodological explorations that unfold in the following sections are an indication of its – hopefully reflexive and productive – open-endedness.

The three themes that unfold in the following paragraphs are reflections of an equal number of issues that emerge as important in theoretical and empirical explorations in this field. They are attempts to (cor)respond to challenges set by diasporic experience, as it unfolds in everyday life and in highly mediated practices that take place in and across various locations and through local and transnational networks. These challenges gain growing importance and relevance in the context of transnationalism and cosmopolitanism. Transnationalism acknowledges the development and sustaining of connections and networks across geographical, cultural and political borders (Schiller *et al.*, 1995), while at the same time it recognizes the interconnection and co-existence of the local, the national and the global. Transnationalism also emphasises the possibility for development of meaningful relations and social formations across borders and through the development of dense networks (Portes, 1997). Next to that, cosmopolitanism recognises the intensification of encounters between people of different backgrounds, cultural origins and orientations, especially in metropolitan, multicultural cities. Cosmopolitanism is also taking a working class direction in the practices and experiences of migrants and diasporas. Working class cosmopolitanism (Werbner, 1999) unfolds in the intensification of networks and sustained relations across boundaries and in working class locations. While it is more humble and less profit-oriented (inevitably) than elite cosmopolitanism, it also takes its shape through localised and transnational ideological, cultural and artefact exchanges that often have consequences for domestic and transnational cultural, political and religious life. Cosmopolitanism will be discussed in more detail in the context of the first theme presented below. I argue that cosmopolitanism is a key concept that both frames the study of media and diaspora and invites conceptual reflection.

The themes below do not exhaust the conceptual and methodological challenges that the field of media and diaspora faces. Important issues such as the state of affairs around formal citizenship and multiple citizenships, the high levels of financial deprivation and social exclusion of migrant and diasporic populations, the policy framework for the management of diversity and participation are not going to be discussed here in any detail. However, a key argument of the paper is that the three themes that are actually discussed (with an emphasis on cosmopolitanism especially) help us engage with further important theoretical, empirical and policy questions in more meaningful ways.

Three epistemological challenges

Media and diaspora are discussed together here and as a vibrant and intimate relation. Diasporas are transnational communities, which extensively depend on media and communication technologies for sustaining relations and connections across distance and across diverse subgroups. Media are becoming increasingly relevant to diaspora as they provide access to images and sounds and expand opportunities for two-way or multiple-way communication between various locations, groups, and individuals. Media are also important when they become alternative/minority media, which present and invite debates, values and interaction often unavailable (if not restricted and self-censored) in mainstream (national or large transnational) media. This powerful and close relation between diaspora and the media needs our attention in order to understand important cultural and political developments in transnational scapes and cosmopolitan times.

I Conceptual Interrogations: Cosmopolitan Explorations

In globalisation studies, but probably more than anywhere else, in grounded research on media and diaspora, nation-centrism is directly challenged. More recently, growing debates on cosmopolitanism and cosmopolitan societies have challenged even further the stability and the coherence of the nation as a political formation but also as a framework for research. Cosmopolitan literature partly reproduces old celebratory discourses from within globalisation studies. In its more useful propositions, cosmopolitanism is a critical interrogation and an operational framework that reflects processes and connections within and across contemporary (western) societies, beyond the linear order and causality assumed in national discourses. Cosmopolitanism does not dismiss old inequalities and struggles though it recognises that they might become more unpredictable. As Beck argues:

> I doubt that cosmopolitan societies are any less ethical and historical than national societies. But cosmopolitanism lacks orientation, perhaps because it is so much bigger and includes so many different kinds of people with conflicting customs, assorted hopes and shames, so many sheer technological and scientific possibilities and risks, posing issues people never faced before. There is, in any case, a greater felt need for an evident ethical dimension in the decisions, both private and public, that intervene in all aspects of life and add up to the texture of cosmopolitan societies (2002: 20).

Beck (2003) argues that within cosmopolitanism the binary of *either/or*[1] is replaced by *this and that*. Arguably, we could even say that often the case is of *neither/nor* – i.e. a choice neither to display loyalties to the country of origin nor to the country of settlement. Research needs to further explore this possibility, next to the possibility of multiple belongings. Amin and Thrift (2002) invite us to think beyond origins and destinations as defining categories for positioning diasporic and migrant people in a research framework. Rather, following Benjamin, they argue for a closer look into the juxtapositions of differences as they take place in everyday urban life. The dual focus on origins and destinations, which has dominated many migration and diaspora studies, has privileged the nation as a core category on one hand, and the western capitalist model as the destination that all cultural groups desire to reach, on the other.

Largely through developments in media and communications, the multiplicity of connections, relations and identities has grown to pose a significant challenge to the centrality of the nation as the political and cultural core of contemporary societies. The growing cosmopolitanization in the experience of diaspora requires an equally reflexive cosmopolitanization in research practice. The cosmopolitanization of conceptual and methodological explorations is a challenge which has only recently started being explored. Studies of media and diaspora require a reflexive revisiting of concepts, methods and research traditions that have inspired them. Developments in the mobility and multipositionality of people, ideas, communications and cultures demand innovative methodological choices[2] that recognize the geographical and symbolic complexity of diasporization and of mediation.

Assumptions about the export of nationalism in the diaspora, about the linearity of diasporic identification in time and space, about the inevitable dependence of diasporic identities upon a *homeland*, and about the evaporation of diasporic cultures through capitalist and national assimilation, have been stubbornly influential. Diasporic studies – and consequently many studies of media and diaspora – have suffered some of the most visible effects of methodological nationalism (Beck, 2002), either as practice or as ideological baggage. The development of theoretical and methodological practice, which is transnational and critical to methodological nationalism, is necessary and more sensitive to diasporic life than nation-centric research assumes.

Inevitably the challenge to the dominant role of the nation-state raises new questions: If the nation provides a misleading and restraining context of research then what would be a more appropriate framework?

Without abandoning the nation-state as a significant category altogether, we need to move away from assuming its centrality, both as regards media systems and as regards mobility, politics and cultural life. Nation-state is central, especially in research that focuses on citizenship and formal politics. Policy is still predominantly national and many of the issues around citizenship and representation, formal discrimination and access to resources are closely related to national policies. At the same time, national politics cannot exist outside an international context anymore (even if this means ignoring it and being in conflict with international or other national players). Policies of migration, citizenship and social services are increasingly shaped through common agendas shared within supranational organisations such as the EU and WTO or conveyed in bilateral agreements between neighbouring states. As a consequence, formal politics, like politics of everyday life, are far from being exclusive affairs of nation-states.

Research on cultural and communication practices and everyday life has been more reflexive in relation to the limitations of the national as a frame for research on diaspora and/or media and communications. Such research, having strong influences from anthropology, cultural studies, media studies and cultural geography, has observed the multiple spheres of activity – this being political, cultural and social – that unravel in overlapping or coexisting spaces. The transnational and the urban domains, the network and the community, have become increasingly useful framing, interpretative and operational categories.

The city

The city is a key location for diaspora, as diasporic populations tend to occupy urban locations (Eade, 2000; Sassen, 1991). The city – especially the cosmopolitan and global city – is also a key location for the production and consumption of the media. Thus, the city – and its visible and invisible elements of life, representation politics, creativity – is probably one of the most useful point of reference. Robins (2001) argues that the city is a more useful category of analysis, especially since it allows us to reflect on the cultural consequences of globalisation from another than a national perspective. 'The nation, we may say, is a space of identification and identity, whilst the city is an existential and experimental space' (2001: 87). The city, in western capitalist societies at least, is an intensely cosmopolitan location. In the city we observe juxtapositions of difference as urban dwellers of diverse backgrounds and particular cultural affiliations live cheek by jowl. Benjamin (1997) has spoken about the unforeseen constellations we observe in the city. When it comes to the cosmopolitan city, we see skyscrapers, which house transnational corporations next to humble and often impoverished multicultural neighbourhoods. The multicultural neighbourhoods might make no impression to a tourist's gaze to cosmopolitanism. However, cosmopolitanism is partly shaped in these urban settings, as their migrant and diasporic dwellers establish a dynamic cultural and financial presence. Often invisibly, diasporic and migrant populations contribute to urban and global economy; more visible, maybe, is their contribution to urban creativity and to practices of (self-)representation. Images and writings on city walls, local community activities, urban music, fashion creations and nightlife cultures often have strong and inspiring links with diasporic and migrant creative practices. This creativity, whose origin often is not easy to track down, relates to juxtapositions and meetings (not always without conflict) that take place in the city (and particularly the humble multicultural neighbourhoods). Many of these forms of creativity are the outcomes of exclusionary processes on the formal political domain. Excluded from citizenship rights, education and Eurocentric and corporate cultures, some migrant and diasporic groups (especially young people) engage in creative, mediated and alternative forms of expression and self-representation. Such creative practices (e.g. music) sometimes allow urban dwellers to develop a common (working-class) cosmopolitan language of communication in the city and in transnational spaces.

The network

Media are produced and consumed in the city; the vast majority of diasporic subjects live in cities. The city is a location where tensions and struggles for control of information, communication and also diasporic ideologies and discourses take place. However, and as Amin and Thrift (2002) propose, in the city the functions and limitations of networks of control are revealed. They name five countervailing tendencies against the network of control in the city: (i) urban life is made up of networks which are longer or shorter but do not reach everywhere and constantly interfere with each other; (ii) all networks look tighter than they actually are; 'a key urban skill is the negotiation of these break-downs' (p. 128); (iii) urban spaces depend on the improvisation of the chance encounter; they often contain within themselves the ability to go beyond routinised responses; (iv) all the systems of governance face the unknown; (v) urban networks are complex: 'they interact and interfere with each other in ways which are not predictable and which produce *emergent* forms of social organization in ways which cannot be foreseen' (p. 129).

The recognition of the existence and role of parallel and competing networks invites a number of key questions: What is the significance of encounters that take place in urban and transnational locations for politics and culture? Are diasporic communities increasingly decentralised as the production and exchange of symbolic content and information follow various directions? Are multi-nodal networks replacing linear one-way flows between the country of origin and each separate diasporic community? How do media form and reform relations and imaginings of community in transnational spaces? The above questions invite further important interrogations for understanding politics and culture in global times and in cosmopolitan societies: Does the growing autonomy of different nodes within diasporic networks increase democratisation within diasporic communities? Does it enable more participation of diasporic communities in the country of settlement or does it further their chosen or enforced exclusion? It is impossible to even attempt to answer these very big questions here. However, addressing them within the growing body of media and diaspora research could further the contribution of this field in important political and policy debates about public spheres and political and cultural participation.

II Media culture beyond the Three-step Process

The divide between media production and consumption, which applied at times when major national and transnational public and corporate media fully controlled media culture, still predominates in media and communications research. The huge gap between media producers and consumers has led to the segregation of the field into three distinct subfields, each focussing (i) on media production, (ii) media text/representations and (iii) media consumption and audiencehood respectively. For decades, scholars constrained themselves in one of the three areas reinforcing the divide of media culture into a three-step media process. While there is still a huge gap (and maybe even a growing one in the case of transnational corporate media) between producers and consumers, the diversification of media cultures requires a reflection on the limitation of this model of analysis. Two-way or multiple-way media that advanced the participation of audiences in content production, as well as the diversification of media consumption that now includes a variety of local, national and transnational public, commercial, community and diasporic media among others, demand further and new analytical explorations.

Diasporas are probably the ultimate transnationals challenging the framing of media as a three-step process. This challenge relates to qualities of the diasporic cultures, which are distinct (e.g. transnationalism; amateur media; role of media in construction of community) but also others, which relate to what is happening within broader national and transnational mediascapes (e.g. interactivity of the media; media literacy; diversification of mediascapes). Of course it is impossible to make any generalisations that apply to all diasporic media cultures. However, there is a number of characteristics which are significant for a large proportion of diasporic media.

Diasporic production and consumption of particularistic media is not a new phenomenon, neither is the important role of long established media cultures in the diaspora. Diasporic newspapers, journals and news bulletins have more than a century's history of circulation, often and for long transnational. Diasporic and ethnic radio has had a vibrant and influential presence in urban multicultural domains for at least thirty years. More recently ethnic, multicultural and transnational diasporic television has in many cases grown as an important competitor to more established and mainstream media. At present, diasporic media cultures have grown in diversity, transnational connections and even political influence (with cases such as Al Jazeera's success and extremist internet media attracting huge publicity). They include media produced locally, nationally and transnationally and consumed locally and translocally.

Transnational diversity

One of the major changes in media cultures relate to the growing diversity of audience practices. Media corporations across the range of commercial, public, and community diasporic are developing the variety of their output as part of their effort to attract audiences in the very competitive contemporary mediascapes. Diasporic media content often becomes multiligual and it regularly combines transnationally and locally produced content. As audiences are dispersed across territories, and linguistic and cultural zones, producers find it more difficult to predict and contain interests and tastes. At the same time, audiences have less ability to imagine other members of the audience compared to media which are geographically contained in their production and consumption. Anderson (1983) suggests that in national media people develop an imaginary sense of commonality across the nation's borders. Transnational media lose part of their power (though not completely) in bringing together people into ideological common zones such as those of nationalism, as described by Anderson. Rather, what is observed to happen more often is a destabilisation of the condition of the three elements of the media circuit. Deterritorialized and dispersed production and consumption redefine the roles of production-text-consumption in a number of ways:

(i)   media production is more diverse and includes corporate, public, community, niche media
(ii) media corporations are less able to predict audiences' interests as they are geographically and culturally dispersed
(iii) content is produced locally and globally, in different languages and by people who might be professional or amateurs
(iv) a growing number of audience members is more media literate than ever. Their consumption includes different media (local, national, transnational; corporate, public, alternative; large and small). Thus, the way they relate with production and text of each medium is far from linear and predictable.

In this context, the production of meanings shifts from being primarily controlled in the production side of the media to being negotiated in an ongoing dialectic relation between production and consumption. Audience research shows that consumers are more critical and detached from the media and thus challenge the linearity of the three-step process. The construction of meanings, research with diasporic and migrant media shows (cf. After September 11 project), does not always take place after the consumption of a particular medium but in the critical and ongoing consumption of a variety of media.

A community role

Another dimension of diasporic media which destabilises the divisions of the three-step model of media analysis is the role of diasporic media as institutions which are not only (or maybe not at all) corporate and which play a community role.

Diasporic media have initiated and participated in the development of spaces for communication in local and transnational level and, arguably, they have contributed to the emergence of local and transnational public spheres.

Most of them are small scale and they do not meet the professional and commercially driven format of large mainstream media. Many diasporic media function as community and alternative media, aiming to provide information and positive (self-)representation unavailable to mainstream media. Others aspire to be commercial and profitable businesses like any other media. Most of them however do not achieve this goal. This is the outcome of a number of reasons including the lack of know-how and the small size of most diasporic audiences. Interestingly, they often fail to become profitable because of the qualities of the diasporic media cultures. Feedback, interaction and participation of the audience is often more direct and more central than in the case of mainstream media. Commercial in their intentions or not, diasporic media depend on their audiences for information and news and for the production of many programmes. This dependence tends to demote profit as a priority. Additionally, as diasporic media extensively depend on interaction between producers and the devoted body of core consumers, they often fail to expand their repertoires and attract more diverse audiences. This results to the alienation of wider audiences, who don't share the interests of the core group of viewers/readers (e.g. young middle class diasporic subjects often have little interest in news about the country of origin, unlike the migrant generation who form the core of a diasporic radio audience, cf. Aksoy and Robins, 2000; Georgiou, 2006). What this widely applied scenario describes is a condition of continuity and interdependence between media and audiences. Diasporic media's relation with audiences sometimes challenges the industry's extreme commercialisation and the divide between an elite of media producers and *the masses* of media audiences.

Diasporic media against exclusion

The three-step media process is further challenged in the meanings that the media take in diasporic subjects' eyes. Ethnographic and intense qualitative research has looked into media practices and further into the cultural and political role given by diasporic audiences to the media. Often diasporic and migrant populations face high level of exclusion in their societies of settlement (Anthias, 1992; Gilroy, 1991, 2004). Exclusion involves the symbolic and cultural sphere and the media in particular. The Parekh report on multicultural Britain (2000) shows a grim picture, with Blacks and Asians being even less represented in the senior decision-making level in the BBC, Channel 4 and ITV in 2000 compared to 1990. According to an Ofcom[3] report, the total volume of multicultural programmes on all main channels, including the BBC's digital services in 2002, was 2.8 hours a week on average, a figure that has gradually reduced – by 21 per cent since 1998. (For the five main channels, 2002 output was 2.0 hours a week – a reduction of 42 per cent since 1998.) Additionally, Ofcom estimates the total spend on such programmes at £5.2 million in 2002, compared with £6.8 million (in 2002 prices) five years previously (www.ofcom.org.uk, accessed 31/05/06). A 2002 report titled *Multicultural Broadcasting: Concepts and Reality*, commissioned by BBC (www.bbc.co.uk/race) shows that significant percentages of diasporic and migrant audiences feel that they are largely misrepresented or invisible in mainstream media.

The sense of misrepresentation or lack of representation in the mainstream media, which is shared across large numbers of diasporic and migrant populations advances further the political and cultural role of diasporic media. Diasporic subjects turn to particularistic media for alternative representations, or for comparing representations between various media systems (After September 11 project, 2002; Iskander and Al-Nawawy, 2002). Also, diasporic populations often use the media as a stable point of reference in their everyday life, as a background but also as an outlet of (self-)representation (Kolar-Panov, 1996; Ogan, 2001). The two kinds of representation – political representation and representation in the media – overlap when diasporic subjects interpret their media representation (or lack of) in highly politicised manners and while making arguments that touch upon issues of citizensip (cf. Georgiou, 2002; Mai, 2005; Siapera, 2005).

The instability of the relation between media production-text-consumption discussed in this section raises important questions about the theoretical and methodological basis of research on media and diaspora. Research needs to reflect further on the assumptions that are so often made about the divide in media process. Case-based and theme-based research has proved to be more productive in understanding if the three-step analysis is relevant to specific media (cultures) or if the boundaries between producers and consumers are blurred and not clearly defined. Starting from exploring what is particular before assuming what is universal in media cultures might leave more space for exploration of commonalities and differences within and across media cultures than research designed to follow the established route of the three-step analysis.

III Empirical explorations and enquiries

A third and consequent area of discussion relates to methodological choice and practice. Methodological choices need to reflect changes in mobility, media practice, growing transnationalism; it needs to surpass old assumptions and habits that reproduce, without consideration of its relevance, the national as a conceptual and methodological framework. Traditions of research design and conduct have long suffered from methodological nationalism. Research often responses to national, top-down enquiries (e.g. national policy related research and commissioned research) and also reflects individual researchers' preconceptions attached to national familiarity, loyalties and affiliations.

Cross-national comparative research, which has predominated in research practice during the last two decades, especially in Europe, has played a key role in the reproduction of the nation-state as a unit of analysis. The design of cross-national comparative research and the expectations of the funding bodies have encouraged large scale and easily translatable into policy studies. Though a number of studies within such programmes have challenged the dominant trends in EU-funded cross-national research (e.g. *Diasporic Media Across the EU: A Mapping; Changing City Spaces*), in many cases, everyday life, experience and transnational media and cultural practices have been overshadowed by quantitative, nationally framed measurements and indicators.

Open methodological and multi-method approaches have proved to be more productive in recording and interpreting media practices and the diversity of migration and diaspora experience that includes discrimination, community and identity construction, creativity and politics of representation, among others. Cross-national research can be one of the most productive research contexts, especially since it benefits from significant funding and academic collaboration across boundaries (Blumler *et al.*, 1992; Livingstone, 2004). Cross-national research can also produce large scale, transnationally relevant data and attract the attention of non-academic users in various locations. As such, cross-national research has enormous potentials for making a contribution. However, cross-national research has to grow beyond the comparison of nation-states that rules at present. Comparison between countries is rarely meaningful and sometimes it can even be counter-productive. In cases when the comparison between national systems (e.g. policy systems) is on the focus of research, this design is productive and fruitful. However in cases when media, cultural and political life of diaspora are on the focus, presumptions about the nation's importance are often irrelevant.

With a whole generation of cross-national comparative research now completed, it's time for explorations of more complex comparative frameworks. Such can be based on themes rather than on national frameworks (e.g. comparison between television systems, or between various urban models of communication, which do not necessarily correspond to nation-states).

Cross-national research is one of the large-scale research frameworks, which can combine various methods – quantitative and qualitative, mapping and collection of descriptive data. Methodological triangulation and collaboration between researchers with different empirical expertise are challenging, yet potentially revealing choices. Combined methods, which do not interpret the cross-national based on vertical national divisions but based on horizontal operational frames and themes, can also contribute to theory. For example, research which looks at politics of representation through a theme-based framework (e.g. using themes such as: formal national politics; formal cross-national politics; urban politics; transnational diasporic politics; mediated politics, etc.) can reveal how different forms of political activity cross and compete with each other within and across local, national and transnational spaces.

Smaller – but also large scale – research practice needs to engage even further with everyday life, experience and communication in and across locations of diaspora. Ethnographic research is a demanding, difficult, yet still probably the most successful methodology for studying and understanding what people actually do with the media, how they actually live their lives, and what interaction (or refusal to interact) with others actually consists of. Experiential and reflexive methods take ethnographic practice further and can reveal unnoticed complexities of diasporic life and media cultures. Levebvre's flanerie and rhythmanalysis (1991, 2003) incite us to study life from the street level and through the senses. Benjamin's transitivity (1997) encourages us to pay closer attention and be open to the juxtapositions of difference and their effects. A number of urban and cultural geographers propose the development of narratives and maps based on wandering in places where everyday unfolds and where the complexity of social relations is unravelled (Amin and Thrift, 2002). Such methods allow the mapping of media cultures in the local and in continuities between the local and the transnational (or the translocal). Such forms of mediation which are integrated in everyday life and which are ordinary, mundane and often invisible in non-ethnographic research unfold some of the complex relations between identity, community and the media. They also reveal important elements of political life in the diaspora, which is very often as mundane as everyday life.[4] In locations where radios and stereos are loud, where satellite dishes point to different directions at different times of the day, where multilingual communication in the street contests monolinguality of mainstream and diasporic media alike, we can observe the symphony and cacophony of diasporic communication practices. A crucial task, of course, remains our analysis; our ability to make sense of it all.

To conclude

This chapter engages with conceptual and methodological challenges in media and diaspora studies; it sides with academic debates that invite reflection on the limitations of current research practice and the potentials for research beyond the still powerful methodological nationalism (Beck, 2002). The proposition of thinking through themes rather than through nations and of diasporic media cultures rather than through the oppositional production/consumption relation framed the discussion. As globalisation, digitalisation and increased population mobility obscure boundaries between production and consumption, linear approaches of the 'sender–receiver' relation become outdated. Similarly, the transnational becomes more than a mere expansion of the national; rather is becomes a conceptual and a methodological challenge to the national perspective. Conceptual and empirical explorations that look deep into the qualities and the particularities of the places where diaspora is lived and where it is communicated allow more reflexive engagement with the politics and cultures of cosmopolitanism. This invite becomes even more of an imperative at times when the politics of difference and of diasporic mobility – physical and imaginary – are in the core of many public debates. The commitment to more reflexive and cosmopolitan research practices can take us further in understanding diversity, imaginary worlds and (re-)imagined communities.

Notes

1. The dilemma of either/or in the case of the diaspora is often asked as an imperative to make a choice of identification between the country of origin and the country of settlement.
2. As will be discussed in the third theme below.
3. Ofcom is the main independent British media regulation body.
4. Political activities and construction of political movements in the diaspora are sometimes the outcome of informal meetings in religious and community centres. Also, political ideologies are partly shaped in the streets of multicultural neighbourhoods where political and social exclusion from the mainstream is experienced.

References

After September 11 Research Project http://www.afterseptember11.tv/ (2002).
Aksoy, A. and K. Robins (2000) 'Thinking Across Spaces: Transnational Television from Turkey', *European Journal of Cultural Studies*, 3 (3), 343–65.
Amin, A. and N. Thrift (2002) *Cities: Reimagining the Urban.* Cambridge: Polity Press.
Anderson, B. (1983) *Imagined Communities: Reflections On the Origins and Spread of Nationalism* (London: Verso).
Ang, Ien (1991) *Desperately Seeking the Audience* (London, New York: Routledge).
Ang, I. (1996) *Living Room Wars: Rethinking Media Audiences for a Postmodern World* (London and New York: Routledge).
Anthias, F. (1992) *Ethnicity, Class, Gender and Migration: Greek Cypriots in Britain.* (Aldershot: Avebury).
Anthias, F. (1998) 'Evaluating "Diaspora"': Beyond Ethnicity', *Sociology*, 32 (3), 557–80.
Anthias, F. (2001) 'The Concept of "Social Division" and Theorising Social Stratification: Looking at Ethnicity and Class', *Sociology*, 35 (4), 835–54.
Appadurai, A. (1996) *Modernity at Large: Cultural Dimensions of Globalization.* (Minneapolis and London: University of Minnesota Press).
Bauman, Z. (1996) 'From Pilgrim to Tourist – or a Short History of Identity' in Stuart Hall and Paul Du Gay (eds), *Questions of Cultural Identity* (London: Sage).
Beck, U. (2000) 'The Cosmopolitan Perspective Sociology of the Second Age of Modernity', *British Journal of Sociology*, 52 (1), 79–105.
Beck, U. (2002) 'The Cosmopolitan Society and Its Enemies', *Theory, Culture and Society*, 19 (1–2), 17–44.

Benjamin, W. (1997) *One Way Street.* (London: Verso).
Berker, T. (2005) 'The Everyday of Extreme Flexibility: The Case of Migrant Researchers: Use of New Information and Communication Technologies' in R. Silverstone (ed.), *Media, Technology and Everyday Life in Europe* (London: Ashgate).
Bhabha, H. (1996) 'Culture-in-between' in S. Hall and P. du Gay (eds), *Questions of Cultural Identity*, (London: Sage).
Blumler, J. G., J. M. McLeod and K. E. Rosengren (1992) 'An Introduction to Comparative Communication Research' in J. G. Blumler, J. M. McLeod and K. Erik Rosengren (eds), *Comparatively Speaking: Communication and Culture Across Space and Time* (Newbury Park, London, New Delhi: Sage).
Boyarin, D. and J. Boyarin (1993) 'Diaspora: Generation and the Ground of Jewish Identity', *Critical Inquiry*, 19 (4), 693–725.
Brah, A. (1996) *Cartographies of Diaspora: Contesting Identities* (London: Routledge).
Castells, M. (1996) *Information Age: Economy, Society and Culture: Rise of the Network Society Vol 1 (The Information Age: Economy, Society & Culture)* (Oxford: Blackwell).
Clifford, J. (1994) 'Diasporas' *Cultural Anthropology*, 9(3), 302–37.
Clifford, J. (1997) *Routes: Travel and Translation in the Late Twentieth Century* (Cambridge, MA: Harvard University Press).
Cohen, R. (1997) *Global Diasporas: An Introduction* (London: UCL Press).
Durham Peters, J. (1999) 'Exile, Nomadism, and Diaspora' in Hamid Naficy (ed.), *Home, Exile, Homeland* (London: Routledge).
Eade, J. (2000) *Placing London: From Imperial Capital to Global City* (London and New York: Berghan Press).
El-Nawawy, M. and A. Iskander (2002) *Al-Jazeera: How the free Arab News Network Scooped the World and Changed the Middle East* (Cambridge, MA: Westview).
Fanon, F. (1986) *Black Skin, White Masks* (London: Pluto Press).
Featherstone, M. (2002) 'Cosmopolis: An Introduction', *Theory, Culture and Society* 19(1–2), 1–16.
Georgiou, M. (2002) *Mapping Minorities and their Media: The National Context: The UK.* http://www.lse.ac.uk/collections/EMTEL/Minorities/reports.html
Georgiou, M. (2006) *Diaspora, Identity and the Media: Diasporic Transnationalism and Mediated Spatialitie* (Cresskill, NJ: Hampton Press).
Gillespie, M. (1995) *Television, Ethnicity and Cultural Change.* (London: Routledge).
Gilroy, P. (1991) *There Ain't No Black in the Union Jack: The Cultural Politics of Race and Nation* (London: Routledge).
Gilroy, P. (1993) *The Black Atlantic: Modernity and Double Consciousness* (London: Verso).
Gilroy, P. (2004) *After Empire* (London and New York: Routledge).
Goffman, E. (1990) *The Presentation of Self in Everyday Life* (London: Penguin, 1959).
Hall, S. (1990) 'Cultural Identity and Diaspora' in J. Rutherford (ed.), *Identity: Community, Culture, Difference.* (London: Lawrence and Wishart).
Hall, S. (1992) 'The New Ethnicities' in J. Donald and A. Rattansi (eds), *Race, Culture and Difference* (London: Sage).

Kolar-Panov, D. (1996) *Video, War and the Diasporic Imagination* (London and New York: Routledge).

Levebvre, H. (1991) *Critique of Everyday Life* (London: Verso).

Lefebvre, H. (1996) *Writing on Cities* (Oxford: Blackwell).

Levebvre, H. (2003) [with Stuart Elden and Elizabeth Lebas] *Henri Levebvre: Key Writings* (London: Continuum).

Livingstone, S. (2003) 'On the Challenges of Cross-National Comparative Research' *European Journal of Communication* 18 (4), 477–500.

Livingstone, S. (2004) 'The Challenges of Changing Audiences: Or, What Is the Audience Research To Do in the Internet Age', *European Journal of Communication* 19, no. 1, pp. 75–86.

Mai, N. (2005) 'The Albanian Diaspora in-the-Making: Media, Migration and Social Exclusion' *Journal of Ethnic and Migration Studies* 31(3), 543–62.

Miller, D. (1988) *Material Cultures: Why Some Things Matter* (London: UCL Press).

Miller, D. and D. Slater (2000) *The Internet: An Ethnographic Approach* (London: Berg).

Morley, D. (1999) 'Bounded Realms: Household, Family, Community, and Nation' in H. Naficy (ed.), *Home, Exile, Homeland: Film, Media and the Politics of Place* (New York, London: Routledge).

Morley, D. and R. Silverstone (1990) 'Domestic Communications: Technologies and Meanings', *Media, Culture and Society* 12 (1), 31–55.

Naficy, H. (1993) *The Making of Exile Cultures: Iranian Television in Los Angeles* (Minneapolis: University of Minnesota Press).

Nightingale, V. (1996) *Studying Audiences: The Shock of the Real* (London and New York: Routledge).

Ogan, C. (2001) *Communication and Identity in the Diaspora: Turkish Migrants in Amsterdam and Their Use of Media* (Lanham: Lexington).

Portes, A. (1997) 'Immigration Theory in the New Century: Some Problems and Opportunities', *International Migration Review*, 31(4), 799–825.

Portes, A. (2001) 'Introduction: The Debates and Significance of Immigrant Transnationalism', *Global Networks* 1(3), 181–93.

Rantanen, T. (2004) *The Media and Globalization* (London: Sage).

Robins, K. (2001) 'Becoming Anybody: Thinking Against the Nation and Through the City', *City*, 5(1), 77–90.

Safran, W. (1991) 'Diasporas in Modern Society: Myth of Homeland and Return, *Diaspora* 1(1), 83–99.

Sassen, S. (1991) *The Global City: New York, London, Tokyo.* (Princeton: Princeton University Press).

Schiller, N. G., L. Basch and C. S. Blanc (1995) 'From Immigrant to Transimmigrant: Theorizing Transnational Migration', *Anthropological Quarterly* 68(1), 48–63.

Seiter, H. (1999) *Television and New Media Audience* (Oxford: Oxford University Press).

Siapera, E. (2005) 'Minority Activism on the Web: Between Deliberative Democracy and Multiculturalism, *Journal and Ethnic and Migration Studies*, 31(3), 499–519.

Siapera, E. (2006) 'Multiculturalism Online: The Internet and the Dilemmas of Multicultural Politics', *European Journal of Cultural Studies*, Vol. 9, No. 1, 5–24.

Silverstone, R. (1994) *Television and Everyday Life* (London: Routledge).

Spivak, G. (1987) *In Other Words: Essays in Cultural Politics* (London: Methuen).

Tsaliki, L. (2002) 'Globalization and Hybridity: The Construction of Greekness on the Internet', K. Karim (ed.), *The Media of Diaspora* (London and New York: Routledge).

Werbner, P. (1999) 'Global Pathways: Working Class Cosmopolitans and the Creation of Transnational Ethnic Worlds', *Social Anthropology* 7(1), 17–35.

2
Diaspora, Multiculturalism and Transnational Media: The Case of Zee TV

Shehina Fazal

Introduction

Debates on issues of multiculturalism and the emergence of diaspora theories and diaspora communities together with the expansion of transnational media have begun to attract the attention of communication researchers. This chapter intends to map the developments around the diaspora, multiculturalism, transnational media and to interrogate the connections made between these three areas. The chapter begins with the evolution and adaptation of the term 'diaspora' from its classical definition to the contemporary conceptualisation that includes recent migrant communities. After that an overview of the multicultural debates in the UK is provided. This is then followed by an exploration of the growth of the concept of transnationalism and transnational media. In mapping these categories of diaspora, multiculturalism and transnationalism, the chapter proposes intersections of these three areas in understanding the growth and implications of transnational media in the diverse, global arena of the 21st century. The chapter uses Zee television as a case study, to illustrate the prevalence of the national framework and the key role-played by the nation-state, in a transnational media corporation.

Diaspora understandings

Early theorising of diaspora used the Jewish diaspora as a model, but the contemporary contextualisation rests on the impact of globalisation and the mobility of migrant communities. The original meaning of the word diaspora originated from Greek language concerning migration and colonisation. The idea of diaspora varies greatly and attempts have been made to provide a typology in the form of categories of the 'victims' (Jews, African and Armenians), 'labour' (the Indian indentured labourers), 'trade' (the Chinese and the Lebanese), 'imperial' (the British) and 'cultural' (the Caribbean abroad) that are helpful. (Cohen, 1997).

However, Cohen's typology does not really take into consideration the late- modern mobility among people of the world. Additionally, it seems that within Cohen's frame, the concept of diaspora is applicable to significant numbers in the population and not quite to the mobility of the smaller groups. Further, it makes a cursory reference to the movement of people through slavery, particularly that of the Africans to the Caribbean and the Americas. Despite these criticisms, Cohen's work provides a range of changing conceptions of diaspora and offers explanations that are concerned more with movement of people rather than capital and commodities.

The diaspora communities studied by scholars towards the end of the 20th century were in some ways quite different to the earlier diasporic identities. (Brah, 1996) The key difference being the new technologies and faster communications experienced by those in the 20th century, compared to the months it took to travel and communicate amongst earlier diaspora groups. The development of the electronic media and faster modes of travel meant that the notions of the 'global village' were attached with new meanings. For instance, there is now greater sharing of events as they occur, particularly through real time satellite transmission. However, interpretation of these events is dependent upon cultural, national and ethnic contexts as discussed later in the chapter. Cheap, long-distance travel and greater mobility also meant that families were able to visit homelands and families and friends in other parts of the world.

Likewise, people from the homelands were able to visit the diasporic communities settled in the 'developed' world. Growth of the Internet and the world-wide-web has resulted in a variety of communities constructed through commonality of interests (Gajjala, 2006). Such developments work against the one-way process of cultural homogenisation. Media and communications play an important role in the social and cultural aspects of the diaspora communities and facilitate the notion of 'diasporic spaces' for communities living away from home. Such conceptualisations of diaspora and diasporic spaces has shifted the diaspora media from the margins into somewhat celebratory status, and where labels of 'fusion' and 'crossover' are frequent in popular vocabulary.

In an overview on the advent of diaspora in a variety of academic disciplines, Braziel and Mannur (2003) state that the explosion in the use of the word does makes it somewhat difficult to confirm why diaspora has become overly popular. They write that the term diaspora, 'is often used as a catch-all phrase to speak of and for all movements, however privileged, and for all dislocations, even symbolic ones' (p. 3). Further, Braziel and Mannur ask the all-important question: 'Why diaspora studies now?' Responding to this question they argue that there are two key issues around which the discourse on diaspora offers justification. Firstly, the theorisation of diaspora compels us re-evaluate the idea of nation and nationalism, while at the same time revising the configurations in the relationship between nation-sates and its citizens; secondly, the diaspora discourse has become a site of resistance to 'hegemonic, homogenising forces of globalisation' (p. 10). Braziel and Mannur emphasize that diaspora and diasporic movements should be framed within the context of global capitalism where the current period of globalisation enables greater economic demarcations between *those who have* and *those who have not.*

The above perspective highlights the major issues that have emerged from the 'diasporic project' over the last 15 years, however, the idea that the diaspora as the site of resistance seems to be somewhat under developed. As this chapter illustrates in the case study later on, that it is difficult to argue that Zee television is a site of resistance to the forces of homogenisation within diaspora communities, particularly as the Zee network emerged within a national framework, in the era of economic liberalization in India.

A synopsis of literature on diaspora is one that is provided by Steven Vertovec. He describes the three general meanings of diaspora that have appeared in the literature. These are: 'diaspora as a social form, diaspora as a hype of consciousness' and 'diaspora as a mode of cultural production'. Vertovec (1999) uses these meanings for 'conceptualising, interpreting and theorising processes and developments affecting South Asian religions outside of South Asia. Vertovec (1999) states that in the meaning of 'diaspora as a social form there are three strands: the first strand concerns the social relationships formed due to common origins and migrations routes; the second strand is one where tensions exist between loyalties to homeland and the host country; the third strand is that some diaspora groups can mobilise collective resources and deploy the economic strategies that enable such collective action. The second meaning of 'diaspora as a type of consciousness' is a fairly recent perspective that offers explanations on the sharpened awareness among transnational communities, where on the one hand there is awareness of issues concerning social exclusion and discrimination and yet at the same time there is intense connection to the histories and heritage of the homeland or current political and cultural forces like religion (Islam). This consciousness is reinforced via cyberspace, where there is the possibility of connecting 'local to the global'. The third meaning is one of 'diaspora as a cultural form' that tends to focus around issues of globalisation where the identities of diasporic communities are perceived to be fluid, with descriptions of 'syncretic', 'crossover', 'hybrid' that are common in the literature. These multiple cultural phenomenon, are helped by the global media and communications that provide access to range of cultures, from whom facets of identity are consciously selected, particularly by young people. (Vertovec, 1999)

This articulation of diaspora towards the late 20th century has enabled the idea of multiple identities and multi-faceted cultural phenomena to be made palatable within mono-cultural environments, where such trends are celebrated with descriptions of 'fusion', hybridity and so on. Additionally, the idea of diaspora spaces as influenced by media and communications, has impacted on the redefinition of locality and the global. In my view, an important question to address is how do these conceptualisations impact upon issues of equality and social justice in the spaces that diaspora communities inhabit?

An attractive perspective is one that is provided by Karim (2003) where he writes that the 'cultural workers' who contribute to the construction of diaspora spaces are not reforming the dominant 'Eurocentric world'. Rather the articulation of co-existence within 'diasporic spaces' enriches the process of remapping, that include issues on ethnicity and religion and their maintenance within existing cosmopolitan structures. Karim's view seems somewhat simplistic, in that it assumes that once the diasporic spaces have been reclaimed predominantly through electronic channels, then the 'cosmopolitan citizenship' that we crave will be a natural outcome on the global terrain. These diasporic spaces have recently been referred to as 'digital ghettoes' in the debate and discussions concerning Muslims in Britain.

A more convincing argument on whether the conceptualization of diaspora has been helpful on issues of equality and social justice or whether it has neutralised the struggles along social, political and cultural arenas, is provided by Virinder *et al.* (2005). They argue that areas where diaspora challenges the traditional views are: belonging and nationhood, transnationalism, and the movement of cultural products. The term 'diaspora' challenges the traditional ideas of belonging and nationhood where the links between those who are outside the national boundaries with those within are articulated through connections that include media channels and cultural products.

On social configurations of diaspora, Virinder *et al.* (2005) argue that the conceptualisation of diaspora has emerged alongside the debates on post-colonialism and globalisation. Further, academic interest has been growing in the area of diaspora, as have the geopolitical positions and conflicts that have in part resulted in movement of people across the globe. By adopting a critical stance on the 'cultural configurations of diaspora', Virinder *et al.* have questioned the usefulness of diaspora as a concept, particularly its recent incarnation:

> If words could change the world, then 'diaspora' is one of those terms that promised much but delivered little. Events have neutralized the purchase of many agreed conceptual staples and today it is transnational networks (often labelled 'terrorist') that have entered into the social science and broadsheet vocabulary. Such a change of terminology-not for the first time-marks a transition in the significance of diaspora for a whole range of cultural, social and political formations (Virinder *et al.*, 2005: 8).

This is indeed a gloomy verdict on the early promise of diaspora that was powerfully expressed by Stuart Hall in the early 1990s. Hall (1992: 310–14) made a significant link between the development of hybridity and the changing nature of diasporas. For Hall, the postmodern world was manifested by two contradictory tendencies: firstly the move towards globalisation with the emphasis on assimilation and homogenisation. Secondly, in response to globalisation there are increasing tendencies to reassert ethnic, nationalistic and religious identities. Within this context, Hall argued that the cultural identities emerging are 'in transition'. These identities are drawing upon the variety of values practices and traditions and that there is the harmonisation of the old and the new without losing the past or assimilating into the new. Hall called this process the development of the 'cultures of hybridity' and closely allied this growth with the 'new diasporas' created by the colonial experience and the resultant postcolonial migrations. Hall's articulation of diaspora was relevant at that point in the evolution of the diasporic project, and it underlined the celebratory aspects of cultural identities that emerged from process.

Like Virinder *et al.*, Brian Axel also provides a critique on the limitation of diaspora theory in that it has not moved the situation any further from the earlier conceptualisation of multiculturalism. Axel offers two models of diaspora community that are constructed by the nation. He categorizes these as the 'settler' and the 'parasite'. (Axel, 2002) The idea of the diaspora as the 'settler' community is one where they are seen to be devouring benefits from the state; second is where they no longer contribute to the nation-state; and third is where the diaspora community has developed its own socio-cultural networks within the nation-state. This latter approach is one where the diaspora community is the 'other' and seggregated from the rest of the population. This explanation echoes with the concerns of multiculturalism as described by Alibhai-Brown below. Axel (2002) also states that the 'parasite' model within the nation-state is not considered in the analysis of the diaspora, but this approach indicates how the 'the nation-state is continually involved in producing its own enemy, an enemy within' (p. 249). It could be argued that the evidence for the parasite perspective provided by Axel can be seen in the narratives of panic constructed in the British press, over the number of refugees and asylum seekers who come to Britain and are allowed to remain in the country. These narratives concerning refugees and asylum seekers have a regular occurrence in the tabloid press where descriptions that the country is 'overwhelmed' with immigrants who are 'sponging' on the welfare state are common

Given the above criticisms, the term diaspora continues to challenge ideas of nation and national identity and also serves as the basis of critiquing binary perspectives that were common currency in the colonial and in some cases post-colonial discourses

Having challenged these traditional perspectives, one cannot fail to question whether they have contributed to greater equality and social justice for diaspora communities. Contemporary diasporas continue to echo with meanings of immigrants, migrants, refugees and asylum seekers and more recently of 'terrorists'. Given this situation, does diaspora continue to be a useful concept? In re-evaluating the conceptualisation of diaspora, Brah (1996) proposes that diaspora does not necessarily have to be used to describe the varying conditions underlying the population movements. Rather, the concept of diaspora signals the understanding of historical and contemporary elements.

From the above overview, two key indicators emerge from the literature and debates on diaspora: firstly that although they have become sites of resistance to the forces of globalisation, discussion on the relationships of historical and contemporary elements of power between diaspora communities and their engagement with the nation-state they inhabit is not prevalent; secondly, the celebratory conceptualisation of diaspora towards the end of the 20th century, seems to have neutralised issues of social justice and equality, as the focus has been on the recognition of multiple identities, exposure to diverse cultures and on the idea of cosmopolitanism that is underpinned by global capitalism. Diaspora offered hope in the early days, but seems to have less currency, in the debates and discussions in the early part of the 21st century.

Multiculturalism

In February 2004, the editor of the *Prospect* Magazine, David Goodhart argued that multiculturalism has failed and that Britain has become 'too diverse to sustain the mutual obligations behind a good society and the welfare state' (Goodhart, 2004). In September 2005, Trevor Phillips, the chairman of the Commission for Racial Equality (CRE) in the UK proposed the integration model where there is equality, participation and interaction. Phillips (2005) goes on to explain:

> Equality: everyone is treated equally, has a right to fair outcomes, and no-one should expect privileges because of what they are. Participation: all groups in the society should expect to share in how we make decisions, but also expect to carry the responsibilities of making the society work. Interaction: no-one should be trapped within their own community, and in the truly integrated society, who people work with, or the friendships they make, should not be constrained by race or ethnicity.

These proposals of integration and assimilation are somewhat alarming, given that the expectations of the earlier policies within a similar framework were so effectively undermined by the critiques in the 1970s and the 1980s. Those earlier frameworks of integration seem to have returned in a somewhat different guise in the UK, at the beginning of the 21st century. Goodhardt's commentary on multiculturalism as a redundant initiative provoked many responses. The underlying theme in debates that followed was that multiculturalism was a failed experiment and that what was required was a new or different understanding of cultural diversity in the (Western) developed countries.

The *open Democracy* website together with the British Council setup a discussion forum on multiculturalism. Ali Rattansi (2004) makes an interesting point on this forum, stating that the idea of assimilation has usually been the project of the Right in Britain, however, the Left now find it attractive, particularly in the context of finding a unitary British national identity. Until recently the left movement in Britain considered the idea of national identity as archaic. As Rattansi (2004) points out four key issues that changed the perspective:

> ... pressures of globalisation, the processes of regionalism and devolution in Britain; the development of a more militant Muslim presence; and the impact of 'people flow' (refugees, asylum seekers and new sorts of economic migrants)-have led to the revival of the project to create a strong national identity.

Responding to criticisms of earlier versions of multiculturalism, the then 'new' Labour government set up the *Commission on the Future of Multi-Ethnic Britain*, with the Runneymede Trust in 1998, and produced what could be argued as a 'new' take on multiculturalism. The Commission produced the document called the Future of Multi-Ethnic Britain (Runneymede Trust, 2000) also known as the Parekh Report after the Commission's chairperson Lord Parekh. The main purpose of the report was to provide a new national narrative for the understanding of Britain as a 'community of citizens' and a 'community of communities'. However, this new take on multiculturalism seems to follow the 'container model' of the nation state where social cohesion, cultural belonging and political participation are confined within the administrative and geographical boundaries of the nation state. The recommendations by the commission for the 'new multiculturalism' were that there should be equal treatment as well as sensitivity to 'real differences of experience, background and perception' (p. 296) and that the concepts of equality and diversity must be part of government strategy at all levels. As mentioned earlier, this vision of multiculturalism that was produced was very much restricted within national boundaries at a time when the impact of globalisation was already being felt by the nation. While there is a large body of literature that critiques the 'container model' of multiculturalism, Kivisto (2002) in attempting to make sense of multiculturalism in the early 21st century says that the:

> enmeshing of information in a global society means that there is a need to reconstitute the idea of nation states. The economic

changes resulting from the expansion of capitalism together with the transformation in relationships of power between the nation-states and the transnational political institutions have been further compounded by the 'intensity of cultural diffusion (p. 30).

In a succinct critique of multiculturalism Alibhai-Brown (2000) states that its limitations are that it is only about 'ethnic minorities and has therefore created a sense of white exclusion, it engages with elites in its models of representation, does not recognise change and creates group barriers and have not connected with globalisation'. She provides a classification on three types of multiculturalisms:

- 'minimalist' where evolution will take its due course and all we have to do is wait and see;
- 'celebratory' multiculturalism which is somewhat positive with 'consumer, sexual, artistic, style' and 'corporate' multiculturalisms, but provides a shallow understanding of diversity in society;
- 'tribal' multiculturalism is one that perceives differences as essentialist and is more exclusive rather than inclusive (Alibhai-Brown, 2000).

The above critique accurately captures the limitations of earlier versions of multiculturalism in Britain in the 1980s and the 1990s. All three types of multiculturalisms have been practised in the UK in various sectors. However in some areas of the country such as Bradford and Oldham, multicultural policies have resulted in segregation and resentment between communities, pointing to the inadequacies of the local and national interpretation of multiculturalism. The state policy at the time was to promote the interpretation of multiculturalism that categorised the ethnic minorities in to the 'other' and subsequent policy issues were led by the binary perspective of 'us' and 'them'. In this scenario, immigrants from other parts of the world were allowed to continue their cultural, religious and linguistic practices provided that they did not impinge upon mainstream society. This take on multiculturalism has excluded minority communities from the mainstream society.

Transnational media

Historically, the idea of transnationalism existed at the beginning of the twentieth century when at the Imperial Press Conference in Ottawa, Canada in 1920, Potter describes the following:

... the proprietor of the London Daily Telegraph, Lord Burnham, declared that 'The British world is a world of its own, and it is a world of many homes.' Burnham used the idea of a British world to reconcile the diverse national, regional and imperial perspectives that characterised the early twentieth century British empire' (p. 191).

Potter explains the construction of the 'British World' via the press in the early twentieth century when newspapers become the medium of imperial mass communication. This explanation on the construction of the British world in the Dominions or settler colonies in the early part of the 20th century was that the press worked within regional, national and imperial regions. In the early 21st century the terms 'British world' could easily be replaced by 'capitalist world' and the key geographical aspects: regional, national and imperial could be reconfigured as regional, national and transnational.

The transnational media such as 24-hour news stations like CNN and BBC World work on the geography of the transnational, where upon the source sends the reports to the headquarters of the news channels where the news is filtered and packaged through a variety of editorial processes, before it is broadcast round the world. This contemporary model of transnational media may reach more consumers, but the material motivations are somewhat similar to the 'imperial' ambitions of the former British empire.

Staying in the contemporary context, Chalaby (2005a) writes that at the beginning of 21st century the shift towards transnationalisation can be described 'as the third phase in a succession of paradigm shifts in the evolution of international communication from the mid-19th century onwards'. The expansion of international communications during the 19th century enabled the colonial powers to extend their influence and control over the empire through the medium of the telegraph. In the middle of the twentieth century technological developments in space, micro-electronics and computing have led to the second stage of international communications. The technologies facilitated the growth of global networks and together with deregulation and liberalisation in communications in the latter part of the 20th century were factors that added to the developments in global communications. A new order is emerging within the international communications arena, the transnational media order. As Chalaby (2005a) states:

A transnational media order is coming into being that is remapping media spaces and involving new media practices, flows and products.

An international reach is no longer the preserve of Western-based conglomerates, as an increasing number of smaller media companies from the developing world are expanding overseas ... (p. 30).

A somewhat different take on transnationalism is provided by Robins and Aksoy (2003) who discuss the idea of 'banal transnationalism', where satellite television programmes from Turkey enables access to the 'ordinary, banal reality of Turkish life to the migrants living in London' (p. 95). The main thrust of Robins and Aksoy's argument is that the reality of Turkish television that is brought to the Turkish community in London shatters the romantic idea of homeland. The expansion of satellite television has resulted in flattening of the romantic idea of 'diaspora-as-exile', as are the idealising memories of homeland. Robins and Aksoy refer to satellite television as 'an agent of cultural de-mytholigisation'.

Issues of identities are receiving more attention due to the expansion of global institutions and trade, the movement of people that has never been seen before as well as the growth of satellite and digital information channels and the increasing domination of global economics and politics by transnational corporations (Gabriel, 1998). These global surroundings have provided a basis for 'white fears and anxieties that have expressed the re-assertion of old identities often based on racialised ideas of the nation' (p. 37). Gabriel goes on to write that these identities are not just connected with anxieties or the cracks in the economic and political structures, but in the everyday routines and symbols such as the 1996 European Football Championships.

In the early part of the 21st century, the crisis in the 'British' national identity continues and the 2006 World Cup Championships became an arena where 'mobilisation and maintenance' of British identity was displayed on the media as well as the football pitch. So strong were the expressions of loyalty to the England football team that Nirpal Dhaliwal, a journalist writing in the London's Evening Standard newspaper on 30 June 2006 stated that Scotland should not be ungrateful to the country that pays for it. The background to this scenario was that during the World Cup 2006, Scotland's First Minister apparently claimed that he would cheer any team that was playing England, meaning that he would not be supporting England in the world tournament. The newspaper article in question lambasted Scotland for adopting such a position and then focused on the financial subsidies that Scotland receives from England. The article reminded Scottish people that they should be supporting England or told 'Go on, have your independence. Let's get shot of you' (Evening Standard, 30 June 2006: 13). Such statements on issues of national identity that seem to be based predominantly around issues of financial subsidies, raise serious concerns over interpretations of diaspora, multiculturalism and transnationalism.

Further away from Western Europe, Melissa Butcher (2003) discusses the idea of transnationalism with the introduction of Star TV in India and how it has impacted upon the changing Indian national identity. Transnational television in India includes overseas as well as Indian enterprises. However, not all content is transnational. Programmes are made in India where 'localisation' has been a key policy among transnational media corporations. What is an interesting development within the Indian television industry is that the Indian-owned and Indian channels of the transnational media corporations such as Zee and Sony broadcast programmes to Europe, USA, Africa as well as other Asian countries. This development has also impacted on the rise in inward migration by the Non-Resident Indians (NRIs) who are returning to work in the industry. In addition, the flow of programmes outwards has also enabled media elements such as advertising to enter the global media landscape. (Butcher, 2003)

Such is the currency of transnationalism in the analysis of national identities and global media, an explanation on the popularity of the concept among scholars is captured by Virinder *et al.* (2005):

> [Transnationalism] It is able to describe wider sets of processes that cannot comfortably fit within the diaspora rubric. Thus we talk of transnational corporations rather than diasporic corporations. The transnational also manages to avoid the group or human-centered notions that diaspora invokes. The term allows a side-stepping of the usual pattern, when discussing diaspora, of having to evoke Jewish or Greek archetypes. At the same time, transnational is a more precise, if somewhat tame, description of the contemporary world of nation-states that might otherwise be called the World System, Imperialism, Empire or New World Order. The transnational describes forces that cross or work across the nation's boundaries but do not necessarily disrupt the workings of the nation-state as executive committee. This lack of disruption does, however, allude to the weakness of the term' (p. 34).

The above points resonate with the proposal that transnationalism has replaced imperialism mentioned earlier in this section. The key point being that the idea of the British World in the late 19th century was replaced by the idea of the 'American World' in the late 20th century. In the 21st century, nations like China and India are in the process of creating this vision, and have many more media channels at their disposal for disseminating such ideas. Earlier in the chapter, it was noted that the term diaspora has failed to deliver what it promised. The limitations of diaspora were noted and an overview on multiculturalism and transnationalism were provided. All three sections have a common theme-that of celebrating influences of globalisation, encouraged by the transnational movement of cultural products.

Having foreground the concepts of diaspora, multiculturalism and tansnationalism, the next section will explore how diaspora, multiculturalism and transnational apply to the Indian television channel: Zee TV. Can Zee TV be diasporic, multicultural and transnational? There is a substantial body of literature on the development of Zee television in India as well as in the global media market (Thussu, 1998, 2005; Page and Crawley, 2001; Singhal and Rogers, 2001; Kohli, 2003). These writers have mapped the first decade of the growth of private channels in India. The following section will provide an overview of Zee television, followed by a discussion on some of the problems concerning the debates on diaspora and transnational media. Zee television was chosen as it clearly illustrates the problems underlying the applications of diaspora, multiculturalism and transnationalism, in understanding the expansion of global television companies.

Zee TV: an outline

The Zee satellite television network was launched in 1992 by an entrepreneur who was one of the first to enter into the private media environment in India in the early 1990s. In its early days, Zee TV relied on recycles from the state channel Doordarshan and Hindi movies (Thussu, 1998). The success of the channel lay in its broadcast of programmes that covered topics from human interest perspectives and the general theme was 'infotainment' rather than information and education, emphasized by the state broadcaster. Currently the channel reaches 225 million viewers in over 80 countries and the corporate website states 'Zee TV has created a strong brand equity and is the largest media franchise serving the South Asian diaspora. Within ten years of its launch, Zee TV has driven the growth of the satellite and cable industry in India' (www.zeetelevision.com). Broadcasting from the BSkyB platform in the UK, Zee claims to be the largest Asian television network with its portfolio of four channels: Zee TV, Zee Music, Zee Cinema, Alpha ETC Punjabi and Zee Gujarati (www.zeetv.co.uk).

Thussu (2005) notes that Zee has also been influential in the development of 'Hinglish', a mixture of Hindi (the main language in north India) and English, the predominant language of international media. The use of Hinglish has been one of the key factors in the success of Indian television beyond the national boundaries and its use is now widespread among the young in India as well as the South Asian diaspora around the world.

The other key issue according to Page and Crawley (2001) that has led to the success of the Zee network and of satellite television in India in general was that it offered a different vision to the one offered by the state broadcaster Doordarshan. The middle class viewers in India were offered channels that promoted consumerism in India, 'where personal choice has become the new ideology' (p. 141).

Writers like Page and Crawley (2001) argue that programmes on the entertainment channels like Zee have helped to create 'South Asian popular culture which transcends national barriers' (p. 139). The evidence gathered by Page and Crawley came from group discussions and interviews. Although impressionistic, their study provides an interesting dimension on the rapid growth of consumerism, children becoming targets for programme makers and advertisers as well as the controversies that are raised around the reconstruction of role models for South Asian women through popular the soap opera genre.

When Zee was launched in 1992, the economic reform was well underway in India and these changes occurred very rapidly. As Sinha (2000) states;

> Based on a rhetoric of socialism, self-reliance, and import substitution, successive Indian governments limited the access of foreign corporations to the India economy. International trade was closely monitored, as imports of foreign goods was severely restricted and the foreign direct investment (FDI) was tightly regulated. However, in 1991 the newly elected Congress Government, under Prime Minister Narasimha Rao, launched sweeping economic restructuring program aimed at loosening trade restrictions, opening the door to FDI, and replacing state control economy with the operation of market forces (p. 23).

The result was privatisation and licensing legislation that created the framework for channels like Zee to set up and compete. As Sevanti

Ninan (2000) wrote, these new proposals were put into place so that the state television network Doordarshan could legally compete in the expanding television sector in India.

Zee TV: diasporic, multicultural and transnational?

The current pattern of understanding of transnational media, like the Zee network takes place within two contexts: firstly it is in the framework of the host country where studies on reception of transnational programmes situates the viewers as 'ethnic minorities'; the second framework is one that is seen in the context of the relationship with the viewers' relationship to their country of origin and the diasporic associations. As Robins and Aksoy (2005) state the general view is that the relationships are examined within 'one or the other national frame, rather than address the difference and distinctiveness of their transnational positioning' (p. 17). In one national frame, Zee network's evolution has taken place within the private sector in India, with the ultimate aim of achieving maximum reach across the world with attempts to occupy every possible niche television market. The other national frame allows for channels within the Zee network to be licensed and to serve the 'ethnic minority' viewers in the UK, as the provision for such communities within the public service frame continues to dwindle (Creeber, 2004).

Within the context of diaspora, two key issues emerge from the Zee TV: is it a site of resistance to the dominant culture and does it offer spaces of empowerment for the diaspora communities in the UK? First, the channel has been successful not only in India, where it has beaten its close rival Sony television in popularity, but also within the diaspora communities in many parts of the world. The predominant content on the Zee network is entertainment-in the form of music, soaps and films. Zee television claims to cater for all segments of the population through programme genres that consist of 'primetime comedy and drama series, television movies, mini-series, theatrical films, specials, children's programs, daytime dramas, game shows, and late night shows (www.zeetelevision.com). Within these narratives it is somewhat problematical to appreciate how these diasporic media, offer 'spaces' of empowerment for diaspora communities. What seems to be offered to the diaspora communities in the UK is the opportunity to 'tune out' of the everyday issues that confront them in everyday life. It could be argued that this 'tuning out' is facilitating digital segregation where there is very little commonality between diaspora and 'host' communities.

In the multicultural context, the diasporic spaces provided by television channels like Zee maybe could be one of the factors that has reduced the collective consciousness among South Asia diaspora communities in the UK. In the 1970s and 1980s, the South Asian communities came together under the political label 'black', (Sivanandan, 1982) but this collective consciousness appears to have fallen apart in the early part of the 21st century, particularly on religious divisions. The result is that on the one hand, there is much more access to the popular culture of the homelands via television channels, yet at the same time, there are sharpened religious and linguistic demarcations in the South Asian communities in the UK. This is particularly crucial if we examine the context within which the Zee network emerged, in the early 1990s. Economic liberalisation in India was implemented with great force towards the end of the 20th century in many sectors and along with the politics of communal mobilisation. These changes set the agenda for the alliance of market forces and the religious influence television programmes. Rajagopal (2001) This influence was notable in news where the Zee news channel adopted a somewhat partisan approach in its coverage of politically sensitive items. For example, during the Kargil war (the conflict with Pakistan in 1999) it has been observed that the private television news channel took a position that was closer to the then state interests than the state broadcaster, in reporting the conflict.

Additionally, within the multicultural frame, diasporic communities continue to be understood within the context of the 'other' and diasporic spaces enables them to be segregated from the dominant culture which is somewhat tolerant of separate cultural practises as long as they do not encroach upon the conceptualisation of the nation and its identity. As mentioned earlier in the chapter, the 'container model' of multiculturalism (Runnymede Trust, 2000) does not recognise that issues of cultural belonging and political participation that extend beyond the administrative and geographical boundaries of the nation state. In this context, rather than allowing spaces of expression within the multicultural frame, the essentialist perspectives prevail with segregation enhanced by the diaspora media. As Thussu (2005) points out, networks like Zee are exposed to the commercial pressures of market-led television and channels that are hardly likely to be viewed by the dominant population in Western countries. Further, Dudrah (2002) in his analysis of the 'pan-European South Asian identity' warns of the exclusive identities being reinforced via the growth of transnational channels that target their programmes to the diverse diaspora communities. What needs to be explored is how these channels raise awareness on issues of equality and social justice for the South Asian diaspora communities living in Europe.

In the transantional frame the argument is that the national borders are no longer seen to be restrictive in terms of movements of people and media and cultural products. However, what is overlooked is that although the 'contraflow' of media products is celebrated, for example, Bollywood films, films from Brazil and various TV and film festivals, what impact do diaspora media like Zee TV have upon the US hegemony of global television?

A key strength of transnationalism is that it prepares us for the role that transnational capital plays in accommodating the movement of diasporic cultural products. As Virinder *et al.* (2005) claim that this role 'cannot be underestimated'. The distinction presented between diaspora and transnational is that transnationalism is coupled with political and economic processes, where as diaspora is attached to the social and cultural. Multiculturalism could become a bridge between diaspora and transnationalism, where politics and economics come together with the social and cultural to provide a holistic perspective on global media. This would connect diaspora to a political relationship with the diaspora communities as well as encourage a materialist critique within diaspora studies. It would also reframe multiculturalism away from the idea of the 'other' and therefore, to be kept at a distance. Additionally, transnationalism would extract multiculturalism away from the container model and into the international arena. Such bridging is essential in the context of re-imagining diasporas, particularly in the context of transnational media as described in the case study. Finally, in diaspora and multicultural perspectives, issues of 'race' and racism have prevailed. Writers and commentators have to foreground such issues, particularly as there is increasing legitimacy given to racist attitudes and behaviour in contemporary times.

Conclusion

The chapter has attempted to outline three key areas that should be embedded in the discourse around transnational media: diaspora, multiculturalism and transnationalism. It is proposed that these three areas have particular resonance in providing an understanding of the diaspora and transnational communities since 9/11 and 7/7. The arguments presented in previous pages allow us to problematize the narrower perspectives on diaspora, multiculturalism and transnational media. They show that the contemporary understanding of trans-nationalism and transnational media has to be considered in the diasporic and multicultural frames. The idea of multiculturalism should not be abandoned in favour of integration. Rather diaspora, multiculturalism and transnationalism perspectives should be considered in parallel, when analysing transnational media.

References

Aksoy, A. and K. Robins (2003) 'Banal Transnationalism: The Difference that Television Makes', in Karim H. Karim (ed.), *The Media of Diaspora* (London: Routledge).

Alibhai-Brown, Y. (2000) *After Multiculturalism* (London: Foreign Policy Centre).

Axel, B. K. (2002) 'National Interruption: Diaspora and Multiculturalism in the UK', *Cultural Dynamics*, 14(3) (London: Sage) pp. 235–56.

Brah, A. (1996) *Cartographies of Diaspora: Contesting Identities* (London: Routledge).

Braziel, J. A. and A. Mannur (eds) (2003) *Theorizing Diaspora: A Reader* (Oxford: Blackwell).

Butcher, M. (2003) *Transnational Television, Cultural Identity and Change: When STAR Came to India* (New Delhi: Sage).

Chalaby, J. (2005a) 'From Internationalization to Transnationalization', *Global Media and Communication*, Vol. 1, No. 1 (London: Sage) pp. 28–33.

Chalaby, J. (ed.) (2005b) *Transnational Television Worldwide: Towards a New Media Order* (London: I. B. Tauris).

Cohen, R. (1997) *Global Diasporas: An Introduction* (London: UCL Press).

Creeber, G. (2004) '"Hideously White": British Television, Glocalisation and National Identity', *Television and New Media*, Vol. 5, No. 1 (London: Sage) pp. 27–39.

Dudrah, R. K. (2002) 'Zee TV-Europe and the Construction of a Pan-European South Asian Identity', *Contemporary South Asia*, Vol. 11, No. 2, pp. 163–81.

Gabriel, J. (1998) *Whitewash: Racialised Politics and the Media* (London: Routledge).

Gajjala, R. (2006) 'Consuming/Producing/Inhabiting South Asian Digital-Diasporas', *New Media and Society*, Vol. 8, No. 2 (London: Sage) pp. 179–85.

Goodhart, D. (2004) 'Too Diverse? Is Britain Becoming Too Diverse to Sustain Mutual Obligations Behind a Good Society and the Welfare State', *Prospect magazine* (February).

Hall, S. (1992) 'The Question of Cultural Identity', in S. Hall, D. Held and A. McGrew (eds) *Modernity and its Futures*, (Cambridge: Polity Press) pp. 273–316.

Karim, K. H. (2003) 'Mapping Diasporic Media Landscapes' in Karim H. Karim (ed.), *The Media of Diaspora* (London: Routledge).

Karim, K. H. (ed.) (2003) *The Media of Diaspora* (London: Routledge).

Kivisto, P. (2002) *Multiculturalism in a Global Society* (Oxford: Blackwell).

Kohli, V. (2003) *The Indian Media Business* (New Delhi: Response Books).

Ninan, S. (2000) 'History of Indian Broadasting Reform' in M. Price and S. G. Verhulst (eds), *Broadcasting Reform in India: Media Law from a Global Perspective* (Oxford: Oxford University Press).

Page, D. and W. Crawley (2001) *Satellites Over South Asia: Broadcasting Culture and the Public Interest* (New Delhi: Sage).

Phillips, T. (2005) 'After 7/7: Sleepwalking to Segregation', speech at the Manchester Council for Community Relations, 22 September.

Potter, S. J. (2003) 'Communication and Integration: The British and Dominions Press and the British World, c.1876–1914', in C. Bridge and K. Fedorowich (eds), *The British World: Diaspora, Culture and Identity* (London: Frank Cass).

Rattansi, A. (2004) 'New Labour, new assimilation', http://www.opendemocracy.net/arts-multiculturalism/article_2141.jsp.

Rajagopal, A. (2001) *Politics After Television: Hindu Nationalism and the Reshaping of the Public in India* (Cambridge: Cambridge University Press)

Robins, K. and A. Aksoy (2005) 'Whoever Looks Always Finds: Transnational Viewing and Knowledge Experience' in J. Chalaby (ed.), *Transnational Television Worldwide: Towards a New Media Order* (London: I. B. Tauris).

Runneymede (2000) Trust/Commission on the 'Future of Multi-Ethnic Britain' (The Parekh Report) (London: Profile Books).

Singhal, A. and E. Rogers (2001) *India's Communication Revolution: From Bullock Carts to Cybermarts* (New Delhi: Sage).

Sinha, N. (2000) 'Doordarshan, Public Service broadcasting and the Impact of Globalization: A short history' in M. Price and S. G. Verhulst (eds), *Broadcasting Reform in India: Media Law from a Global Perspective* (Oxford: Oxford University Press).

Sivanandan, A. (1982) *A Different Hunger: Struggles for Racial Justice* (London: Pluto Press).

Thussu, D. K. (2005) 'The Transnationalization of Television: The Indian Experience' in J. Chalaby (ed.), *Transnational Television Worldwide: Towards a New Media Order* (London: I. B. Tauris).

Thussu, D. K. (1998) 'Localising the Global: Zee TV in India', in Thussu, D. K. (ed.), *Electronic Empires* (London: Arnold).

Safran, W. (1991) 'Diaspora's in modern societies: myths of homeland and return', *Diaspora*, Vol. 1, No. 1, pp. 83–99.

Vertovec, S. (1999) 'Three Meanings of "Diaspora", exemplified by South Asian Religions', *Diaspora*, Vol. 6, No. 3, pp. 277–300.

Vertovec, S. (2001) 'Transnational Challenges to the "New Multiculturalism"', paper presented to the ASA conference at University of Sussex, March.

Vertovec, S. (2001) 'Transnational Challenges to the "New Multiculturalism"', paper presented to the ASA conference at University of Sussex, March.

Virinder, S. K., R. Kaur and J. Hutnyk (2005) *Diaspora and Hybridity* (London: Sage).

3
Art in the Age of Siege

Nikos Papastergiadis

Introduction

The metaphor of flight has dominated the era of globalization. Even those who have never left home are affected by the movements of others and by the arrival of new messages. The flows of traffic in this new network have accelerated to new levels, and the directions of movement have multiplied and leapt across the well-worn paths. The movement of ideas, capital and people is faster and wilder than at any point in history. In this massive race to pass on information, to circulate symbols, to move from one place to another, no culture can exist in isolation. However, as nation-states welcome the advances of capital and new technology, paradoxically, they are fortifying their borders against migrants.

Between the fall of the Berlin wall and September 11, visions of the immediate future were dominated by images of free movement. The global hype of 'no frontiers' pumped oxygen into the old dreams of free trade as economic paradise. Commodities could arrive with minimum cost and maximum speed. However, this fantasy of uninhibited mobility hides the violence of penetrating boundaries, and imagines the world as a flat grid, in which all distances and objects can be calibrated according to a single value system.

This idealised map of global trade sits uneasily with contemporary migratory patterns and the dispersal of new communication networks. Here the fantasy of mobility discovers links but also encounters new monsters, viruses and barriers. As Saskia Sassen has argued, while a greater proportion of the economy is dematerialised and circulating within digital networks, there is also an uptake in cross-border communication initiatives in poor and marginal communities (Sassen, 2001).

However, unlike digital transactions on foreign money exchanges, or re-distributed commodity production, human movement and communication has unintended and multi-directional consequences. The cultural dynamics of globalisation challenge our existing models for explaining contemporary patterns of exchange and forms of belonging. Complexity and contradictions unwind at every point. In every moment of human communication, as in every journey, there is a process of change.

After September 11, the general fear of the unknown has itself become more mobile – and has spawned its own 'monsters': terrorists in our midst and refugees on the move. However, the horrors of terrorism do not compare to the minor burden of settling a few strangers. And yet, these two events are transposed onto the same paranoid level. Fear has become a force that is experienced viscerally, framing our suspicious glances at our neighbours, and extending into the gleeful approval of the state's use of violence.

To understand the psychic, social and political dimensions of fear we need to not only excavate its origins and measure its consequences, but also consider the way it circulates in the 'body politics'. Organization was once the driving force of modernity, enabling companies, gangs and unions to gain power and build a new kind of social order. Today the old bonds holding people together have loosened and fragmented. There is a growing fear that structures are tenuous, and that the turbulent forces driving the world are producing chaos and devastation. Fear, I will argue, grows in the metaphors of flow and containment. Its self-fuelling momentum enables it to blur its sources and consequences. Fears are now most vivid in the way we describe mobility and belonging.

Mapping mobilities

Modern power cannot control global flows largely because it has not addressed the complex patterns of mobility. The turbulence of global migration requires a new conceptual framework. Traditional frameworks assumed migration was a uni-directional movement – the migrant left one bounded space, entered another through the front gate, then slowly began acquiring rights. Since the 1970s, there has been profound change in the volume and trajectories of global mobility. The complexity of current patterns hinges on five factors:

1. More people on the move than at any point in history. Between the two world wars migrant numbers doubled. By 1965 there were

75 million migrants; in 2002 there were 175 million, of which 16 million were refugees. While migrant numbers grow, refugee figures appear to have peaked in 1993 and declined steadily since. However, these figures omit vast numbers of undocumented migrants and internally displaced people. The UNHCR estimates that 20–25 million refugees have left home without finding refuge in another country.[1]

2. Multiplicity of directions. The contemporary migrant does not necessarily 'Go West', taking a finite journey in a single direction, but traces more complex patterns, including seasonal, itinerant, recurrent and incessant movements (Zlotnik, 1998: 429–68). No one structural force, or singular set of co-ordinates, governs those movements. Labour migration now heads for both developed and developing countries. Contemporary migratory flows are multiple and turbulent.

3. Diversification of migrants. The classical sociological image of an uprooted, lonely and poor man has lost currency. The classical image of the migrant centred on the 'marginal man', a psycho-social type, and Simmel and Schutz's more ambivalent figure of the 'stranger' – an image that suggested migration could broaden cultural horizons and introduce critical perspectives. By contrast, the contemporary figure of the migrant is loaded with stigmatic associations of criminality, exploitation and desperation. In reality, migrants now include men from all classes and status groups, and growing numbers of educated women.[2]

4. Complex forms of agency and spatial affiliation. Migration is not always economically driven. The recent acknowledgement of social, cultural and political factors as active in the *whole* migration process has a dramatic impact for understandings of spatial attachment. Complex migration networks are emerging. Many diasporic communities channel their media services through satellite networks, creating complex new links and a sense of adjacency across vast distances. Mass air transportation and new communication networks have also transformed spatial relationships. Migrants often choose their destination according to personal knowledge, networks and available transport, not geographic proximities (Massey *et al.*, 1998: 12).

5. Governance of transnational flows. In 1976 only a small minority of countries had policies to lower immigration levels, while a slightly larger number aimed to raise them. By 2001 almost a quarter of all countries saw immigration levels as too high, and almost half the

developed countries sought to restrict flows by dismantling official migration recruiting agencies, limiting access to asylum claims, introducing new sanctions, detention and deportation practices, and the 'safe country of origin' and 'safe third country' principles. These measures have proven ineffective, or worse. Many legitimate refugees must now rely on illegal people trafficking networks – alongside which flourishes a sex slave trade as lucrative as the drugs and arms trades.[3] The UN High Commission for Refugees and the International Organization of Migration argue that migration is a global issue, but the nation-state circumscribes their capacity to act, and there is still no global regulative authority. This regulative void between global and local exposes refugees to criminal networks and exaggerates fears on cross-border movements.

This level of interconnection is overlooked in mainstream political discourse. Governments do not admit that the history of migration controls is a catalogue of failures, or that migration is a driving force and product of globalization. Historical evidence and economic data now demonstrate the dynamic role migrants play.[4] Yet the populist fear endures that migration threatens society, and the link is seldom made between stigma against migrants and an inherent ambivalence towards mobility in broader cultural frameworks for representing belonging.[5]

Mobility in art and culture

The political discourse on migration has become the focal point of defensive reactions against globalisation and the aggressive reassertion of cultural nationalism. For a more affirmative and critical response to issues of mobility, we must turn to the new transnational and anti-nationalist practices of contemporary artists. I will focus on some select examples that challenge the mainstream political discourse, explore the complexities of cultural difference, represent the hidden forms of contemporary violence, and propose ethical alternatives through interpretative strategies emerging from collaborative practices in specific communities.

Artists have also seized the new communicative technologies to transform modes of production and interaction with their work. While some use new technologies to create site-specific projects, others argue that neither the context of their practice, nor the meaning of their work, is necessarily bound by an exclusive locale. As new technologies foster and mediate the growth of transnational networks, other artists are creating new 'bridged' spaces, ambiguous territories that traverse, transcend and link disparate sites. However, the common desire to be globally visible or participate in transnational dialogues does not mean that all contemporary artists embrace the logic of global capital. On the contrary, they have been among the most outspoken critics of both contemporary neo-nationalism and globalization's homogenising tendencies.

The events of September 11 and the global refugee crisis have sharpened the ethical demands in cross-cultural communications, and re-defined the politics of transnational exchanges. Art cannot stand outside of these challenges. In the diverse artistic responses I will examine, we can witness strategies that oppose the border politics of exclusion, offer alternative perspectives on cultural identity and initiate a new ethical quest for community. Artists pursue these social ends by aesthetic means. The aesthetic holds attention beyond the act of interpretation, then turns this appreciation into a different form of social, ethical, political and cultural knowledge.

What sort of alternative does this knowledge produce? These examples reveal a diversity of struggles: some operate in isolation, others are interlinked by different media. They are concentrated in very specific sites, but also connected to parallel events or like-minded agents in distant locations. These collective ventures contest particular historical and political constructions, but also draw on a broader discourse of cultural exchange and human rights. We can see these flashes of resistance as individual dots that spin deeper into a terrain, or as clusters of diverse entities that work within a locale, while drawing in information, support and motivation from a broader network.

The difficult question now arising is whether all these dots and clusters are connected in a way that offers an alternative response to dominant fears. This is not necessarily answered by an empirical calculation of the sum or scope of resistance. Large-scale popular protests against the Iraq War and sporadic symbolic skirmishes over the consolidation of globalization have dented the authority of political and economic elites. But they have not spawned new ideological opposition movements, or provided a platform for a new form of leadership.

What has emerged is a complex amalgam of diverse nodes, within which like-minded agents make tactical alliances. These fragmentary pockets of interaction sporadically produce intense bursts of resistance that rise like flares, then fade into the horizon. These entities do not consolidate within formal structures, but have the dynamic of cluster. Near and distant elements form loose configurations, and throw out signs that loop into other systems. Creative juxtapositions, unstable identities, non-linear feedback – these are some features of these new clusters. The complexity of this cultural resistance is another indicator of the collapse of the ideological opposition between Western capitalism and Soviet socialism, and a marker of the decline of US geo-political hegemony. This struggle cannot be grasped in terms of two rival discourses in conflict over supremacy. Similarly, the increasing scepticism and outright hostility to US unilateralism has produced some peculiar social and political alliances. The cultural struggles evident in the artworld – in large-scale exhibitions like Documenta[6] and the Venice Biennale, major international surveys like ARS in Kiasma,[7] and even modest artist-run initiatives – are all symptomatic of this complex process of local resistance and global feedback. The energy sustaining these events cannot be explained within the old binarisms of centre versus margin, or the oppositional discourses of class struggles. The paradoxical alliances now being forged defy the classifications of conventional models of analysis.

The shock of difference

September 11 triggered a chain reaction in the American political discourse. As Judith Butler observed, rather than pausing to reflect on the trauma, there was immediate hunger for revenge and escalating steps to justify 'heightened nationalist discourse, extended surveillance mechanisms, suspended constitutional rights, and developed forms of explicit and implicit censorship' (Butler, 2004: xi). The violence of terrorism produced violent responses, including both a novel form of infinite retaliation and vigilance against anonymous enemies. Threat, we are warned, no longer takes the form of an invading army, but enters by more covert means and incites chaotic consequences. Images of warfare are now framed by terrorist networks that could be anywhere. Killing has become an invisible and irregular business (Mbembe, 2003: 30). To pursue these boundless goals and faceless enemies, America exempted itself from the full range of civil and international laws. The 'land of the free' suspended its own liberties – including, as Butler noted, the freedom of dissent. Opponents to the 'war on terror' were threatened with the charge of treason, or mocked as juvenile idealists and anachronistic obscurants blind to the fact that the 'world has changed'.

September 11 provided a stark reminder of the need to re-think the connections between art and politics. However, this task met considerable resistance in the mainstream artworld. Many critics and curators responded with disdain towards art that they perceived as either point-less activism or tedious literalism (McEvilley, 2002: 82). Perhaps the deep rifts in the international artworld were exacerbated by September 11. Cosmopolitan fantasies were challenged by ambient fears. Against this growing atmosphere of uncertainty and paranoia, numerous artists, curators and theorists sought to comprehend how art could intervene in public debates. The Australian curator/artist Mary Lou Pavlovic noted the urgency for an alternative, because the govern-ment's response was confined to 'a discourse of racism and revenge' (Pavlovic, 2003: 35). There was a renewed self-belief that art could expand our consciousness of the political and psychic dimension of tragedy.[8] The curators of *Slanting House/Statements by the Artists in Japan since 9/11* sought to go beyond the image of apocalypse and examine the deeper notion of ruin. The exhibition's title expressed both a lament for collapsing structures, and a reflection on the crisis that is not simply a relay of political messages. This redemptive task was powerfully expressed by participating artist Tadasu Yamamoto:

> We can probably assume that we entered a new century on September 11, 2001. The commencement was announced in inverted form through an overwhelmingly eschatological scene. The incident distinctly divided time into before and after. What used to be hidden became visible... What had been silently in progress some-where deep in the world suddenly emerged in an apocalyptic specta-cle. And ever since that incident, all acts of expression appear to have had a huge hole cut through by an absurd spectacle to the extent that they are so deeply wounded that they suffer a feeling of helplessness. ... Although there is no telling how certain the terror-ists were about the effect such an image would have in carrying out those attacks, it is obvious that the sight of those planes crashing into the WTC and other buildings proved far stronger a weapon that a patriot missile, cluster bomb and daisy-cutter. People all over the world were attacked by the sight of those attacks broadcasted on television. I intend to convert the image shot into me into an artwork and throw it back to the world together with a premonition of catastrophe (Yamamoto, 2003: 93).

For curator/theorist Okwui Enwezor, the image of Ground Zero pro-vided an even broader metaphor for recognising the crisis of globaliza-tion. He argued that the old 'dead certainties' of East versus West, and

Bush's cowboy rhetoric, would only inflame further violence. For Enwezor, September 11 marked a moment of critical transformation: the problems of modernity were brought 'home'. Tensions previously relegated to the margin were now being played out in the centre (Enwezor, 2002: 47). This profound challenge requires us to recognise that both political forces and cultural identities are caught in turbulent patterns of interconnection and displacement. As people move across boundaries, they bring different ideas and values. Interactions may commence along old pathways, but quickly bifurcate and develop within new networks.

Critical responses to these issues are now being driven from within the cultural domain. These contradictions and tensions in the deterritorialisation of cultures and people demand new theories of flow and resistance. There is an urgent need for a new vocabulary in art discourse to make sense of the complex forms of representation now emerging in the world – forms that incorporate images from different locations, and activate multiple signs, each embodying contrary or competing codes. Artists have set out to find new ways to explore mobility and attachment, and create new perspectives on both the refugee crisis and the war on terror. In these practices we can witness both a loss of faith in the official political discourses, and an exploration of different modalities for expressing hope and developing ethical relations with others.

Artists in opposition to border politics

In times of crisis and conflict, artists are among the first to protest against authoritarian tendencies and propose alternative ways for relating to social issues. In Australia, for instance, artists quickly showed their solidarity with the asylum seekers in the wake of the *Tampa* crisis.[9]

The government's response to the *Tampa*'s arrival signalled a shift in public values and attitudes toward refugees.[10] There was no public debate about the causes, volume and trajectories of global migration – instead, there was a vilification campaign against refugees, fuelled by rumours of a possible 'flood' and devastation of the 'lucky country'.

After whipping up hysteria over a coming invasion, Australian political leaders switched our immigration and asylum policies from being some of the world's most benign, to being global standard-bearers on violent exclusion and deterrence. Military and intelligence agencies were mobilised to intercept and destroy 'people smuggler chains', prevent refugees from landing and forcibly repatriate them. The state excised remote islands from national migration laws, enforced the mandatory detention of all refugees, and exempted detention centres from civil codes. Children born in detention are denied citizenship. Even refugees eventually deemed legitimate after years of waiting are merely issued with a temporary protection visa, a marker of anxious limbo. If the state deems they are no longer at risk of persecution in their homeland, whole families can be repatriated without consent.

The cultural and social opposition to Australia's refugee policies has been loud and varied. Church leaders, anarchists, public intellectuals, student activists, senior statesmen, the judiciary and leading health and welfare representatives have raised their voices in protest.[11] They have demanded that this crude and cruel exclusion mechanism should be dismantled, because it fails to deter new arrivals, creates profound harm and is based on an exaggerated fear of invasion. The horror of the system is an open secret, and its persistence is seen as a humanitarian scandal.

While the two major Australian parties do not differ on refugee policies, border politics has divided the nation. The media has used attitudes towards refugees as indicators of the depth of our internal values and perspective onto the outside world. The 'moral majority' is clearly opposed, but a larger electoral majority favours this use of violence. In one national survey 68 per cent of respondents agreed that 'refugees should be put back to sea'. The representation of a moral position is split from the construction of violence as an expedient political force.

One prominent artistic response to the refugee crisis was Juan Davila's *Woomera*, 2002, a series of paintings and drawings depicting the asylum seeker's plight through the frontier myths of Australia's colonial history. While the government actively prevented the media from interviewing and photographing the asylum seekers, to block them from public consciousness, Davila deliberately depicts their struggle as part of the national mythology. He stages the drama of detention camps against the background of the outback. To intensify the parallels between Aboriginal displacement, colonial settlement and contemporary migration he portrays the 'monstrous' figure of the refugee in the physiognomy of the dominant race.

In the painting *Detention Place* (2002), two figures dominate a desolate, turbulent and parched landscape. At the centre a middle-aged man is kneeling – perhaps as a sign of penance, or in stunned exhaustion. Behind him is the glow of an industrial city. The atmosphere is dominated by whirling remorseless skies and a wind that has stripped the trees of vegetation. In the foreground is a strong, beautiful and naked woman. There are signs of blood smeared on her arms and thighs. She holds the shutter cable for a camera that faces the viewer. The image of violence, turned awry, points only to the outsider: the one not inside the camp.

Almost three years after this painting was completed, a story emerged of the incarceration of a former Qantas airline crewmember in an Australian immigration detention centre. Cornelia Rau, a German-born Australian citizen, suffered a mental breakdown and became delusional over her origins. Convinced that she was ill, the northern Queensland Aborigines who found her delivered her to the police. She was detained along with the other 'illegals'. After ten months of searching, her family found her in tatters. She was eating dirt, refusing to wear clothes and did not recognise her own sister. The story sparked a national scandal: on the basis of her 'foreign', uncooperative and clearly schizoid testimony, the Australian government had falsely imprisoned one of its own citizens, and made numerous efforts to deport her to Germany. One commentator noted that this ordeal gripped national attention and provoked unparalleled protest against the detention system – but only when it was revealed that, like the figure in Davila's painting, she turned out to be one of us (Marr, 2005: 27).

In Mike Parr's performance *Close the Concentration Camps* (2002), the artist sewed his lips and eyelids together, as a gesture of solidarity with the refugees and an attempt to expose the inhumanity of a system the Australian government was shielding from public view. Before the performance, art critic David Bromfield dismissed the idea as 'false realism' and questioned the vicarious motivation. Writing to Parr, he remarked: 'We both know that it is no good simply becoming a glorified stand-in for a camp inmate' (Geczy, 2003: 45). Parr replied that doing something 'bad' might have a greater social effect. Before the performance Parr underwent a rigorous preparation involving fasting and sleep deprivation, seeking to 'violently split off whole zones of my body', and perhaps mimic the state of bodily objectification implicit in the trauma of self-mutilation.

Parr's re-naming of government detention centres as 'concentration camps', and his imperative to close them, were both a political pro-test and an act of symbolic shifting, catapulting the seemingly sterile discourse of detention into the history of state barbarism. He deliber-ately challenged the state's terminology, which evoked a false bene-volence and concealed its own violence. Suspended in the hell of 'concentration camps', isolated from the outside world, many desperate individuals committed acts of self-harm, stitching shut their eyes and mouths with crude instruments and coarse string. The government dismissed this gesture as moral blackmail. Parr's performance didn't catch the public imagination like the 'real story of Cornelia Rau', but those who paused to reflect saw he had used his body as a metaphor for the disfiguration of civic space.

Alongside these individual works were numerous collective responses to Australia's 'refugee crisis'. The exhibition *Borderpanic* was a powerful guerrilla-styled response. In Hossein Valamanesh's arresting photographic installation *Longing Belonging*, the absence of a preposition in the work's title launches these two terms into orbit: drawn to each other, but separated by an invisible, perhaps unbridgeable distance. This work represents neither the exile's nostalgic longing for belonging, nor the citizen's slothful belonging in longing. The photograph shows a clearing in the bush, a Persian carpet hovering magically just above the ground, and a campfire that seems drawn by the carpet's uplift. Is this an unhomely arrival, or the co-existence of two types of landing in a strange landscape?

These tense juxtapositions between place and meaning are echoed in *Legislation Affecting Aliens 1895*, a collage by Vivienne Dadour. This work combines images from the artist's own family history, archival family wedding photographs, a small gathering of people squatting together, an early Christian building and an historical document declaring that Chinese and Syrian people should be excluded from Australia because they carry unwanted parasites and intransigent customs, posing biological and cultural risks to the integrity of the yet-unformed nation. The racist texts are juxtaposed against images of community and hospitality. At the centre is the peculiarly inviting gaze and gesture of a man looking up, which immediately focuses the viewer's attention and offers 'us' the position of guest in his scene. It is an ancient, unequivocal invitation to share in food and drink, the arms open to embrace and receive. This gesture moves beyond the photographer into the future of the unknown viewer. Generosity is declared, despite the subject not knowing who is on the other side of the photograph, and it prefigures similar gestures made across the wire by refugees in Woomera: 'Tell them we are human, we are not animals'.[12]

Carlos Capelan's sculpture *My House Is Your House* (2005) is a stark reminder that hospitality is not unlimited hotel service. Capelan's installations have repeatedly used the chair and a glass of water as a symbol of the minimum offering we can make to strangers. As part of his exhibition *Only You*, at the National Gallery of Uruguay, he tied two stakes to the legs and back of an old fold-up chair. These prosthetic legs transform the chair so it resembles a tent frame, but the sculpture also carries the more sinister echo of a body thrust rigid by shock treatment. The invitation to share a house is a precarious gesture, for it splices the guest's acceptance onto the host's tensions.

Jacques Derrida has stressed that hospitality, unlike charity or other forms of investment, is made without any expectation of return. The 'gift of hospitality' is not offered with any expectation of gaining economic security or social status. 'Let us say yes to who or what turns up, before any determination, before any anticipation, before any identification' (Derrida, 2000: 77). However, such an open-ended 'gift' can never find a place within legal or political structures. As Derrida argues, the gift is also held together with strings. An unconditional welcome, a concept that he concedes is practically inaccessible, is also posed against its opposite, the imperative of sovereignty. The right to mobility must be positioned alongside the host's right to authority over their own home. 'No hospitality, in the classic sense, without sovereignty of oneself over one's home, but since there is also no hospitality without finitude, sovereignty can only be exercised by filtering, choosing, and thus by excluding and doing violence' (Derrida, 2000: 55).

When two rights are posed as both legitimate and incommensurable, the task of negotiation becomes urgent. The competing rights are unrankable. You cannot decide by putting one above the other. To betray hospitality in order to secure sovereignty is a moral loss. To denounce sovereignty for total hospitality is a political catastrophe. In this conundrum, relativism is no help. Decisions must made, and as curators Maria Hlavajova and Gerardo Mosquera argued, by virtue of its 'dialogic concept', art can play a vital role in participating in, rather than merely observing, the conduct and content of these debates (Hlavajova and Mosquera, 2004). Artists in exhibitions like *Cordially Invited* and *Borderpanic* have used the spaces of art not only as a tool for public discourse, but as stages to reinterpret the boundary between sovereignty and hospitality. No nation can ever totally open its borders, but the current hostility towards refugees signals a deeper ambivalence towards our own sense of place, and the repression of exilic narratives from the national imaginary. This 'unknown history' is excavated by photo-monteur Peter Lyssiotis in his *The Great Wall of Australia*, a fictional documentation of a timber and brick fence stretching across the infinite suburbia of Southern Australia. Lyssiotis probes the smug, self-contained architecture of suburban life, while linking this to paranoid fantasies of border control. In contrast with the Arabic mythology of paradise as a walled garden, Lyssiotis represent suburban garden walls as a block out. The wall limits topographic associations, excludes the ghosts that an indigenous artist like Darren Siwes would summon from the land, and protects the fragile forms of homely affection. The wall becomes a metaphor of our insecurity.

Artists as border shifters

Between the USA and Mexico is a real Great Wall: the place where the two Americas meet and one bleeds. For decades, migrants have been slipping between the gaps of the wall, or going beneath it and travelling in the sewers. Others cross the sea on leaking boats, and even inflatable toys. The border between Tijuana and San Diego is a place of intense violence and creativity. During the 1980s the artist collective *Border Arts Workshop* mimicked and celebrated the hybrid imagination of the itinerant border crossers. Perched on the Tijuana hills were illegal Mexican radio stations that declared themselves 'border busters', beaming their own blend of music that formed a bridge across Chicano-California. The artist collectives shared this energy – which they defined as a 'formal and intellectual hybridism' – and set out to show that even the most fortified zone can be penetrated, and that ultimately cultural survival requires circulation and exchange (Grynstejn, 1993: 23–58).

However, a decade later, the optimism of border crossing and vitalism of cross-cultural exchange is supplanted by a far more despairing vision of the journey. There are more guards on the border. On one side are those who live – but, as revealed in Chantal Ackerman's multi-screen installation 'From the Other Side', (2002) at Documenta XI, there are those who dream of leaving, but face a road of death and disillusionment. The installation is structured around the countless stories of migrants who seek to cross the frontier but fail, and by the silence of those who disappear. Alongside video footage of guards pursuing migrants with helicopters and night vision cameras, Ackerman recorded the stories of those who crossed and returned from the other side. The survivors' voice is not one of conquest, but of guilty solitude. It contrasts the heroic stories of proud migrants who see the border-crossing journey as the decisive turning point, at which one makes something of one's life. The border is represented as an irresistible yet fatal encounter. Before the border are slogans warning 'stay out and stay alive'; closer by are shrill pitch police alarms; and on the 'other side' is the monstrous portrayal of 'wetbacks' on Californian road signs – a man running and a mother pulling her child in flight.

Driving from Los Angeles to San Diego, the Thai curator Apinan Poshynanada contemplated the meaning of this monstrous sign. After considering the various imperatives of vigilance and courtesy he mused on a more revealing possibility: the sign mirrors America's desperate past. 'These illegal travellers might escape the authorities to become sojourners and settlers in communities where their status would change to that of housemaids, waiters, teachers, labourers, bartenders, masseurs, chauffeurs, security guards, robbers. ... Their status one day might be that of American citizens, later driving on that same LA–San Diego motorway to see the signs of their past' (Poshynanda, 2004: 182).

Artists often identify new trends long before they are articulated in mainstream debates. In a prescient video installation for ARS 01, '3-minute survival attempt' (2000), Anna Jermolaewa simulated both the destabilizing effects of conflict, and the anxiety over the faceless aggressor. The social order's fragile balance is played out through interacting toys shaped like pendulum figures. Accompanied by an ominous soundtrack of jackboots, one piece suddenly falls onto another, precipitating a cascading effect. As the pieces tumble and fall in a multitude of directions, the only certainty is that disaster is imminent. Each toy is uniform in shape, and at first appears stable, but their movement leads towards a chaotic fall. The displacement effect is compounded by another unseen force that creates a swirling motion. The toys spin and fall into a vortex. Eventually even the surface tilts and everything falls off the edge. But the aggressor who precipitated the fall is never shown.

Documenta XI included several collaborative projects and installations that worked with the thesis that power is as evident in the new mechanisms for controlling flows as it is in the occupation of territory. Michael Hardt and Antonio Negri have argued that in the networked and globalised world, sovereign power takes a deterritorialised form, and is increasingly defined in the ability to regulate movement and exclude rivals (Hardt and Negri, 2000: xv). 'Multiplicity', an Italian-based collective of artists, architects and activists, presented an installation, *Solid Sea* (2001) on the 'ghost ship' that sank off the coast of Sicily in 1996. A handful of survivors tried to convince authorities of the tragedy in their waters, but the incident was ignored until fisherman discovered bodies in their nets and the identity papers of the dead began to wash ashore. 'Multiplicity' then began its own investigations. By examining Italian Navy surveillance records, and metereological department satellite footage, they demonstrated that the State had callously turned a blind eye to drowning refugees. At one level, this act of exclusion confirmed Etienne Balibar's prediction, made almost a decade earlier, that after the Berlin Wall collapsed, 'fortress Europe' would erect a new invisible wall in the Mediterranean to exclude the South. At another level, it was an index of the way social life is dominated by 'borders, walls, fences, thresholds, signposted areas, security systems, check points, virtual frontiers, specialised zones, protected areas and areas under control' (Multiplicity, 2005: 173). This proliferation of 'border devices' has not merely extended the function of sub-division, but also shattered the utopian dream of an urbane conviviality based on the co-existence of cultural differences.

Politicians are now increasingly caught in a negative competition: who will flex the biggest authoritarian muscle by exerting the greatest ever 'crackdown' on migrants. While seeking to bolster a flagging sense of sovereignty, this 'crackdown' also re-draws the boundaries of social responsibility. Artist projects like *Solid Sea* refuse to accept the declaration that refugees in international waters are in no-mansland. They prefaced the work with the caption: 'An Italian community in Tunisia, an African community in Sicily. The fishing activities in the Strait of Sicily have blurred the border between the two continents: each population can see its counterpart reflected as in a mirror. One landscape crossed by 150 miles of solid sea.' The project's title, *Solid Sea*, refers to the blockage of an historical process, and the fluid networks that previously enabled coastal Mediterranean populations to share the view that they possess a common sea. Today this space is fraught with tension and striated by exclusive zones that regulate mercantile flows, and national boundaries are patrolled with heightened military vigilance. The common sea is now channelled into separate zones for immigrants, tourists, fishermen and soldiers.

As refugees attempt to leave one place and enter another, they enter a bridged space that includes both places. This ambiguous bridge does not sit comfortably within the ever-narrowing administrative categories of civic entitlement, and is being increasingly weakened by the undermining of international human rights laws. Globalization collapses old distances as it produces new intimacies, compels new platforms of convergence but also bypasses obsolete stations. Yet for all the experimentation between internal and external forces, there is an increasing effort to regulate flows into the antagonistic logic of capital and exclusive categories of cultural identity.

Waiting for the Barbarians

Just over a hundred years ago Constantine Cavafy wrote the poem 'Waiting for the Barbarians'. Cavafy received a classical education in England and lived in the cosmopolitan merchant quarters of Alexandria. He may have had some premonition of the expulsion of foreigners, but was deeply aware of the general sense of unease in the city. In ancient Greece the mark of the barbarian was linguistic. Greeks considered their language to be the only sign of a civilised human. All other tongues were indistinguishable: mere sounds, to their ears no different from the bar-bar-bar bleating noises of animals. Of course, barbarians could be admitted inside, once they learned to speak Greek. Nevertheless, the barbarians that remained outside were always something to be feared. How could you negotiate without language? What do they want? If not to destroy our precious civilization, their aim must be to exploit our goodwill? Cavafy describes the foreboding that precedes an invasion, revealing how internal fears are spread by rumour, provoking panic and a dread of devastation. In this state of alert, the city braces itself for the worst. However, he does not end his poem with an apocalypse. On the contrary, there is an ironic twist:

> Why are the streets and squares emptying so rapidly
> everyone going home lost in thought?
> Because night has fallen and the barbarians haven't come.
> And some of our men just in from the border say
> there are no barbarians any longer.
> Now what's going to happen to us without barbarians?
> They were, those people, a kind of solution.
>
> (Cavafy, 1984: 5)

The people had come together for defence, ready for a fight. But then, after all the waiting, nothing happens: neither conquest nor defeat. Cavafy does not follow this realization with the exhalation of relief: he intimates that something else has occurred. The city had become dependent on the barbarians – if not addicted to the fear they inspire, at least affirmed by the desperate stance of defensive hostility. The barbarians had served a purpose. They helped bring a focus into the city. By closing up the city, needs could be simplified, loyalties resolved and identities separated. 'Those people' were indeed 'a kind of solution'. The barbarian could be seen as a mirror of the internal fears. We need them to see ourselves. However, this narcissism is also a form of self-seduction. Waiting for the barbarians we created a mirror that not only reflects our fears, but also deflects a deeper encounter with the hate in our self. In this state of defensive preparedness, there is already a justification of violence towards the other. With the barbarians outside, it is convenient to avoid asking the question: is the barbarian already inside us?

In the context of refugees and global terror, it is both easier and harder to see power as multi-directional. The ambient fears of global terror suggest that the faceless terrorist could be anywhere. However, while we realise refugees also utilise complex information networks and transportation systems, we still tend to think of them as passive victims caught up in persecution and exploitation. They are stuck in a no-mans-land. Dropped into a lawless void, blocked from returning home by fear of persecution. When there is a sympathetic image of the refugee, it is no longer an image of the homeless drifter, but a trapped person, unable to move forward or back. The image of refugees held in detention, cowed by heavily armed guards, their movements recorded by elaborate surveillance technologies, confirms that the state is in control. The reality is more complex. The refugee knows of the state's power to exclude, but also maintains faith in his or her capacity to gain entry.

After September 11, the violent impact of the hijacked planes and the repeated screenings of their explosive consequences did little to undo US hegemony – but it produced an audacious image of the 'implacable hatred' of its enemies and an equally perplexing revelation of vulnerability. A vertical city accommodating over 150,000 daily workers and visitors was reduced to a few tortured girders and a pile of smouldering rubble. Most subsequent commentaries and editorials claimed these events marked a 'clash of civilizations': a dreadful illustration of the perversity of tyranny and the precariousness of contemporary life. However, the violent clash had nothing to do with civilization. When civilizations encounter difference they do not clash, but search out new avenues for dialogue and negotiation.

In this era of rising neo-nationalism and creeping fear, the ethical challenge for art lies in contesting this oppositional discourse of 'clashing civilisations' and seeking more affirmative modes of aesthetic and critical engagement with issues of mobility, cultural difference and belonging. Art must face the question: in waiting for the barbarians, what do we sacrifice? What is the true cost of this hyper-vigilance and suspicion – and what are the alternative responses? In the context of global complexity, artists are approaching this project by various means: through collaborative practices sited in specific locales, via the technology-mediated clustering of like-minded but diverse agents across distant locations, and in the weaving of broader cross-cultural communities and networks between these local dots and transnational clusters. These new alliances are by nature fragmentary, ephemeral and loose, often operating beyond or on the margins of institutions and in opposition to formal structures. These flashes of creative resistance do not offer simple or even unified solutions. But within this complex system of local resistance and global feedback, we can glimpse the potential for new discourses of hope.

Notes

1. The US has the highest number of immigrants, but the heaviest percentage of migrants and refugees arrive in select parts of Africa, Pakistan and Iran, and overall most migrants live in the South (*International Migration Report*, 2002).
2. In the Philippines, the second largest 'exporter of labour in the world', women migrants vastly exceed the men, and their remittances have prevented the national economy from total collapse. (S. Go, 1998: 147).
3. As one pimp boasted, drugs and guns can only be sold once (Pope, 1997: 38). There are no uniform international laws against the trafficking of women by prostitution rings. A recent international trafficking report estimated that between 800,000 to 900,000 people are forcibly moved across borders every year (*Migration News*, 2003: 34).
4. In the USA, there is a historical correlation between trade growth and immigration, and a correlation between recent immigration restrictions and the USA's declining international trade rates (Massey and Taylor, 2004: 377). British migrants earn an estimated 15 per cent more than their native-born counterparts, contribute more to government revenue, and are less reliant on welfare and state support (Sriskandarajak *et al.*).
5. As an introduction to the range of accounts of how fear has been manipulated in contemporary politics, see Mamdani, (2004), Roy, (2004) and Lapham, (2005).
6. Documenta is a major international art exhibition held every five years in Kassel, Germany.
7. ARS Kiasma is another major international art exhibition, run by Kiasma Museum of Contemporary Art in Helsinki.
8. For example, the exhibitions *Fallout* and *Slanting House*; for a record of public art interventions in New York, see *Quaderns* (2002).
9. In August 2001 the *Tampa*, a Norwegian container ship, rescued 433 refugees from a sinking Indonesian fishing boat and headed for the nearest port, in the Australian territory of Christmas Island. This conventional maritime rescue triggered an international crisis: the Australian, Norwegian and Indonesian governments refused to accept the refugees, and the ship was ordered not to enter Australian waters. A violent response unfolded, involv-

ing military interception, the re-drawing of Australia's borders, the mandatory incarceration of refugees, an aggressive backlash against humanitarian refugee policies, and the so-called 'Pacific Solution' – the forced incarceration of refugees in purpose-built detention centres in countries such as Papua New Guinea and Nauru.

10. I use the term 'refugee' to bridge over the quasi-legal and moralistic distinctions between different kinds of asylum seekers. I have also used the term 'migrant' in a generic way, because I believe that the distinctions promoted in the popular discourse have a spurious conceptual basis, and often conveniently reduce complex forms of connection to, and complicity with, the forces that compel people to move. The new vocabulary of 'qualified' types of migrant and asylum seeker reflects a need to categorise people and promote a false sense of order and control.

11. Notable examples include Archbishop Peter Carnley, Governor General Sir William Deane, and the former Prime Ministers Bob Hawke and Malcolm Fraser.

12. Reported in the tactical media lab held at the Museum of Contemporary Art, Sydney, to coincide with the exhibition *Borderpanic* at Performance Space, September 2002 (www.borderpanic.org).

References

Borderpanic, Performance Space, September (London: www.borderpanic.org).

Butler, J. (2004) *Precarious Life* (London: Verso).

Cavafy, C. P. (1984) 'Waiting for the Barbarians', *Collected Poems*, transl. E. Keeley and P. Sherrard, ed. George Savidis (London: The Hogarth Press).

Derrida, J. (2000) *Of Hospitality*, transl. Rachel Bowlby (Stanford: Stanford University Press).

Enwezor, O. (2002) 'The Black Box', *Documenta XI*, Catalogue (Kassel: Hatje Cantz Publishers)

Fallout (2001) VCA Gallery, Melbourne, 13–20 December.

Geczy, A. (2003) 'Focussing the Mind through the Body: an interview with Mike Parr', *Artlink*, Vol. 23, No. 1.

Go, S. (1998) 'The Philippines: a Look into the Migration Scenario in the Nineties', *Migration and Regional Economic Integration in Asia*, Organization for Economic Cooperation and Development, Paris.

Grynstejn, M. (1993) 'La Frontera/The Border: Art About the Mexico/US Experience', in *La Frontera/The Border: Art about the Mexico/US Experience*, exhibition catalogue, (San Diego Museum of Contemporary Art).

Hardt, M. and A. Negri (2000) *Empire* (Cambridge, Mass.: Harvard University Press).

Hlavajova, M. and G. Mosquera (curators) (2004) *Cordially Invited*, BAK, Utrecht, October.

Lapham, L. (2005) *Gag Rule: On Suppression of Dissent and the Stifling of Democracy* (New York: Penguin).

Mamdani, M. (2004) *Good Muslims, Bad Muslims* (New York: Pantheon).

Marr, D. (2005) 'Odyssey of a Lost Soul', *Sydney Morning Herald*, 12 February.

Massey, D. *et al.* (1998) *Worlds in Motion* (Oxford: Clarendon Press).

Massey, D. and J. E. Taylor (2004) *International Migration* (Oxford: Oxford University Press).

Mbembe, A. (2003) 'Necropolitics', *Public Culture*, Vol. 15, No. 1.

McEvilley, T. (2002) 'Documenta 11', *Frieze*, Issue 69, September.

Migration News (2003) 'Global Trends', Vol. 10, No. 3, July.

Mosquera, G. and M. Hlavajova (curators) (2004) *Cordially Invited*, BAK, Utrecht, October.

Multiplicity, (2005) 'Borders: the other side of globalization', *Empires, Ruins and Networks*, (eds), Scott McQuire and Nikos Papastergiadis (Melbourne: Melbourne University Press).

Parr, M. (2002) *Close the Concentration Camps*, performed at Monash University Museum of Art, Melbourne, 15 June.

Pavlovic, M. L. (2003) 'Fallout', curator's statement, *Artlink*, Vol. 23, No. 1.

Population Division, (2002) Department of Economic and Social Affairs, UN *International Migration Report* (New York: United Nations).

Poshynanda, A. (2004) 'Desperately Diasporic', in Gerardo Mosquera and Jean Fisher (eds), *Over Here: International Perspectives on Art and Culture* (Cambridge, Mass.: MIT Press).

Pope, V. (1997) 'Trafficking in Women', *US News & World Report*, 7 April.

Quaderns: New York Notebook (2002) No 232, Barcelona, January.

Roy, A. (2004) *Public Power in the Age of Empire* (New York: Seven Stories Press).

Sassen, S. (2001) *The Global City* (rev. edn) (Princeton: Princeton University Press).

Slanting House (2002) Museum of Contemporary Art, Tokyo, November.

Sriskandarajak, D., L. Cooley and H. Reed 'Paying their Way: the Fiscal Contribution of Immigrants' (London: www.ippr.org).

Yamamoto, T. (2002) *Slanting House/Statements by the Artists in Japan Since 9/11*, curated by Michiko Kasahara (Museum of Contemporary Art, Tokyo), and Miwako Takasuna (Saison Art Program), Tokyo.

Zlotnik, H. (1998) 'International Migration 1965–96: An Overview', *Population and Development Review*.

4
Re-Imagining Diaspora Through Ethno-Mimesis: Humiliation, Human Dignity and Belonging

Maggie O'Neill

> Here abroad nothing is left, we have been catapulted out of history, which is always the history of a specific area of the map, and we have to cope with, to use an expression of an exile writer, 'the unbearable lightness of being'.
>
> (Czeslaw Milosz 1988: 1–3)

Introduction

This chapter builds upon the author's work on renewed methodologies for conducting ethnographic research with asylum seekers and refugee groups in the UK and explores the political implications of 'ethno-mimesis' as critical theory in practice. Concepts of 'diaspora', 'humiliation' and 'dignity' will be problematised and explored through the analysis of hybrid texts (art forms) produced by refugees and asylum seekers in the inter-relation/inter-textuality between art and ethnography – as ethno-mimesis. The author's concept of 'ethno-mimesis' is defined in this chapter through a combination of participatory action research (PAR)[1] and participatory arts informed by the work of Adorno and Benjamin. Ethno-mimesis draws upon 'feeling forms' such as photographic art, performance art and life story narratives, and engages dialectically with lived experience through critical interpretation, towards social change. Ethno-mimesis as critical theory in praxis seeks to counter negative stereotypes in the public imagination and facilitate the production of refugee and asylum seekers self re-presentations of lived experiences through visual and biographical texts that speak of the utter complexity of lived relations through 'feeling forms' as 'sensuous knowing'.

'Diaspora' is re-imagined within the context of the current law in the UK, the asylum-migration nexus, and new labour 'governance' on this issue especially discourses of public participation and inclusion. Concepts of 'humiliation' 'belonging' and 'identity' are examined both theoretically and experientially through ethnographic accounts and ethno-mimetic texts.

This chapter argues that the articulation of identity and belonging for those situated in the tension that is the asylum-migration nexus[2] can helpfully be understood within the context of: (a) renewed methodologies for social research that are participatory, interpretive and action oriented; (b) a deep understanding of the economic and political relations of humiliation, inclusion and exclusion that includes the role of the mass media (print and broadcast); (c) and the related issue of governance at national, European and international level. The focus for the work discussed here is research undertaken by the author with Bosnian and Afghan refugee communities in the UK and new arrivals (asylum seekers and economic migrants from various countries) to the East Midlands between 1999 and 2002.

At the centre of this work is the importance of renewing methodologies in the process of re-imagining diaspora especially within the context of the asylum-migration nexus, globalisation, analyses of human rights and the impact of humiliation (Linder 2004).

Re-imagining diaspora: the asylum–migration nexus

Stephen Castles (2003) and Zygmunt Bauman (1998) both focus theoretical attention on the global dimensions of forced and economic migration. 'Migration in general and forced migration in particular are amongst the most important social expressions of global connections and processes' (Castles 2003: 17). Bauman quoted in Castles (2003: 16) adds: '"mobility has become the most powerful and the most coveted stratifying factor ... the riches are global the misery local"'.

Analyses of the asylum-migration nexus should necessarily acknowledge the wider global and political context in which mobility and migration (both inward and outward) take place. What is very clear, even in the most rudimentary exploration of the literature, is that migration, particularly in the context of globalisation, is on the increase; as is the emergence of transnational identities.[3]

Marfleet (2006) urges us to think about transnational communities in relation to 'circuits of migration' and diasporas (scatterings) as 'networked communities.' Within the context of migration research he argues that three developments have been crucial to the growth of transnational communities. First, changes in new technologies of mass transport (international tourism, mass air transport); second, changes in the means of communication (virtual communication, satellite, internet and cyber environment), and finally 'the generalisation worldwide of ideas about human entitlement' or human rights that 'require new frameworks of understanding' (Marfleet 2006: 216). Moreover, one dimensional analyses focusing upon push–pull factors in relation to economic need and the demands of the market are now too limited and linear. The complex movements of migrants involves undertaking multiple journeys 'which may involve repeat, shuttle, orbital, ricochet and yo-yo migrations' in attempts at settlement and return (Marfleet 2006: 216).

A number of key themes emerge when exploring the asylum-migration nexus, not least of which is what Castles describes as the complexity of this 'transnational and inter-disciplinary undertaking' that include analyses of globalisation, legislation, policy and border controls, processes and practices of settlement and belonging, the development of transnational communities.

Castles (2003) outlines the foundations for a sociology of forced migration, as a development of his work in this area over a number of years. He suggests a shift in focus from a sociology of the nation-state to a transnational sociology, arguing also for a renewal of social theory 'taking as its starting point the global transformations occurring at the dawn of the 21st century. The key issue is transnational connectedness and the way this affects national societies, local communities and individuals' (Castles 2003: 24). Castles urges us to examine networks and global flows as the key frameworks for social relations 'in which "global cities" with dualistic economies form the key nodes' (p. 27) and transnational communities are the focus 'for social and cultural identity for both economic and forced migrants' (p. 27). Castles suggests integrating various levels of analysis into a new global political economy from local ethnographic to global political economy including dynamics of mobility, settlement, community and identity. Moreover, methodologically the underlying principles should take into account interdisciplinarity, historical understanding, comparative analysis, transnational social transformation, local, regional and national patterns of social and cultural relations, human agency *and* the need for participatory methods.

The remainder of this chapter takes up Castle's suggestion of integrating the ethnographic with the political aspects of sociology of forced migration. This is achieved by exploring the concepts of 'diaspora', 'humiliation' and 'belonging' as well as a methodological approach to research that incorporates participatory action research and participatory arts; the inter-relation/inter-textuality between art and ethnography as *ethno-mimesis*, as critical theory in practice.

Diasporic identities: humiliation, identity, and belonging

Today militancy in the Middle East is fuelled ... by a pervasive sense of humiliation and helplessness in the region. This collective feeling is driven by a sense that people remain helpless in affecting the most vital aspects of their lives, and it is exacerbated by pictures of Palestinian humiliation (Shibley Telhami [2002] quoted in Lindner 2004: 28)

The opening up of communications and travel, global connections and processes alongside the erosion of national boundaries and cross border flows make understanding processes and practices of globalisation crucial to analysis of the migration-asylum nexus. Moreover, forced migration is 'not the result of a string of un-connected emergencies but an integral part of North-South relations' (Castles 2003: 9). Forms of expression emerge from global inequalities, societal crisis and social transformations in the South, as well as what Marfleet calls 'the impact of the entire migratory framework' upon our understanding of community beyond the boundaries of space, place and the nation state. 'New networks themselves play a role in shaping global movements, drawing in and re-circulating migrants as part of a process of flux and flow' (Marfleet 2006: 218).

Kushner and Knox (1999) write that the identity of the label 'refugee' can be both a source of pride and shame. As 'outsiders' asylum seekers and refugees as 'others' cope with 'scapegoating' and 'othering' within the context of dis-location and attempts at re-location. 'Catapulted out of history' (Milosz 1988) it is very difficult to feel at 'home' in the new environment. Finding new rhythms in time and space, quelling the anxiety of the unfamiliar and the loss of orientation takes time. Drucilla Cornell drawing on Stuart Hall's work describes cultural identity as a matter of 'becoming' as well as 'being' belonging to the future as much as to the past and subject to the continuous play of history, power, culture. She tells us:

far from being grounded in mere recovery of the past, which is waiting to be found and will secure our sense of ourselves in eternity, identities are the names we give to the different ways we are positioned by, and position ourselves within the narratives of the past (2000: 55).

In the following narrative, (an excerpt from an interview conducted in 2000[4]) Leyla's experiences of humiliation, loss of dignity and respect are wrapped up in the experiences of forced migration, dislocation and the temporary nature of being an asylum seeker in the UK.

Leyla's brother was killed and she was forced to flee because of a well founded fear of persecution that included possible death at the hands of the authorities. She arrived in Britain using a visa and claimed asylum when the visa expired. She was dispersed to a city outside of London.

> They didn't explain anything that night. That night they decide to take us to X from X. That night they just took us in the bus and then we didn't know where we had to go and then we arrived to X. ... It was the middle, midday and then we arrived about night-time. There were people from somewhere else they dropped them from other towns and places. The one important thing is that the main thing is that they didn't explain us where we had to go. ... And then they separate everybody and we just see women left because they, our names weren't on the list, our names weren't on the list and other people they had accommodation ... we are speaking very little English and then I ask them why, where I am going for. And I tried to hit the person because my temperature was over and then I called my sister on the phone ... I forced a person to call my sister to communicate ...

She describes being very scared and humiliated by this experience. Her asylum claim took one and a half years to be processed and her application was refused. She appealed against the decision and at the time of the interview was awaiting news of the appeal. During this time she tried to kill herself twice. In her home country Leyla was a journalist writing for a Kurdish women's newspaper. She said:

> We are scared to go back to our country ... can we stay or not and psychologically we are under pressure on this because we don't know what our future will be ... we don't know what will happen to us.

A concept that is becoming a key focus in interdisciplinary research related to the asylum-migration nexus is *humiliation*. A global network, founded by Evelin Lindner, has emerged around the need to address, understand and move beyond the experiences of humiliation, non recognition and lack of respect through transformative social action underpinned by the need for human dignity globally and locally. For Lindner (2004) there has been a shift (*we could call it from modernity to late modernity or postmodernity*) in global relations, 'from a world steeped in Honor codes of unequal human worthiness to a world of Human Rights ideals of equal dignity' Influenced by anthropological texts Lindner writes:

> in the new historical context (of equal dignity for all/Human Rights legislation), the phenomenon of humiliation[5] (expressed in acts, feelings and institutions), gains significance in two ways, a) as a result of the new and more relational reality of the world, and b) through the emergence of Human Rights ideals. Dynamics of humiliation profoundly change in their nature within the larger historical transition from a world steeped in Honor codes of unequal human worthiness to a world of Human Rights ideals of equal dignity. Dynamics of humiliation move from honor-humiliation to dignity-humiliation, and, they gain more significance (2004: 4).

For Lindner the human rights revolution 'could be described as an attempt to collapse the master-slave gradient to a line of equal dignity and humility' that she defines as 'egalization'. Lindner writes that feelings of humiliation may lead to (a) depression and apathy, (b) the urge to retaliate with inflicting humiliation (she gives the example of Hitler, genocides, terrorism, or (c) they may lead to constructive social change (she gives the example of Mandela). Lindner is committed to research and action that helps to foster new public policies for driving not only *globalization* but also *egalization* and helping to create a peaceful and just world and she writes that three elements are necessary for this to be progressed.

> Firstly, new decent institutions have to be built, both locally and globally, that heal and prevent dynamics of humiliation (see *Margalit*, 1996). Secondly, new attention has to be given to maintaining relationships of equal dignity. Thirdly, new social skills have to be learned in order to maintaining relations of equal dignity. We need not least, a new type of leaders, who are no longer autocratic

dominators and humiliation-entrepreneurs, but knowledgeable, wise facilitators and motivators, who lead toward respectful and dignified inclusion of all humankind as opposed to hateful polarization.

Lindner calls for a *Moratorium on Humiliation* to be included into new public policy planning. The need for new decent institutions and leadership to heal and prevent the dynamics of humiliation, othering, de-humanization and an examination of governance both nationally and globally.

Governance in the UK

Nationally, in the UK, a commitment to international Human Rights legislation is overshadowed by a focus upon protecting borders and strengthening legislation to reduce the flow of people seeking asylum and refuge. There are many examples of the humiliation of those seeking asylum and protection from the British State in relation to a general lack of welcome and fear of the stranger perpetrated by some sections of the mass media; and the raft of asylum and immigration legislation from the 1990s through to current day that makes it very difficult to gain refuge in the UK. The operation of governance in this area does not operate in a clear way with internal integrity but rather is deeply problematic in offering a mixed message of 'welcome to Britain' and 'Go Home'.

O'Neill and Harindranath (2006) write that in relation to forced migration and asylum discourses around the exclusion of the 'other' (involving criminalisation, detention and deportation) and the maintenance and control of borders (developing ever more tighter controls on entry and asylum applications) exist in tension with discourses that speak of human rights, responsibilities and possibilities for multi-cultural citizenship especially in the community cohesion literature.

There is a conflict at the heart of New Labour's approach to asylum policy linked to the 'alterity' of the asylum seeker that promulgates hegemonic ideologies and discourses around rights to belonging and citizenship, perceived access to resources (redistribution) and misrecognition fostering suspicion of the 'stranger'. Alongside discourses of fairness and rights to enter and seek refuge, there exist regressive discourses that water down the vitally important actual and symbolic 1951 UN convention, and foster a split between 'bogus' and 'genuine' refugees, making it extremely hard to seek asylum in the UK.

In the 1990s a series of asylum and immigration acts were passed in the UK that served to increasingly restrict the rights and choices of asylum seekers and refugees, and ultimately lowered benefits. In January 2003 support was further eroded by section 55 of the 2002 Asylum and Immigration Act. Asylum seekers who do not put an application in at the point of arrival will receive no support. 2004 saw an additional asylum and immigration act with the implementation of sections 2 and 9 in particular adding to the hardship and humiliation experienced by asylum seekers both on arrival and at the end of their claims. Section 2 criminalises those who arrive without a passport and without reasonable excuse[6] and under Section 9 of the Asylum and Immigration Act 2004:

> families who have reached the end of the asylum process and exhausted all their appeal rights can have their financial support and accommodation removed if they 'fail to take reasonable steps' to leave the UK. In the event that families are made destitute, they can face having their children removed and taken into the care of social services. During the passage of the bill, the government said their aim was not to make victims of families with children but to encourage them to take up voluntary return packages. (http://www.refugee-council.org.uk/downloads/rc_reports/Section9_report_Feb06.pdf)

Increased use of detention is a further issue of major concern. Tim Baster, Director of Bail for Immigration Detainees (BID), presented an update on detention to a conference hosted by the Refugee Council in March 2006:

> By October 2005, 2929 people had gone through super fast track at Harmondsworth of whom 2424 had been refused and about 1500 removed. The average length of detention was 53 days. Eleven had been granted asylum and 67 had successfully sought bail. The rest were passed through an unjust system at speed and released. However, their appeal rights were already exhausted. There are no automatic bail procedures for families, and it is estimated that 2000 children are detained each year. Often this is as a result of early morning swoops with no warning, and then detention for indefinite periods. As many detainees have no access to legal help, they cannot access the 'elective bail' procedure. It is BID's understanding that currently half of those going through the new fast track procedures have no legal representation when they arrive in court for their appeal. (http://www.refugeecouncil.org.uk/eventsandtraining/conferences/archive/policy.htm)

Research conducted by Save the Children in 2001 '*Young Separated refugees in the West Midlands*' found that young separated refugees experience considerable anxiety over the asylum process, brought about by the difficulty of contacting legal representatives in distant cities, problems with the Home Office, and a general lack of information and support.

> Section 20 of the 1989 Children Act, which identifies when children in need should be looked after by the local authority, is rarely used in the assessment of young separated refugees. Almost all young separated refugees are housed in inappropriate accommodation. In some cases this raises child protection concerns. Young separated refugees reported that social services were often unable to help them with their problems. 58% had no named social worker. Standards varied widely between different social service teams. Young separated refugees prioritised the need for better access to appropriate education, in particular English language courses. Many 16–17 year olds have no access to education; some under 16s were not attending school full-time. Many young separated refugees, although physically healthy and with good healthcare access, are suffering the combined effects of home country trauma and loss, and isolation and boredom in the UK. (source: http://www.icar.org.uk/?lid=4397).

Research conducted nationally throws up a number of key themes in relation to the impact of dispersal managed by the National Asylum Support Service (NASS – a government office) including the impact of destitution, housing, health, mental health, and education needs. The literature provides evidence of fragmented services, serious language and communication issues, a need for orientation and information about the dispersal area for new arrivals, and emerging tensions between established and new arrival communities. The latter appears to be fuelled by perceived differential access to limited resources.

Certainly, it can be argued that the phenomenon of humiliation is expressed in acts, processes, feelings and institutions at local, regional and national level when we examine through ethnographic methods the experiences of those seeking a place of safety, settlement and belonging. This phenomenon is embedded in the practices, processes and institutions that make up the network of agencies involved in dealing with immigration. As I complete this chapter a national newspaper documents the case of a Zimbabwean refugee, the victim of rape and violence, who is the target of sexual bullying and exploitation by an immigration officer based in the IND (Immigration and Nationality Directorate) at Croydon, who has demanded sex in exchange for help processing her asylum claim.

Governance in relation to the asylum-migration nexus appears to be in a state of crisis that includes extending the processes of humiliation experienced by new arrivals to include the enforced lowering of a person or group through a process of subjugation that damages or strips away their pride, honor or dignity.

Re-imagining the asylum–migration nexus through a politics of representation

How can we address these processes of 'othering' and subjugation? How can we foster processes of dignity and egalization in our institutions, policies and practices towards people seeking safety?

New arrivals in communities impact upon the richness of social and cultural diversity. Integration (settlement) via supporting micro community development and fostering routes across diversity is a key theme of much of the work conducted in the UK in this area by mutli-agency fora, local and regional integration strategies and academic and policy oriented research.

We need innovative methodologies to analyse the new governance, the dynamics of forced migration, humiliation, and processes of exile, displacement and belonging. In this chapter I argue that combining arts based methods with ethnographic methods is one route to facilitating transformation in this area. More specifically, I will talk about the contribution that 'ethno-mimesis' (O'Neill, 2001) can make under the rubric of PAR. I developed the concept of ethno-mimesis[7] in the process of imagining a methodological process that might bring together sociology (ethnographic social research) with artistic methods – creative art processes in challenging and changing sexual and social inequalities – towards social justice. Ethno-mimesis (a combination of ethnographic work and artistic re-presentations of the ethnographic developed through participatory action research) is a process and a practice, but it is ultimately rooted in principles of equality, democracy, and freedom, as well as what Jessica Benjamin (1993) describes (drawing on Hegel, Kant, and Adorno) as a dialectic of mutual recognition.

In a recent article O'Neill and Harindranath (2006) explore the use and importance of taking a biographical approach to conducting participatory action research (PAR) with asylum seekers and refugees in order to better understand lived experiences of exile and belonging; contribute to the important field of Biographical Sociology; provide a safe space for stories to be told; and in turn for these stories to feed in to policy and praxis.

> Recovering and re-telling people's subjectivities, lives and experiences is central to attempts to better understand our social worlds with a view to transforming these worlds. ... Biographical work represented poetically, visually as well as textually can help to illuminate the necessary mediation of autonomous individuality and collective responsibility. (O'Neill and Harindranath, 2006: 49)

The authors also ask how do we come to understand the lived experience of 'asylum', exile and processes of belonging in contemporary western society? They answer by offering examples such as the mediated images and narratives of mass media institutions; advocacy groups and networks; and academic research. Moreover, the authors argue that the media politics of asylum can be interpreted through the weaving together of legal, governance and media narratives/messages for general consumption. Examples are given such as 'the relentless repetition and overemphasis of precisely those images that reinforce particular stereotypes and a failure to source more diverse images to illustrate the many other aspects of the asylum issue'.

Bailey and Harindranath (2005: 28) illustrate that in media representations there often takes place a 'discussion of policy issues in an outwardly reasonable language, but one using words and phrases that are calculated to carry a different message to the target audience' (Bailey and Harindranath, 2005: 28). The asylum seeker is represented as an undesirable alien, occasionally represented as a possible threat to national sovereignty and security. This appears to be humiliating at the level of lived experience, re-presentation and embedded in the institutional processes of media production.

The combination of the biographical and visual can be potentially powerful in providing alternative re-presentations and challenging such limited and limiting imaginings in relation to individuals, groups and micro communities and that may ultimately impact upon practice and policy.

Participatory action research and artistic/visual methodologies can create a reflectively safe space for dialogue, thinking through issues, and representing the voices of refugees and asylum seekers that speak of loss, mourning, shame and humiliation as well as mutual recognition and the importance of publicness/public sharing for democratization and egalization.

Participatory, creative methodologies also help to counter processes of 'postemotionalism' that Stefan Mestrovic (1997) writes about in his work and that may underpin the contradictory approaches to asylum-migration taken by the new labour government. Mestrovic writes about how in contemporary 'me dominated' (*Western*) society rooted in consumption and commodification our emotions lose their genuineness. Thus, we reach a state of 'compassion' fatigue and cannot/ or choose not to connect with the pain and suffering of others. So, in relation to forced migration and the plight of people we turn over the page or reach for the remote control to switch off the images or words.

The image in (Figure 4.1) helps the observer/participant to engage with the flesh and blood young people whose lives were transformed by war in Bosnia. Two young men re-present their memories of the refugee camp, of living in cramped containers, of land mines, guns and bombs; all symbols of their lived experiences. The inclusions of a walkman and toy car provide symbols of their life before the war *and* they reveal their ordinariness as young people who, like their British counterparts, had access to toys, technology and music. The inclusion of these images was a direct resistance to the way they were defined by some of their peers at school as 'peasants'. Just as the images in Figures 4.2, 4.3 and 4.4 are representative of a peaceful family oriented childhood devastated by the gathering forces of war and humiliation. The young woman's family and life were turned upside down, forced into hiding, shunned by friends and neighbours, they eventually reached safety in a UN refugee camp in Croatia and were sent to England under the Bosnia Programme in the mid 1990s (Figure 4.5). In Figure 4.6, the young woman's life in England is marked by the letters from family and friends in other countries, representing her life as part of a transnational community/network – but also the joy of surviving of being alive is present here too in the shiny newness of the image.

Shierry Nicholsen (2002) draws comparisons with postemotionalism (Mestrovic) and normotic illness (Bollas). In her reading of Mestrovic she says emotions 'lose their genuineness and become quasi emotions. The emotional spectrum becomes limited and individual emotions blurred'. In defining 'normotic illness' Shierry states that for the normotic individual subjectivity recedes and the person experiences him/herself more as a commodity object – describing flatness of emotions and an absence of affective links between people and in relationships.

84

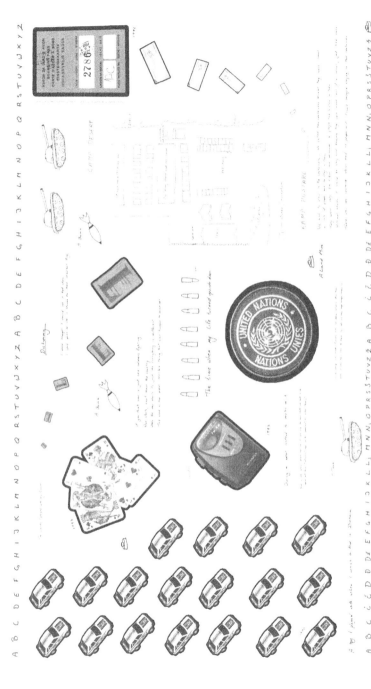

Figure 4.1 'Timeline'

Figure 4.2   House of cards

Nicholsen (2002) further develops the analysis by drawing on Adorno to argue that normotic illness and postemotionality cannot be understood separately from war.

Death-dealing violence and social domination are the agents of the destruction of experience, and thus inextricably linked to the phoniness and propaganda quality of postemotional society – not

Figure 4.3 Family life

the war of the Good Americans a vs Bad Germans, but rather the inextricable presence of killing and war-making in the society of domination (p. 11).

To counter postemotionalism and the administered society (in our lived experience but also in building, creating our social worlds) the interrelation between thinking, feeling, and doing is crucial (Tester,

Figure 4.4 The gathering forces of war

1995). Moreover, the interplay between critical thought, artistic praxis, and social action is one source of resistance to and transformation of the disempowering and reductive social and psychic processes that Mestrovic (1997) speaks about so clearly in his work.

In the process of developing intertextual research with refugees and asylum seekers, it is important to counter the forces of humiliation and shame by helping to open up multiple, practical spaces for new

Figure 4.5   My life turned upside down

arrivals, asylum seekers, refugees, economic migrants to speak for themselves. This work, as a work in progress, as 'micrology,' aims to create intertextual social knowledge as ethno-mimesis (O'Neill, 2001; 2004) and can help us avoid accepting reified versions of reality, re-presents the complexity of lived experience and lived relations as a counter impulse to 'postemotionalism'. The research also supports processes of community development (social regeneration, social

Figure 4.6 A sense of belonging

renewal) and cultural citizenship in collaboration with the individuals and groups.

In PAR with Bosnian and Afghan communities life history narratives, biographies were re-presented in visual and poetic form. The participants in the research are the co-creators of the research. The life story narratives and photographs produced represent three key themes that emerged from the life stories of those involved in the research:[8]

1. Experiences before the war – dislocation marked by post communist citizenship in Yugoslavia that reconstituted citizenship on a kinship or community basis, that is, for the Serb leader only Serbs were allowed citizenship and the protection of law.
2. Experiences during the war – displaced and abstracted from history, citizenship, and the law, humiliated, separated from families and friends – living in refugee camps, and for some, concentration camps.
3. Experiences of living in the UK – relocating and rebuilding lives and diasporic communities

The research is both transgressive and regressive. Working together with the Bosnians in the Midlands through participatory action research (PAR) proved to be transgressive across three levels of praxis. The first level is textual, performed through documenting their life stories as testimony to the humiliation, suffering, and genocide they encountered at the hands of the government, army, police, employers, hospitals, medics, and former friends and neighbours. The second level is visual, performed through the production of art forms to re-present their life stories with the help of freelance artists, saying the unsayable. The third level combines the visual and textual elements shared with others – audiences in community spaces, gallery spaces, civic centres and universities, and supports and fosters dialogue, understanding and processes of community development.

Challenging and resisting dominant images and stereotypes of refugees and asylum seekers and making this work available to as wide an audience as possible can also serve to raise awareness, as well as educate and empower individuals and groups. Dominant images and stereotypes of refugees include those of victim, passive, and dependent and do not reflect the courage or resistance, as well as the need for building self-esteem, self-identity, and cultural identity, in the face of tragedy and loss (see Adleman 1999; Harrell-Bond 1999).

The PAR project with the Bosnians (funded by AHRB) proved to be both critical and reflexive. By both narrativizing and re-presenting/ reimagining history and lived experience the vital importance of opportunities for social renewal, for creating citizenship, for re-imagining identities and communities against the backdrop of British law (and at local level the mediated structures and processes of statutory and voluntary organisations both horizontally and vertically) emerged. The role and purpose of PAR, the vital role of the arts in processes of social inclusion, the civic role and responsibility of the university and the vital importance for creating safe spaces for dialogue that might support processes of restorative justice and reconciliation were also explored.

In summary, there is clearly an urgent need to develop interventionary strategies based on collective responsibility and what Benhabib (1992) has called a 'civic culture of public participation and the moral quality of enlarged thought' (1992: 140) in relation to work in the area of understanding diaspora/transnational communities and identities, circuits of migration. How can ethno-mimesis address this?

The experiences of the people concerned must be listened to and acknowledged, and advocacy networks developed to operationalize their voices through participatory action research. Recovering and retelling people's subjectivities, lives, and experiences is central to attempts to better understand our social worlds with a view to transforming these worlds (see O'Neill and Harindranath, 2006). Such work reveals the resistances, strengths, and humour of people seeking asylum, as well as knowledge of and a better understanding of the legitimation and rationalization of power, domination, and oppression.

Drawing on Shierry Nicholsen's work, the photographs presented here have the capacity to arouse our compassion while not letting us forget that what we are seeing is socially constructed meaning. Through re-presenting the unsayable, the images help to 'pierce' us, bringing us into contact with reality in ways that we cannot forget – ways that counter the 'postemotionalism' of contemporary 'me' dominated society that Mestrovic (1997) details so carefully in his work.

Within the context of the work of the humiliation and human dignity network research undertaken using participatory and visual methods envisions/imagines a renewed social sphere for asylum seekers and people seeking asylum and refugees as global citizens, with our eyes firmly fixed on the 'becoming' of equality, freedom, and democracy, through processes of social justice, cultural citizenship, egalization and mutual recognition and renewed social and public policies – in the spheres of polity, economy, and culture. PAR as ethno-mimesis is both a practice and a process aimed at illuminating inequalities and injustice through socio-cultural research and analysis. In addition, it also seeks to envision and imagine a better future based upon a dialectic of mutual recognition, ethical communication, and respect.

Acknowledgements

The images were created with the support of artists Simon Cunningham (Figure 4.1) and Maggy Milner (Figure 4.2–4.6) on the Global Refugess project based at Staffordshire University and City Arts Nottingham and funded by the AHRB.

Notes

1. Temple and Moran (2006: 6) argue that participatory approaches can help to maximise local participation, (which is especially significant for people who speak little English and/or do not access services); lead to a sense of ownership, responsibility and self esteem; recognize and value people's skills and capacities; and lead to community development processes and capacities. Additionally, because the research methods used involve rigorous checking and cross checking of interpretations a deeply embedded reflexivity emerges in the research design, process and outcomes.

2. This is the complex relationship between migration (the movement of people across borders) and forced migration (forced movement, for example as a consequence of civil war, natural disasters, decolonization). The distinction between forced and economic migration has become blurred and there are complex factors and outcomes operating that link the local with the global.

3. See for example the web-based site- www.saemp.org.uk a Somali European Media Project, based in Leicester (a nodal city) that are global in reach but have particular links with the Netherlands, Norway, where some of their members first gained refugee status before deciding to make Leicester in the UK their home.

4. The interview was conducted as part of an AHRC funded research project examining experiences of exile and integration led by O'Neill and Staffordshire University.

5. Lindner writes:
   Humiliation means the enforced lowering of a person or group, a process of subjugation that damages or strips away their pride, honor or dignity. To be humiliated is to be placed, against your will and often in a deeply hurtful way, in a situation that is greatly inferior to what you feel you should expect. Humiliation entails demeaning treatment that transgresses established expectations. It may involve acts of force, including violent force. ... Indeed, one of the defining characteristics of humiliation as a process is that the victim is forced into passivity, acted upon, made helpless (2004: 29).

6. According to Home Office statistics, more than 100 people were charged under Section 2 between 3 July and 9 October 2005; three quarters of these were convicted and imprisoned. The prison term is usually 2–5 months if the person pleads guilty. However, it is only after the term has been served that the person can enter the asylum determination process and the actual strength of the case for asylum can be considered. The case may then have to be pursued from detention, which means it will be harder to get legal advice; and the Section 2 prosecution has to be taken into account in determining

credibility in the initial decision and any appeal. Jawaid Luqmani (2006: 5) 'Working with change, meeting the challenge: an asylum policy and legislation update' March 2006 Conference Report.

7. Following Adorno, 'mimesis' does not simply mean naive imitation, but rather feeling, sensuousness, and spirit in critical tension to constructive (instrumental) rationality; reason; the 'out-there' sense of our being in the world. Mimesis is not to be interpreted as mimicry but rather as relationally deeper – as sensuous knowing. Taussig understands 'mimesis as both the faculty of imitation and the deployment of that faculty in sensuous knowing' (1993: 68). Ethno mimesis is both a practice (a methodology) and a process aimed at illuminating inequalities and injustice through sociocultural research and analysis; but it also seeks to envision and imagine a better future based on a dialectic of mutual recognition, congruence, care, and respect for human rights, cultural citizenship, and democratic processes.

8. See O'Neill (2004) 'Global Rights (Human) Rights, Citizenship and the Law' in Cheng, S. (ed.), *Law, Justice and Power: Between Reason and will* California: Stanford University Press.

References

Adleman, H. (1999) 'Modernity, globalization, refugees and displacement'. In A. Ager (ed.), *Refugees: Perspectives on the Experience of Enforced Migration*. (London, Continuum) pp. 83–110.

Bailey, O. and R. Harindranath (2005) 'Racialised "othering": the representation of asylum seekers in the news media'. In S. Allen (ed.), *Journalism: Critical Issues* (Maidenhead and New York: Open University Press) pp. 274–87.

Bauman, Z. (1998) *Globalization: the Human Consequences* (Cambridge: Polity Press).

Benhabib, S. (1992) *Situating the Self* (Cambridge: Polity Press).

Benjamin, S. (1993) *The Bonds of Love: Psychoanalysis, Feminism and the Bonds of Domination* (London: Virago).

Castles, S. (2003) 'Towards a sociology of forced migration and social transformation', *Sociology*, Vol. 37, No. 1, 13–35.

Cornell, D. (2000) *Just Cause: Freedom, Identity and Rights* (Maryland and Oxford: Rowman and Littlefield).

Harrell-Bond, B. (1999) 'Refugees' experiences as aid recipients'. In A. Ager (ed.), *Refugees: Perspectives on the Experience of Enforced Migration* (London: Continuum) pp. 136–68.

Kushner, T. and K. Knox (1999) *Refugees in an Age of Genocide* (London: Frank Cass).

Lindner, E. G. (2004) *Humiliation in a Globalizing World: Does Humiliation Become the Most Disruptive Force?* (New York, NY): paper prepared for the 'Workshop on Humiliation and Violent Conflict', 18–19 November at Columbia University.

Luqmani, (2006) *Working with Change, Meeting the Challenge: an Asylum Policy and Legislation Update*, Report of Conference Organised by the Refugee Council and Supported by the Immigration Law Practitioners' Association (ILPA), Regents College, London, 9 March (London: Refugee Council).

Accessed at: http://www.refugeecouncil.org.uk/eventsandtraiming/conference/ archive/policy.htm.

Marfleet, P. (2006) *Refugees in a Global Era* (London: Palgrave Macmillan).

Mestrovic, S. (1997) *Postemotional Society* (London and New York: Sage).

Milosz, C. (1988) 'On exile'. In Koudelka, J. (ed.), *Exiles* (London: Thames and Hudson).

O'Neill, M. (2001) *Prostitution and Feminism: Towards a Politics of Feeling* (Cambridge: Polity Press).

O'Neill, M. (2002) 'Renewed methodologies for social research: ethno-mimesis as performative praxis', *Sociological Review*, 50, No. 1, Feb.

O'Neill, M. (2004) 'Global refugees (human) rights, citizenship and the law' in Cheng, S. *Law, Justice and Power: Between Reason and Will* (California: Stanford University Press).

O'Neill, M. and R. Harindranath (2006) 'Theorising narratives of exile and belonging: the importance of Biography and Ethno-mimesis in "understanding" asylum', *Qualitative Sociological Review*, Vol. 11, Issue 1, 39–53.

Nicholsen S. (2002) *'Adorno's' Minima Moralia: On Passion, Psychoanalysis and the Postemotional Dilemma, in the Alliance* Forum on Passion (Seattle: Washington).

Refugee Action and the Refugee Council, (2006) *Inhumane and Ineffective – Section 9 in Practice* (London). (http://www.refugeecouncil.org.uk/downloads/rc_reports/Section9_report_Feb06.pdf)

Taussig, M. (1993) *Mimesis and Alterity* (London: Routledge).

Temple, G. and R. Moran (2006) *Doing Research With Refugees* (Bristol: The Policy Press).

Tester, K. (1995) *The Inhuman Condition* (London: Routledge).

Weber Nicholsen, S. (2002) 'Adorno's Minima Moralia: On Passion, Psychoanalysis and the Postemotional Dilemma' (from personal communication with the author).

Part II

Diasporic Politics: Tensions and Promises

5
Transnational Islam and the Internet

Eugenia Siapera

Introduction

This chapter will attempt to contribute to the theorisation of the articulation of Islam with the internet and its transnational aspects. Islam is here understood as dynamic, internally diverse and structured along different ethnic, class, culture, linguistic and so on lines – it is an expansive term encompassing those who understand and define themselves as Muslim. Studying its articulation with the internet is important in many respects. First, as an apparently 'odd' combination of 'tradition' and (hyper) modernity, that may end up modifying our understandings of both; second, as a means of understanding how communities/agents 'shape' the technology in practice; third, as a case study for understanding how spaces interact with identities. It is the last element that will be at the centre of this chapter: the way in which the space created by the internet gives rise to certain ways of articulating Islam and its links to territories or localities.

The focus on transnationalism reflects the increased interest generated by recent work (c.f. Smith and Guarnizo, 1998; Vertovec, 1999). Theorists have drawn our attention to the ways in which human mobility has led to a new kind of experience with territoriality, understood as an in-between transnational or more broadly translocal way of being. To human mobility, we can add the mobility of ideas and more generally communication – what Appadurai (1996) has called ideoscapes and mediascapes. Experiences, ideas and images are increasingly mediated, thereby foregrounding the media as a protagonist in the shaping of trans/local experiences. Within this context this chapter will focus on the internet, whose defiance of geography makes it a transnational medium *par excellence*. From the point of view of transnationalism the empirical question is to find the kinds of transnational experiences/practices fostered by the internet. The main, empirically oriented part of this chapter is therefore concerned with identifying the types of transnational practices associated with different internet genres. The final section will examine the role played by the internet in fostering a transnational Islam. The findings suggest that although transnationalism exists as an imaginary, action and experience are very much localised. But how can we use these findings to understand the internet and its relationship to a variable Islam? There are two possibilities: one is to view the internet as an expanded public sphere, which includes several smaller ones, including a (transnational) Muslim public sphere. In this manner, a transnational Islam is created through an internet-supported public sphere. This argument does not fare particularly well when it comes to accounting for both the imaginary and the local/experiential elements encountered online. Another possibility is to view online Islam as a site for the antagonistic creation of identities and discourses, which have both an imaginary and an action-oriented component; this site can be understood as a space for the creation of new significations where new imaginaries offer new impetus for action, and where new experiences give rise to new imaginaries. In ideal-typical terms, whereas the public sphere can be thought as contemplative/deliberative with a legitimating function, this public site can be understood as generative/creative with an oppositional/critical function.

Multiple transnationalisms and Islam

Talk on transnationalism gained momentum in the field of the sociology of migration, when theorists and researchers became dissatisfied with existing concepts and their ability to capture the dual or multiple orientations, lives, and experiences of migrants. In a well-known definition, Basch *et al.* (1994: 8) defined '"transnationalism" as the processes by which immigrants forge and sustain multi-stranded social relations that link together their societies of origin and settlement'. At the same time, the concept acquired currency in the field of cultural theory, when theorists such as Arjun Appadurai (1996) and Ulf Hannertz (1996) attempted to describe an experience stemming from occupying simultaneously two or more spaces or localities. These sociological and cultural approaches were complemented by explorations highlighting the multiple transnational flows of capital (e.g. Sklair,

1998) and an emerging transnational political system (e.g. Held, 2003). Despite their different foci, most of these approaches agree that the nation becomes relativised as one of the multiple locations that people experience rather than the central unit of analysis.

But what are the implications of transnationalism for Islam? Grillo (2004) has identified three versions of transnationalism, when it comes to Islam in particular. First, transnational Islam as operating in transnational circuits: an example is that of some Sufi orders which often follow saints from their homelands as well as local leaders (Riccio, 2001). The second conceptualisation is of a transnational Islam operating in a binational or plurinational framework: examples here include the British Pakistani Muslims, the French Algerian Muslims, and the German Turkish Muslims, who are often engaged in the politics of their 'original' countries, but who live and work elsewhere. A third understanding of transnational Islam is that of the *umma*, the community of believers united by common beliefs rather than ethnicity, language or culture. Grillo refers to the 'transethnicisation' of Muslims, as the emergence of a Muslim supra-identity that unites Muslims beyond religious, ethnic and cultural differences. An example here would be the emergence of the category 'British Muslims' comprised of those British citizens understanding themselves primarily as Muslim, and secondarily as members of an ethnic community, such as Pakistani, Arab, or English. Others, such as Pnina Werbner (2004), argue that any movement towards such a transethnicisation will have to confront existing divisions along ethnic and linguistic lines.

Elaborating on the same theme, John Bowen (2004) argues that Islam is developing more and more along transnational lines, drawing upon Islam's history and universal message. But this universal message is associated with figures of authority, Islamic scholars whose knowledge of the Qur'an, and Arabic language is deep and beyond question. In these terms, argues Bowen, the transnational orientation of Islam is not towards a broad and general *umma*, but rather towards a more specific source of authority. For example, scholars such as Yusuf Al-Qaradawi have risen to prominence and Muslims across the world have gathered around them. The point here is, according to Bowen, that transnational Islam revolves around the idea that regardless of where they are Muslims must listen to the most learned. Transnationalism for Islam is therefore linked not to the migration of people but to the migration of ideas, to communication and debate across boundaries, in short to the development of Islam as a transnational public space, 'based on a set of extra-national social norms – the many interpretations of the *sharia*,

"God's plans and commands"' (Bowen, 2004: 883). This for Bowen means that transnational Islam must be thought 'beyond migration', but also, from the current perspective, it must be thought as highlighting the struggle for authority in this public space, as well as the many exchanges and interactions between localities and the transnational meaning and message of Islam. Finally, if we accept that transnational Islam is linked through ideas, communication and debate, then the role of the (new) media becomes even more pronounced.

Taking the above into consideration, transnationalism emerges both as an in-between category, bringing together or bridging different localities, but also crucially as a supra-category, subsuming and containing other identifications. At the same time, we see that the media's importance is central both as a bridge and as providing a platform that connects people from across the world. From this perspective, the importance of the internet is even more crucial as a medium that defies geography. At the same time, it is accessible to people in a manner that differs from the traditional mass media: rather than being audiences, people can participate online. This leads to the formulation of several questions on the role of the internet in transnationalism: does it support the creation of a supranational *umma*? How is locality treated in a space that is virtual? And in connection with the medium itself, how is it appropriated and used by diasporic/transnational Muslims? The following section will therefore seek to discuss the role of the internet in more detail and through empirical examples.

Locating transnational Islam online

A brief discussion on matters of method needs to precede the presentation of the empirical material. Given the enormity of the internet and 'online Islam'[1] certain limits must be set. First, 'online Islam' will be discussed here through short case studies, through references to a few websites. These are not meant to be representative, but rather suggestive of some of the issues involved. In terms of the transnational aspect, the focus here is on the 'British Muslim internet', that is on sites that clearly operate from the UK and are run by people who define themselves as Muslim. In terms of the internet, we propose the use of the concept of 'internet genres' as a means by which we can approach the vast expanses of cyberspace. The Oxford English Dictionary defines genre as: 'A particular style or category of works of art; esp. a type of literary work characterized by a particular form, style, or purpose.' The usefulness of the concept of genre is threefold: first, it is attentive to the diversity of communicative forms found in the media; second, it enables an analysis of how communication is organised in different ways; and third, it allows for an examination of the different implications this formal organisation may have. Chandler (1997) points to the sharedness and conventionality of genres, which operate on the basis of shared codes that position authors and readers in certain ways. In this chapter, the focus will be on four internet genres, namely: websites, portals, blogs and discussion fora. These will be analysed from the point of view of the current problematic, centring on notions of locality, Muslim identity and the *umma*. Different sites will be used as examples or short case studies. The analysis does not claim representativeness of all that there is out there; rather it aims to be suggestive of some of the issues involved in the interaction between Islam, the internet and locality.

Websites: interpellating the Umma

Wikipedia defines websites as:

> 'a collection of webpages, that is, HTML/XHTML documents accessible via HTTP on the Internet. [...] a website will often be the work of a single individual, a business or organization, or dedicated to a particular topic or purpose'.

In ideal–typical terms, website as a genre organises communication in a 'traditional' way, of one source communicating to multiple audiences. This is the main means by which the typical general website communicates: it may be using the internet hyperlinked architecture, but its communication can be still understood as one-to-many. In formal terms, this organisation of communication privileges the 'source' as the originator of communication. To the extent that the 'source' has a particular communicative goal, then this is also indirectly privileged. The 'identity' of the communicator and their goals are therefore central to this internet genre.

The website chosen here for analysis is that of the Muslim Public Affairs Committee (MPACUK: www.mpacuk.org); this choice reflects its relative prominence in the British public space. MPAC achieved notoriety when it featured in a Channel 4 documentary.[2] MPACUK has a very clear identity explained in detail in their 'about us' section. It is an activist organisation defining itself as: 'the UK's leading Muslim civil liberties group, empowering Muslims to focus on non-violent Jihad and political activism'. Its actual geographical location is immediately recognizable as the UK, which also appears in the url of the site. All actions proposed by this activist organisation are located in the UK, even if they refer to other parts of the world. At the time of writing, there was an 'action alert' about a planned BBC Panorama documentary on a pro-Palestinian charity. MPAC denounced this as anti-Muslim and asked visitors to write to the BBC and complain. Another 'action alert' invites visitors to write to their MP complaining against the discontinued aid for Palestine.

Although action is localised, the rhetoric is not. MPAC makes reference to no other ethnic group apart from 'British Muslims', but it makes constant references to the *umma*, as an imagined transnational community of believers: 'MPACUK are aiming to bring the community together, disunity among Muslims has been our biggest downfall in recent years. This will not, however, stop us from holding Muslims and their leaders to account'. This imagined community is embroiled in controversy: MPAC has several articles condemning terrorism but also recognising that some terrorist activity can be linked to some part of the Muslim community. The *umma* is also thought as being misrepresented: MPAC's remit is to counter what they see as the negative representation of Islam in the media. Finally, the *umma* is understood as disempowered: MPAC argues that Muslims are victimised because of their beliefs and relative powerlessness. Action is then justified in the name of this transnational community, in order to address and ultimately resolve the problems facing it. The transnationalism that emerges in this site is therefore one that interpellates the *umma*, it calls it into existence and seeks to materialise it through localised action in a concrete place: that of the UK.

The formal organisation of the website as a genre places the communicator or source at the centre, and places emphasis on what they communicate: in the case of the MPAC website, the communicative goals include the actual creation or materialisation of the *umma* as a united community through actions in the specific locality of the UK. There is no bridging or in-betweeness in this conception of the transnational: rather it is the imagining and the acting on behalf of this imagined community that creates a mode of being that rather than transcending locality, it acts upon it with a view to change it. The extent to which this reflects the particular rhetoric of MPAC or is more widely shared remains an empirical question. However, from the point of view of the website as a genre it can be argued that the privileging of the source of communication in websites can be linked to a prioritisation of the element of interpellation: of the calling into being of audiences or readers, who may or may not respond to such invitations. The way in which the internet is involved in this is by enabling the issuing of such calls: and if indeed a transnational *umma* is to emerge, it will emerge as part of such efforts to call it into being.

Portals: controlling the *umma*

> Wikipedia: A *web portal* is a web site that provides a starting point, a gateway, or portal, to other resources on the Internet.

This definition is in fact ambiguous when it comes to Islamic portals: it refers to websites acting as portals to Islam, offering information on Islam as a religion. It may also refer to websites offering a Muslim perspective of the internet, with resources and so forth which may be of interest to Muslims. At the same time, it can be a directory and a gateway to other Islamic sites. All three versions of portals share one main characteristic: they seek to define and circumscribe the Internet from a Muslim viewpoint, or put differently: to provide an entry point to online Islam. In terms of the conventions of the genre, the definition provided by Wikipedia points to the gatekeeping function of portals, in turn pointing to their attempts to set borders and controls. The emphasis here is not so much on the communicator but rather on the areas or themes covered (and conversely left out): if a portal acts as a gateway to some information, then it is important to find out what this information might be. The portal selected here for analysis is the main UK Islamic portal: salaam.co.uk. In its site Salaam describes itself as: 'a Muslim community portal launched in 1997 and owned by Webstar Plc, a London-based Internet service provider and software house. The Salaam site's mission is to serve as the leading trusted source of information of relevance to the British Muslim community'.[3]

Salaam acts as a gate first to Muslim religious/spiritual matters. Specifically, Salaam has an 'advice' section, where advice on *fiqh* is provided is by a relevant expert; a 'knowledge' section with information about religious aspects, such as the Hajj, the Quran and Quranic studies; a set of downloads including MP3 files with sermons; and a tool for locating a Mosque in different locations in the UK. This latter tool is the only link to locality; in the remaining religious information, the transnational element is obvious: the *umma* is addressed in religious terms beyond location. This religious aspect is central to online Islam, but keeping in mind the diversity and multiplicity of Islam, it is one of the most contentious elements. Through this provision of fatwas, advice and opinion, Salaam is demarcating the perimeters of Islam. In other words, it marks appropriate or inappropriate behaviour, and declares what is acceptable and not in Islam by advising what people should or should not do from an 'Islamic' or 'Muslim' point of view. Here the findings of Gary Bunt on the internet and religious authority are crucial: for Bunt (2003), the popularisation of fatwas through the internet has meant first that the traditional Islamic authorities are undermined, and second that there is an ongoing struggle for 'authoring' Islam. Both aspects seem to be associated directly with portals, rather than with websites, since websites clearly state their purpose and hence their partisanship. Portals, on the other hand, present a generic template for those interested in online Islam. The religious aspects of online Islamic portals can therefore be seen as attempts to define and author(ise) Islam. This element shows the struggle involved in the creation of a united *umma* as a community of believers.

A second, often more obvious, entry point is that of news: news items that concern Muslims are a consistent part of the portal provision, and are given a prominent place. The transnational aspect of online Islam is very apparent here: news items seem to have a transnational character, including items from both Muslim majority countries and from Muslim communities across the world. The idea here is that the *umma* is interested in the news, both news concerning Muslim issues as well as more broadly important news of the world. In providing such news, Salaam evidently has a gatekeeping function: it presents news filtered both for relevance as well as for contents or perspective. What is important for the *umma*, and how it is presented are both relevant decisions here. These journalistic elements involved here are closely linked to classic conceptions of the public sphere in its informational dimensions. But the gatekeeping function equally points to the ways in which control is exercised over this 'public sphere' and its public(s).

Salaam further provides entry points to social and cultural elements: here we see information about social matters, about families, and parenthood, about marriage, sex and children, as well as about cultural aspects, such as books and book reviews, films and other cultural events. In a similar fashion to the news function, this element provides articles and suggestions for Muslim everyday life. In doing so, it circumscribes and delineates the boundaries around acceptable behaviours. Again the transnational character of the *umma* more broadly is evident: Muslim life is characterised by the same concerns more or less across national contexts: how to raise children, how to overcome temptation, how to appreciate life more and how to live in accordance with Muslim beliefs regardless of location. The question of authority is present here too: articles are signed by authors whose biographies and credentials also published: both the force of their argument as well as their credentials are meant to persuade readers that they speak authoritatively about contentious matters.

Finally, Salaam acts as a gate to the Muslim community more broadly: it provides information and link to Islamic businesses, to a 'Who Is Who' directory, with biographies, and to other Muslim sites on the web. At the time of writing, Salaam included advertisements for Sharia banking services and halal restaurants: these are businesses operating in the UK. The 'Who Is Who' directory is divided into two: one including the profiles of important Muslims throughout history, and a second directory of 'Who Is Who' among contemporary British Muslims. The website directory of Islamic/Muslim sites offered by Salaam is a comprehensive one, spanning across several categories, and including sites from across the world. We see therefore a dual orientation both towards the *umma* in general, but also towards the British Muslim community specifically. In fact, Salaam has a section devoted entirely to 'Muslims in Britain', which includes history, statistics, laws affecting the community, schools, and so on. The question of control is apparent here too: Salaam controls the visibility of this community: parts of the community not on these directories are excluded or 'excommunicated'. It should be noted however, that Salaam offers readers the opportunity to submit information, although it must be cleared and checked by its editorial team.

This discussion on Islamic web portals has argued that these can be understood as a genre which seeks to circumscribe and delineate online Islam, whilst at the same time competing for authorship and visibility. We have also seen that the transnational dimension is clearly present in the provision of 'Muslim news', in the religious and 'Muslim lifestyle' information, in the 'Muslim history' sections, and in the 'Muslim online links'. At the same time however, the local British dimension was equally present: the businesses, the particular Muslim persons, the immediate and pragmatic action-oriented context of life is clearly located in the UK.

Blogs: reporting on the 'Muslim' experience

Wikipedia: A *weblog* (usually shortened to *blog*, but occasionally spelled *web log*) is both a web application used for entering, modifying and displaying periodic posts (normally in reverse chronological order) as well as the totality of content constituted by these posts.

In practice blogs are online diaries kept by a variety of people and for a variety of purposes. Mostly, however, they just seem to contain the author's personal commentary on events of everyday life. This personal perspective, along with the predominantly informal way of writing, and the eclectic mix of comments, make blogs a very particular form of communication, a bottom-up one, that whilst making no claims to authority it nevertheless 'authors' a particular version of reality and experience. In its informality and personalisation, the blog constitutes the other side of the instrumental and authoritative websites and portals: the perspective of everyday life, of personal experience, of subjective interpretation of events and information. In this respect, blogs are crucial for online Islam as they provide a means by which we can find out the actual experiences, thoughts, and online practices of the much invoked *umma*.

The blog chosen here is called 'Opinionated Voice', and is run by Jamal, describing himself as '*A Muslim twentysomething with a dislike for injustice and oppression*' (http://opinionated.blogsome.com/). The personal, the religious and the topical are all mixed in this blog, with Jamal commenting from a personal perspective and inviting other readers to comment upon his comments and interpretations. Rather than claiming authority and power by 'authoring' texts on Islam Jamal is doing the very opposite: he seeks to co-author or rather collaboratively describe his experiences as a Muslim in London, but also to comment on matters and news concerning Muslims elsewhere – he does this not only through offering news and comments, but also through providing links to other blogs, news outlets and other sources he finds relevant. The collaborative element is crucial for blogs: although entries are authored by the blogger, readers are invited to comment on what they read. And it should be noted here that comments can come from anyone: they are not confined to Muslims. In these terms, rather than authoritative, strategic and instrumental, this blog may be considered as a collaborative attempt to write (Muslim) experience. In so doing, it represents an attempt to express lived experience and opinion, and in this sense to provide an outlet for the everyday. The diary format of blogging lends itself perfectly to this, and to the collaborative aspects and elements of this enterprise.

But this expressive function of blogging is not without its political repercussions and ramifications: first, a blog like Opinionated Voice contains an overt political dimension; he campaigns against the war in Iraq, and against Guantanamo Bay which leads him to provide evidence, facts, and other means to justify his viewpoint. Second, the expressive dimensions of the blog may be seen as close to the function of culture and art, which constitute a significant source of meaning and interpretation. This, in turn, may have a double political function: the first would be, following Adorno,[4] to stand both outside and inside in relation to society which in turn enables a particularly insightful commentary. This commentary must subsequently be taken seriously for political change to actually occur: as it is now, i.e. expressed online, it provides an impetus for change, and it may contribute to the creation of momentum. A second political function stems from the possibility offered by this expression of views to act as a form of political participation in the sense of enabling, fortifying and preparing persons for entry to the domain of politics proper – understood as becoming involved in the allocation, administration and management of power.[5]

In terms of the *umma*, however, the main implication of this expressive and subjective dimension is to pluralise it, and to give an outlet to its multiplicity. Rather than seeking a unity in commonality of purpose and action, as in the MPAC website, or to control the *umma* as in the Salaam portal, the Opinionated blog is individualising the 'Muslim' experience, points to its broader commonalities with other communities and with other individuals: similarities and agreements are commonly reported in comments, but crucially so are differences and disagreements. The blog format not only allows but relies on this type of comment: they are the lifeline of the blog. But it is precisely this pluralisation that shows the difficulty and perhaps also ultimate impossibility of a 'united *umma*'. In terms of the question of transnationalism, the subjective element of the blog is both bound to location, as the source of experience, as well as moves beyond it, in extrapolating from the local to the more general, from the specific experience and opinion, to the broader principles and reasons. Posts draw on personal experience, but unless one can read something more general in them, then no comments will be posted. As such, this genre can be thought as a bridge between the local and the 'translocal'.

Forums: debating the *umma*

> Wikipedia: An *Internet forum* is a web application which provides for discussion, often in conjunction with online communities.

This format is one of the most familiar online, and it is often found at the centre of arguments seeking to resurrect, or recreate deliberative democratic politics using the internet as a tool. The ideas behind deliberative democracy, at least the one advocated by Habermas (1999), are taking the theory of the public sphere further by holding that for a public opinion to form, citizens must be able to deliberate, i.e. to discuss in depth arguments, to consider positions, to weigh the pros and cons, and to reach decisions based on the validity of arguments, on their ability to address the issue at hand, rather than on preformed impressions, or attitudes, or identity-based positions. In (some forms of) deliberative democracy every citizen should be able to participate in decision making through deliberation; the internet, in its interactive, widely accessible (in principle) and user-friendly character is placed at the centre of deliberative democracy, since it can link citizens, it can provide a virtual public space in which people can meet and discuss. Such views led to a prioritisation of the online forum as the political internet genre par excellence. This is not the space to consider either the validity of the deliberative democratic model or the extent to which these fora actually contribute to democratic politics, deliberative or not.[6] Rather, it is to point out to some of the characteristics of the genre: its general inclusiveness and openness, and its political significance.

The forum on which I will focus is the one found on www.ummah. com – its forum is be a very popular one, with a vibrant community, which posts often. The administrators describe the site as 'the UK's number 1 Muslim discussion forum'. The ummah.com domain name is registered in the UK, but the participants seem to come from across the world: users report several locations, ranging from East London to East Europe, from the US to undisclosed locations, such as 'the waterfront'. What is immediately striking is the variety of topics covered, which range from the idiosyncratic and the personal to general announce-ments, to political issues, to the Qur'an and so on. A second, equally striking observation is that the language used is a mixture of argument, opinion and description, peppered with emoticons; additionally, although English is the language used, it is very often complemented by Arabic, written in both Latin as well as in Arabic characters.[7] The style of language is very informal, often with typos, or online conven-tional abbreviations. Rather than the informed argumentation at the centre of deliberative democracy we see here an informal exchange of views, with agreements and disagreements more stated than argued, with religious and spiritual language and arguments (e.g. the Prophet said ...) often accompanied by secular, and 'rational', as well as by emotive and passionate discourse. Users mostly employ 'nomes de plume', and the information they offer about themselves is minimal. In this particular forum, however, information about religion is required: most users report themselves as Muslim, but there are also a significant number of non-Muslim participants: for instance, a user describe him/herself as a 'back pew Catholic', another as a 'token Buddhist', yet another reports their religion as 'Judistianslam'. This shows the wide range of people participating in this forum, but this anonymity more generally is an important aspect of online forums and it evokes questions of trust and credibility.

The four elements that emerge from this description include first, the many locations of participants, the wide ranges of themes and topics covered, the mixed language used, and the multiplicity and anonymity of users. These elements point to the difficulties with which the forum can be made compatible with a deliberative democratic politics; nevertheless, to discount the political relevance of this forum for online Islam would disregard its important contributions. First, the transnational dimension is overtly present here as in the former three genres: the forum can then be seen as a site bringing together Muslims from across the world. Secondly, the varied themes point to the wide interests and experiences of the users. The anonymity offered to users points to the relative ease with which people can write their opinions, although the forum is moderated and requires registration. And the multiplicity of the users points to the overall inclusiveness and openness of the forum. Taken together these aspects contribute to the development of a controlled but accessible area for the exchange of ideas and experiences, for discussion and disagreement about issues, and more broadly speaking of the 'thematization' of Muslim life: putting forward and discussing aspects of Muslim life and beliefs.

In terms of the current problematic, this genre seems to have a dual function, first to express the *umma* from the bottom-up, in the same way that the blogs give voice to the subjective experiences of Muslims; and second, to provide a space where people can come together in dialogue, in the exchange of opinions and experiences, as well as in disagreement and in conflict. The range of topics covered in the fora indicates the significance both of localised experiences as well as of broader translocal aspects of 'being Muslim'. But what is crucial is that the discourses encountered here are not of the authoritative type found in websites and portals, but rather of the subjective, personal type such as those on blogs. It is this bottom-up and collaborative aspect, as well as the room to disagree and voice different opinions that are politically significant. Rather than interpellating the *umma* from the top-down, the online forum allows for the development of a space to negotiate what it means to be part of an *umma*, a community of believers that 'exists' in both a localised manner and in a translocal way.

Conclusion: locating transnational Islam

The survey of the four internet genres showed that the articulation of Islam and the internet, and of locality and translocality, is more complex than initially assumed. First, the discussion here broadly supports Bowen's (2004) arguments of Islam as a transnational public space. In these terms, it exists and develops in a manner more or less independent of locality whilst entailing struggles of authority and authorisation. The internet seems to support the development of a transnational Muslim public, bound by common beliefs rather than by location. Second, however, we have seen that locality is important both in terms of action and in terms of experiences. However, rather than interpreting these findings as entailing a contradiction or a paradox, it will be argued here that transnationalism and locality in fact correspond to different planes of existence which are differentially articulated on the internet: transnationalism corresponds to imagination and thought and locality to experience and action. Rather than being mutually exclusive, in other words, they lead to the articulation of different relationships between imagination and experience, thought and action. This argument will be pursued through a critique of some of the existing frameworks for thinking Islam and the internet, and through formulating possible alternative ways of approaching Islam online.

The most well-known theorising is linked to the concept of the public sphere. Theorists such as Jon Anderson (2003; Eickelman and Anderson, 1999), as well as Bunt (2003) and Mandaville (2001) speak of the emergence of an internet supported Muslim public sphere. This Muslim public sphere brings together the discourses of science and technology with those of Islam, and leads to a new class, that of the new Muslim intellectuals, whose role in Islam is pivotal, leading to a widening of Islam, to a rearticulation of religious with other discourses, and to a move away from the traditional Islamic centres and authorities. This democratisation of Islam through the internet leads to a questioning of traditional religious Islamic authorities, to a broadening of the participatory basis of Islam when it comes to interpretations of *fiqh* or the issuing of *fatwa*. This online Muslim public sphere is therefore characterised by a new middle class of educated and relatively affluent mostly diasporic Muslims, with a transnational orientation, and who are seeking to formulate a novel Muslim identity incorporating new experiences, views, practices and politics. In terms of offline Muslim politics, this public sphere has been linked to the potential democratisation of illiberal Muslim majority countries (Mandaville, 2001).

But to what extent can online Islam be understood through the prism of a theory that was suggested in order to capture a very specific moment of European history, and which is inextricably linked to the nation-state as a form of governance? It may be that the concept is used without the theory; however, as soon as the public sphere becomes linked to politics, its position as a legitimating device is evident. This is the original argument put forward by Habermas (1962/1989). And in order for the public sphere to operate as a legitimating device, it must be open to all, characterised by rational discourse, by a relatively homogenous public, and who must make informed decisions based on facts. As we have seen the discourses encountered online are authorial, controlling, expressive and subjective, and only to a small degree can they be thought as 'rational/argumentative. The broader question here concerns the status and function of this online public sphere. In addition, the idea of a public sphere does not allow for the struggle for authority and control or the fragmentation and multiplication that we have seen online. I suggest that the discourse of the public sphere is already heavily burdened with assumptions that may hinder than contribute to understanding online Islam. Rather, beginning with online Islam, we might then help develop an understanding of a multiple Islam operating in a transnational, and perhaps for some post-national, and agonistic world.

Indeed the above findings suggest that online Islam is concerned both with the articulation of a common Muslim identity in accordance with the requirements of religious authorities, which then forms the centre of the *umma*, as well as with the articulation and expression of experiences, of problems, of solutions, of practices and actions. In practice, these articulations are always contested. More broadly, online Islam has a dual orientation: one towards the imagination, towards imagining what the community is or might be, and one towards action and practice, towards acting, experiencing and practising. This points to the internet acting not as a public sphere, that is, a sphere that constructs/expresses public opinion, but as a space that articulates imagination with experience, and thought with action. The translocal dimension may be seen as corresponding to the element of imagination and thought, and the local to that of action and experience. These two aspects interact with one another in various ways. We have seen for example that the blog operates in an inductive manner: extrapolating from localised experience to a broader imagined community/ *umma*. Conversely, in the MPAC website, action is justified in the name of an interpellated/imaginary *umma*. The portal shows the struggle involved for controlling or delimiting the imagined *umma*, whilst also pragmatically limiting or localising its actual manifestation, in the directories of local business and so on. The forum, on the other hand, provides a platform for the articulation both of different, and often conflicting, imagined *'ummas'* as well as for the expression of different experiences and proposed actions. All these point to a conceptualisation of the internet as a generative space, a space which actively constructs or articulates imaginaries, through allowing both the top down interpellation and control of a differentially imagined *umma*, and the bottom up inductive extrapolation of an imagined community drawing on localised experience and actions/practices. It further points to the antagonistic existence of these imaginaries: there may be some agreement and coincidence of opinion, but mostly the internet allows for the proliferation of a multiplicity of imaginaries surrounding the *umma*. From this perspective the function of the internet is not to legitimate but to provide a space for the formulation of critical and often antagonistic and oppositional imaginaries. Transnational Islam is therefore located in the different and often competing imaginaries found in the various internet genres.

A note of caution should however be inserted here. It may be tempting to see in the new technologies the harbinger of a new, more inclusive world. To an extent this follows from the above analysis; in addition, theorists such as Peter Mandaville (2001) have pointed to the importance of the internet in reforming Islam from a critical perspective, and for giving voice(s) to alternative formulations, but have perhaps underestimated the extent to which this imagination may be a conservative, traditional and top down, authoritarian one, as well as the great diversity of the internet. Indeed, in our brief discussion the attempts to control and set boundaries emerge as immanent in the two genres of website and portal. The bottom-up genres of blog and forum allow for a negotiation between positions and for variable input, and could be thought as inherently more 'democratic'. However, the fragmentation involved in the multitude of blogs and fora point to problems with this formulation. This fragmentation and proliferation of opinion may be thought as inimical to democracy insofar as this requires a demos that comes together to think and decide upon matters of common concern. From this point of view, the political

efficacy of transnational online Islam in existing multicultural democracies is necessarily limited and equivocal.

Notes

1. Google returns 150 million results for 'Islam', almost twice than for
   'Christianity' (84 million). Search conducted on 11 May 2006.
2. Operation Muslim Vote was broadcast on 16 May 2005, following the UK
   2005 general election. The documentary followed the efforts of MPACUK to
   influence Muslim voters: MPACUK first wanted to get British Muslims to
   vote in the election, and second to vote in a manner that reflects their
   interests.
3. See: http://www.salaam.co.uk/exposure/exposure.htm
4. This is Adorno's (1996) argument for art in relation to society: it must be
   inside to know its subject matter, but also outside so that it can provide a
   different perspective and viewpoint. This is what makes art the source of
   major change and innovation, as well as of insight, which then enable
   society to remain dynamic.
5. On the role of the community sites as preparatory for entry in politics, see
   Siapera (2005).
6. For a set of reviews of the role of the internet in radical democracy, including deliberative democratic models, see Dahlberg and Siapera (forthcoming).
7. Consider for instance the following post: – e.g. 'Assalamualaikum
   jazakaAllah for posting that, i will take time out to watch it inshaAllah.
   Walaikumusalam'.

References

Adorno, T. (1999) *Aesrhetic Theory*, trausl. Rovert Hullot-Keutor (Minneapolis:
   University of Minnesota Press).
Anderson, J. W. (1999) 'The Internet and Islam's New Interpreters'. In
   D. F. Eickelman and J. W. Anderson (eds), *New Media in the Muslim World:
   The Emerging Public Sphere*. (Bloomington: Indiana University Press) pp. 41–56.
Anderson, J. (2003) 'New Media, New publics: Reconfiguring the Public Sphere
   of Islam', *Social Research*, 70 (3), 887–906.
Appadurai, A. (1996) *Modernity At Large*, (Minneapolis: University of Minnesota
   Press).
L. Basch, N. Glick Schiller and C. Szanton Blanc (1994) *Nations Unbound: Trans-
   national Projects, Postcolonial Predicaments and the Deterritorialized Nation-State.*
   (New York: Gordon and Breach).
Bowen, J. (2004), 'Beyond Migration', *Journal of Ethnic and Migration Studies*,
   30(5), 879–94.
Bunt, G. (2003) *Islam in the Digital Age*, (London: Pluto Press).
Chandler, D. 'An Introduction to Genre Theory' [WWW document] **URL**
   http://www.aber.ac.uk/media/Documents/intgenre/intgenre.html [Produced in
   1997, last accessed 16 May 2006]
Dahlberg, L. and E. Siapera (eds) (forthcoming) *Radical Democracy and the
   Internet*. (Basingstoke: Palgrave).

Eickelman, D. and J. Anderson (1999) 'Redefining Muslim Publics'. In D. Eickelman and J. Anderson (eds), *New Media in the Muslim World: The Emerging Public Sphere* (Bloomington: Indiana University Press), pp. 1–18.

Grillo, R. (2004) 'Islam and Transnationalism', *Journal of Ethnic and Migration Studies*, 30 (5), 861–78.

Habermas, J. (1989) *The Structural Transformation of the Public Sphere: An Inquiry into a Category of Bourgeois Society*. (T. Burger with F. Lawrence Trans.) (Cambridge: Polity Press).

Habermas, J. (1999) 'Three Normative Models of Democracy'. In C. Cronin and P. De Greiff (eds), *The Inclusion of the Other: Studies in Political Theory* (Cambridge: Polity Press), pp. 239–52.

Hannertz, U. (1996) *Transnational Connections: Culture, People, Places* (London: Routledge).

Held, D. (2003) *Cosmopolitanism: A Defence*. (Cambridge: Polity Press).

Mandaville, P. (2001) *Transnational Muslim Politics: Reimagining the Ummah*. (London: Routledge).

Riccio, B. (2001) 'From Ethnic Group to Transnational Community? Senegalese Migrants' Ambivalent Experiences and Multiple Trajectories', *Journal of Ethnic and Migration Studies*, 27 (4), 583–89.

Siapera, E. (2005) 'Minority Activism on the Web: Between Deliberative Democracy and Multiculturalism', *Journal of Ethnic and Migration Studies*, 31(3), 499–519.

Sklair, L. (2001) *The Transnational Capitalist Class* (Oxford: Blackwell).

Smith, M. P. and L. E. Guarnizo (1998) (eds) *Transnationalism from Below*. (New Brunswick: Transaction Publishers).

Vertovec, S. (1999) 'Conceiving and Researching Transnationalism', *Ethnic and Racial Studies*, 22(2), 447–62.

Werbner, P. (2004) 'Theorising Complex Diasporas: Purity and Hybridity in the South Asian Public Sphere in Britain', *Journal of Ethnic and Migration Studies*, 30 (5), 895–911.

Websites cited (last accessed 5 September 2006):

www.mpacuk.org; www.salaam.co.uk ;
http://opinionated.blogsome.com and www.ummah.com/forum

6
The Sámi Media, State Broadcasting and Transnational Indigeneity

Lia Markelin and Charles Husband

Introduction

There is now an extensive literature which explores the relationship between ethnic identities and the media. A specific sub-set of this academic and policy debate has addressed the unique status of indigenous peoples and their relationship to the media and systems of communication (Langton, 1993; Browne, 1996; Alia, 1999; Hartley and McKee, 2000; and Molnar and Meadows, 2001). In seeking to explore the development of the Sámi media it is appropriate to acknowledge the salience of post-modernism as a theoretical position within academic and public discourse, and its impact in now making it normative to recognize the complexity of subjectivities and collective identities in the contemporary world. The transnational reach of biographic and political affiliations, encapsulated in the concept of diasporic identities, extend and transform our understanding of ethnicity. At the same time, recognizing the significance of the current debates around globalisation and the impact of late modernity we are urged to recognize the capacity of new communication systems to contribute to the fragmentation of identities nurtured by a super abundance of communicative choice. The current academic fascination with the vanishing possibility of stable identities, suggested by a world defined by the 'liquid modernity' of postmodernist analyses (Bauman 1997, 2000; Elliott and Lemert, 2006), sits awkwardly in relation to the necessary certainties of identity politics. As historically oppressed peoples contest their rights in the context of nation state media regulation and minority policy there is a rhetorical requirement of certainty and confidence in asserting identity based claims. Asserting the – 'endless possibilities of hybrid-diasporic identities in forming the elusive and transient sense of possessing an ethnic identity' – is folly on a grand scale when dialoguing with state agencies over resource allocations. The logistics of competing for resources and recognition within state policies of managing ethnic diversity have been recognized as generating the use of pragmatic collective categories that are shaped by that context of competition; with consequent distortions of the routinely employed ethnic categories in play within the communities being represented (Anthias and Yuval-Davis 1992, Solomos and Back 1995).

Academic concerns regarding the dangers of essentialising diasporic, and indigenous, identities are well founded (Cunningham and Sinclair, 2000; Brown, 2003). However, an integral claim of indigenous identity is the recognition of a tie between people and territory over time. The social imaginaries that provide the deep roots of a shared culture (Taylor 2003, p. 23) have for indigenous peoples a historical and territorial rootedness that may be all too elusive for majority populations transformed by modernity and its more recent variants. Indeed, as Brown (2003, p. 67) has suggested it may well be this claim to a grounded existential authenticity which makes majority 'modern' populations vulnerable to the claims of indigenous peoples. He suggests that the certainty implicated in the grounded and continuous identity claims of indigenous peoples may appear deeply attractive to contemporary national identities that are so richly fragmented by the hybrid dynamics associated with late modern capitalism. Somewhat provocatively he proposes that, for example,

> Today, white Australia needs Aboriginal Australia to keep alive the dream that there exist, somewhat not impossibly far away, forms of lived experience that retain the magical holism shattered by modernity. (Brown, 2003, p. 67)

The analysis offered in this chapter is framed by the international political discourses surrounding indigeneity and the rights of indigenous peoples; and more specifically by a Nordic perspective on this issue (Aikio and Scheinin, 2000; Ivison *et al.*, 2000; Oskal, 2002; Anaya, 2004; Cant *et al.*, 2005). The multiple and overlapping identities available to the Sámi actors in this account can be seen as offering different negotiating positions within the overall political economy that determines the Sámi media environment. Simultaneously these identities provide a context of collective affiliation and political mobilisation that may conjure forth a variety of priorities.

This chapter provides an account of the development of the Sámi media system in the Nordic Arctic. It draws upon extensive fieldwork carried out throughout 1999–2003. In that time interviews were held with key persons in the Sámi media system, the Sámi political system and the majority structures in Norway, Sweden and Finland. Several individuals were interviewed more than once and this research is deeply indebted to the openness and generosity of the many people who gave of their time and expertise.

Indigenous peoples, worldwide, have been the subjects, and objects, of social scientific study. Their shared experience of having been exploited as 'grist to the academic mill' rightly has made them cautious of the external gaze. Equally, for those non-indigenous scholars who wish to engage with indigenous communities, ignorance of the potential pitfalls of ethnocentrism and insensitive reporting is not an option. The dynamic relationship between subjectivities and institutional forces in relation to the Sámi media system, discussed below, are still very much in play in relation to current developments (as of May 2006). Since we have shared the initial analysis with a range of our original respondents we feel comfortable in presenting this analysis. We do not believe, however, that we are qualified to contribute to current sensitive political and professional debates within the Sámi media world. It is, therefore, a deliberate choice that the argument developed below preponderantly reports the situation as outlined in detail by Markelin (2003 a,b).

The setting: Sámi and the Sámi media in the Nordic states

The Sámi are the indigenous peoples of Norway, Sweden, Finland and the Kola Peninsula. Having inhabited large parts of Finland and the Scandinavian Peninsula before the emergence of state borders, the Sámi are today divided between four different countries. Sámiland stretches from southern central and northern Norway over Sweden and northern Finland into the Kola Peninsula in Russia. However, a sizeable part of the Sámi population lives outside of this area, not least in the capitals of the Nordic states.

Sámi organisations and representative bodies today present the Sámi as one people, and Sámiland (or *Sápmi*) is represented *inter alia* through its own flag, a national anthem and common cultural symbols. The Sámi have actively participated in the international Indigenous people's movement, not least through the Sámi Council, a non-govern-mental umbrella organisation for Sámi organisations in the four countries. Although sometimes referred to as one language, there are ten Sámi languages,[1] some of which are mutually unintelligible. With four different majority languages involved, three of which are similarly mutually unintelligible, there is no one language common to all Sámi. However, North Sámi is the most widely used Sámi language, and it is the Sámi language most widely used in the Sámi media. An estimated one third of the Sámi population speaks Sámi (or at least one of the Sámi languages). The symbolic meaning of the language, however, also remains strong amongst many non-speakers (Svonni, 1996).

The history of the Sámi media stretches back to the late nineteenth century. With the growth of broadcast media in the middle of the twentieth century, Sámi media became a more permanent presence in the area. Sámi radios were established in the late 1940s in Norway and Finland, in the 1950s in Sweden and in 2003 in Russia.[2] Today the Sámi Radio and Television broadcasting units form the main media services in Sámi. In addition, two newspapers are published in North Sámi and one in Norwegian in Norwegian Sámiland, and a number of magazines are published across Sámiland. The Internet has also become a medium increasingly used by the Sámi media as well as other actors.

Below the situation of the Sámi broadcast media will be discussed in greater detail.

Identities and the logics of media development

The brief description above reveals the multiple and overlapping identities which are in play within Sápmi. All Sámi may legitimately call themselves indigenous peoples, and this immediately invests the small populations of the Sámi communities with the global status of authenticity that has become associated with indigeneity (see, for example, Brown 2003). More specifically, the debates around the international political recognition of the status of indigenous peoples, and the legal instruments developed around this, provide a mechanism of leverage against the current ambivalence of individual nation states in their relationship with their own specific indigenous populations. This is a stratagem the Sámi have been adept at employing.

At the same time, all Sámi are citizens of a specific state; Norway, Sweden, Finland or Russia, and as will become apparent, the differing legal status accorded to the Sámi in each country has contributed to the development of the Sámi media system.[3] However, it would be naïve and simplistic to assume that location within a national territorial space has only political–juridical implications for individual Sámi. It is quite possible to be affectively both Sámi and Swedish, Finnish or Norwegian. Nationalist sentiments are not alien to the interactions of colleagues from different Nordic countries as they seek to develop trans-national Sámi media systems.

As we have seen above, the Sámi are also internally fragmented into language groups with their own territorial reach. The more localised territorial and cultural claims of being, for example, a Skolt, Inari or Kildin Sámi have implications for each person's entry into their understanding of being a member of the Sámi within Sápmi; or living in a national capital far from the homeland. Given the different size of the different Sámi populations, and the critical viability of some of the Sámi languages, there must inevitably be a range of political priorities in play as each Sámi population develops their wish list for state intervention: including the provision of Sámi media.

The international language of recognition of indigeneity provides a robust discourse within which the Sámi and the national majority populations may negotiate each others identity and status. For the national majorities it provides a homogenizing conceptual framework within which 'their Sámi' can be recognized: and even valorized. For the Sámi themselves such inclusiveness could potentially be both helpful and problematic; for whilst it may furnish an identity that is viable in international and national political fora, it does not highlight the specificity of community and individual Sámi identities.

Sámi broadcast media and media co-operation

Because of an early monopolisation of frequencies and a continued strong tradition of public service broadcasting in the Nordic states, Sámi broadcasting emerged within the framework of national public service broadcasting. The main Sámi broadcasting centres today remain part of the national public service broadcasting companies. There is a Sámi Radio unit within the public service broadcasting companies (PSBs) of Norway (NRK), Sweden (SR) and Finland (YLE) that in Norway and Finland also produce other forms of electronic media including television. In Sweden, where radio and television are separated into two different companies, Sámi radio and television form separate units (SR Sámi Radio and SVT Sápmi).

Co-operation between the Sámi Radios has long formed an important aspect of Sámi broadcasting. The long-term plan for the Sámi Radios has been to develop one common full-time Sámi Radio channel across the borders. Although the channel has not yet materialised as planned, sharing, exchange and co-production of programming have become important characteristics of Sámi radio broadcasting. A significant milestone in the development of Sámi broadcasting and broadcast co-operation was the introduction of daily news on television in 2001. The news, which could be seen as a significant development for indigenous broadcasting worldwide, is jointly produced and broadcast weekdays in all three countries. Sámi is the main language of the programme, which is subtitled to the respective majority languages before being aired in Norway, Sweden and Finland respectively.[4]

In many ways, Sámi broadcast media provide a unique and strong case for the possibilities of media co-operation as a way of strengthening and sustaining a common identity and language. Partly as a result of co-operation, Sámi broadcasters have managed to develop and sustain a range of Sámi media and programming that otherwise might not be possible. Co-operation can perhaps also be seen as a natural and desirable element of media production within a shared culture, even though its inhabitants live in different countries – a view that was voiced by workers within the Sámi media (Markelin, 2003a). However, as revealed in this research (Markelin, 2003a,b), a shared language or identity might not be enough to sustain a common public sphere. There are a number of factors potentially affecting collaborations within the Sámi media world. We shall have a closer look at some of these here.

The political economy of Sámi media

Media structures, just as ethnic relations, emerge and develop within particular economic and political frameworks. As far as media regulation is concerned, it is still largely within the borders of the state that decisions regarding frequencies, content and competition between the media are made. Importantly for smaller groups, it is also within national borders that possible public support for the media is distributed *inter alia* in the form of public service broadcasting or press subsidies for the printed media.

Although three of the four states in which the Sámi live belong to the family of the Nordic countries, a group of Northern European countries with similarities in political, social and cultural traits, Sámiland exists within four separate national frameworks. This is relevant if one considers the ways in which national contexts have been seen to affect national responses to multiculturalism (e.g. Heckmann and Bosswick, 1995; Koopmans and Statham, 2000). How the relationship between the state and the Sámi has developed within four separate contexts is not irrelevant for the development of the Sámi media. On the contrary, as demonstrated in Markelin (2003a,b), the national position of the Sámi in terms of legal, political and economic frameworks, as well as the perceived legitimacy of Sámi claims, is reflected in the strength and size of the Sámi broadcast media.

Among the aims of the 2003 study was to map the actual situation of the Sámi media, and find some explanations for the differences in development that the Sámi media have experienced over the years. The situation of the Sámi broadcast media in Norway, Sweden and Finland has over the past few decades differed significantly in terms of size, output and resources. While the development of resources for Sámi broadcasting in Sweden and Finland remained fairly stagnant for most of the 1990s and into the twenty first century, Norway has seen a fairly steady development of Sámi media. In 2004, the budget and size of the Norwegian Sámi Radio was many times greater than that of its Swedish or Finnish counterparts.

However, in 2004, it was YLE Sámi Radio in Finland who had the longest daily broadcasts, broadcasting for about eight hours every weekday. NRK Sámi Radio broadcast about six hours, and SR Sámi Radio in Sweden one and a half hours on weekdays. The Finnish Sámi Radio has had access to its own separate analogue channel, albeit a regional channel, since 1991, whereas the Sámi Radios in Norway and Sweden have been dependent on slots of broadcasting time within majority channels. Without the resources to fill the channel, however, a large part of the Finnish YLE Sámi Radio broadcasts are produced by NRK Sámi Radio, or co-produced with the other two countries. In Sweden, by contrast, the limited access to broadcasting space available for Swedish Sámi Radio has meant the station has had no space to include the available programming of the other two states. For a period of time, SR Sámi Radio was not able to broadcast all of the programming that it itself had been part of producing, due to a lack of broadcasting space. At the time, even a channel manager within the Swedish Radio, of which SR Sámi Radio forms part, judged this a waste and a 'destruction of capital' (Markelin 2003a, p. 185).

The starting point of the research was that such discrepancies between the Sámi stations were difficult to understand without looking at the political economy of which the Sámi media form part. This included looking not only at the historical, political and demographic developments of the Sámi and of state-Sámi relations in the three countries, but also at how power relations and policies of multiculturalism have emerged and developed within the three states, and how these might have affected the development of the media and thus, in extension, the development of a common public sphere across borders.

Development of state policies towards the Sámi

Historically, all three of the Nordic states in question have seen similar developments in their relationship to the Sámi. Despite evidence of early recognition of Sámi rights,[5] processes of appropriation have taken place across the Scandinavian peninsula. In the late nineteenth and early twentieth centuries in particular nationalist sentiments favoured unfavourable, and in Sweden and not least in Norway, explicitly assimilationist policies, towards the Sámi. As both attitudes and policies started changing in the twentieth century, particularly after the end of the Second World War, policies towards the Sámi too began to change.[6]

In Norway, there was a radical shift in Sámi policy particularly from the beginning of the 1980s onwards. This development, a process aided by the widely publicised struggle over the damming of the River Alta in the late 1970s early 1980s (Brantenberg 1985; Minde 2005), pushed Sámi issues to the centre of national political attention in a way not seen in the neighbouring countries. From a multicultural perspective, this apparently aided a separation of Sámi issues from issues concerning other minority ethnic groups in the country. Although Norway encompasses other historical minority groups and had been receiving foreign labour for some time, a clear policy distinction emerged between Sámi issues on the one hand, and migrant and later minority issues on the other.

In Sweden, by contrast, a major country of immigration in Western Europe in the twentieth century, immigration and integration took centre stage in multiethnic policies for decades. In fact, immigration appears to have been so dominant that in the 1970s no clear distinction was necessarily made between minority groups and immigrants, rather everyone who was not 'an ethnic Swede' was easily perceived as an immigrant (see, for example, comment in Markelin 2003a: 174). Within the context of national multicultural policies, consequently, the Sámi (as well as national minority groups) appear to have been left in the shadows of immigration and integration concerns.

In Finland, on the other hand, a country of emigration until the late 1980s where the number of immigrants is still comparatively small, a lot of attention has historically been given to the Swedish-speaking

Finns. As an officially bilingual country where the smaller official language group consists of around 5.5 per cent of the population, Finland always had to deal with issues of minority rights. Although not thereby pushing Sámi issues onto the centre stage of politics, this can be seen to have created a different starting point for Sámi and minority rights than that of Sweden.

Though radically simplified, this short description points to certain significant differences in the historical development of the three countries as multiethnic states, and to the way in which the Sámi have been 'ranked' within these states in relation to other groups who find themselves in positions of being a minority. This becomes relevant when considering the way in which resources are divided between groups; or the level of legitimacy awarded Sámi claims today.

Legal and political framework

Both Norway and Finland today recognise the rights of the Sámi at a constitutional level. According to the Norwegian constitution it is the responsibility of the State 'to create conditions enabling the Sámi people to preserve and develop its language, culture and way of life'. The Finnish constitution in turn states that the Sámi, as an indigenous people, have the right to maintain and develop their own language and culture. Sweden in turn does not mention the Sámi in its constitution. Thus the basic legal framework of Sámi rights, and the basis on which to develop one's life and society as Sámi, depends on the national borders within which this is to happen. Other significant differences in Sámi rights too can be found between the legal frameworks of the three countries (see, for example, Myntti, 1998). Significant issues of land ownership and rights to natural resources remain unresolved in all three states. Sápmi, as the imagined collective territory of all Sámis, sits uncomfortably within the different political jurisdictions of individual Nordic states.[7]

In terms of political rights and state policies, further differences emerge. Although all three countries have their own Sámi Parliaments, the legal bases of these parliaments and the extent of their mandate, as well as their funding base, differ from one country to another (cf. Myntti, 2000). While the Norwegian Sámi Parliament has comparatively enjoyed the greatest resources over the past years, the resources of the Finnish Sámi Parliament have clearly been more limited than that of particularly its Norwegian but also its Swedish counterpart. A more coherent Sámi policy started to develop within the Norwegian government in the 1980s; something that at the beginning of the twenty first century seemed to start to develop in Sweden. Sámi policy in Finland, on the other hand, still remained more fragmented at this time. All three of these states officially recognise the Sámi as indigenous in their own country. The level of this recognition, however, and what the position of the Sámi as indigenous means or perhaps should mean, remain questions of debate. Whereas the official rhetoric at the highest level of Norwegian politics in the 1990s was that Norway is a country based upon the land of two peoples, Norwegians and Sámi, this did not at the time of the research appear to be familiar language in the other two countries. Though all three countries obviously struggled with the concept of indigeneity, Norway appeared to have come the furthest in recognising the consequences of this concept, including in relation to the media. In Finland, and Sweden in particular, Sámi issues or claims were more easily put on a par with other minority ethnic group issues (Tuulentie 2001; Markelin 2003; cf. Lawrence 2005).

Media political framework

Perhaps not surprisingly, reflections of the above differences in the legal and political frameworks can also be found in state media policies towards Sámi initiatives. By 2003, Norway was the only country of the three to have included Sámi media needs in national media policy, not only through public service broadcasting, but also in terms of press subsidies for Sámi print media, obligations on commercial broadcasters to produce programming in Sámi, and support for Sámi film. In Sweden and Finland, by contrast, support outside of the public service broadcasting companies has been limited. There have been no public subsidies for a printed Sámi news media, or pressures on commercial channels to serve the Sámi population. Instead, the main responsibility has, as in Norway, been handed over to the public service broadcasting companies.

The public service broadcasting companies in all of the three countries have, in other words, been given a clear responsibility for Sámi programming as part of their public service mandate. How this responsibility has been formulated in regulations, however, and how these have been interpreted within the companies, differs from one country to another.

In Norway, as seen above, there has been a significant increase in support for Sámi broadcasting over the past decade and a half in particular. According to the former Director General of the Norwegian NRK, this was the result of a clear priority made by the company. In the early 1990s NRK Sámi Radio became a separate division within the company, and the head of NRK Sámi Radio part of the company management. The head of Sámi Radio is thus not only in charge of the Sámi programming, but also takes part in forming company policy more generally. The Norwegian broadcasting company NRK has in its past policy documents mentioned its responsibilities towards the Sámi language on a par with Norwegian. According to the regulations that guided the Norwegian public service broadcaster NRK from 1996 (revised in 2004), one of the core tasks of the company is to develop and convey both Norwegian and Sámi culture and language.

In Sweden in contrast, as demonstrated above, fairly little happened to the growth of Sámi broadcasting in the country during the 1990s. One reason for this, according to the companies themselves, was the sheer number of minority ethnic groups that the broadcasters have been responsible for serving. Resources in Sweden were, in other words, seen to be stretched between too many groups to be able to make such investments in Sámi programming as has been done in Norway. This could be seen to reflect a failure to define the Sámi as having distinctive claims as an indigenous people. In the late 1990s and early twenty first century, however, as interviews were carried out at the companies, some development was taking place and there was a sense within the companies that they were doing what they could; perhaps even more than was required from them by their regulatory authorities. Sámi programming was seen as a priority – or at least as one priority amongst many. One significant problem at the time was a lack of broadcasting space: the analogue channels were full, and to radically alter the programming of the analogue channels to fit in more Sámi broadcasting was not seen as a viable option. Throughout the 1990s the Sámi units in both Swedish Radio and Television also found themselves low on the organisational hierarchical scales of the companies, with little institutional influence within the highest echelons of management.

In Finland, a period of great development was seen in the late 1980s and early 1990s, as a separate regional analogue radio channel was opened for Sámi programming in the northern part of Finland. This remains the only analogue Sámi broadcasting channel within the public service system in the Nordic states. In the decade that followed, however, little development was seen in terms of an increase in resources. In the late 1990s it was rather services for other groups, such as the Russian population, that appeared most problematic by company management, while views towards the development of Sámi broadcasting appeared relaxed–not dissimilarly from state policies towards the Sámi as a whole. The fact that Finland has two main language groups to service to start with (Finnish and Swedish) was also perceived as a problem by the management, providing 'much less flexible programming possibilities' on television (Markelin 2003a, p. 196). As in Sweden in the 1990s, YLE Sámi Radio has been treated as a local radio within the company, low on the hierarchical scale.

Most central to the developments that have taken place within all Sámi broadcasters over the past decades has naturally been the activism of the Sámi themselves. However, the support structures in place for facilitating these efforts have been significant in determining their success. As seen above, the support frameworks outside of the media vary from one state to another. As the Sámi media depend on public funding and support, at least in their present form and with the audience bases known today, these are of central importance.

It should also be noted that the medium for a majority of the Sámi media co-operation is the North Sámi language. Some of the smaller Sámi languages are spoken mainly within the borders of one state, and thus have limited support to gain from cross-border co-operation. This, and the fact that a large number of Sámi do not speak any of the Sámi languages, also puts pressure on national structures to provide basic services irrespective of the potential additional strength gained through co-operation. Thus the internal diversity of the Sámi populations, and their linguistic diversity, has implications for the media logics of optimizing audience size which may cut across parallel concerns with deploying the media as active agents of language maintenance.

The fact that the main responsibility for Sámi broadcasting has been handed over to the national public service broadcasting companies in the three countries could possibly be viewed as a problem, considering that the public service companies of the three states in question are majority-ethnic owned and driven companies. There did not appear to be a sense within the companies of common resources to be shared between the different groups in the country, but rather the PSB organisations appeared to be majority resources shared with minority ethnic groups on terms decided by the majority. How the rights of the Sámi are viewed then becomes a central issue. At the time of the research there was no Sámi representation within the highest decision-making bodies of the public service broadcasting companies of any of the three countries, and only in Norway was the head of Sámi Radio represented in the company management. Institutionally speaking, there was thus limited Sámi influence over the main Sámi media in all three countries, and the development of Sámi broadcasting becomes at least in part dependent on the support of non-Sámi individuals within company management.

Simultaneously, however, national public service broadcasters are sizeable companies with strong infrastructures capable of providing support for smaller production units such as the Sámi. None of the companies voiced negative views towards Sámi broadcasting during the research. On the contrary, one could say it has been the companies themselves, rather than the states that have assumed greatest (financial) responsibility for Sámi media development (as argued in Markelin 2003a, p. 262 in particular). However, how this responsibility is realised is related not only to perceptions within company management, but also to the development of multicultural relations outside of the companies, and the resources and respect awarded Sámi representative bodies. As the former director general of NRK commented, in order to understand the investments in Sámi programming made by the Norwegian broadcasting company they had to be put in relation to the development of Sámi issues in Norway from around the early 1980s, and the process of awareness regarding the Norwegian responsibility for Sámi language and culture.

Consequences for Sámi broadcasting and broadcast co-operation

The aim of the Sámi broadcasters remains the development of a full-service alternative for the Sámi population. The way to achieve this, respondents of the research seemed to agree, was through co-operation. Today, however, the Sámi broadcasters cannot engage in co-operation from an equal footing. The differences described above provided the Sámi broadcasters with different starting points from which to engage in co-operation: whereas one has a media organization of closer to eighty staff, the others are still working on building up their own infrastructures. And whereas a lack of broadcasting space in Sweden was seen as a major obstacle for co-operation in both Finland and Norway, the limited broadcasting space on analogue radio in both Sweden and Norway was perceived as a problem by respondents in Finland.[8] In addition, the head of the Norwegian Sámi Radio questioned the commitment by the public service management in Sweden and Finland to common projects.

In 1997 the director generals of the three public service radios in question agreed on the establishment of a common Sámi Radio channel. However, in 2005, it could be observed that it was only in Norway that the plans had been adhered to or been exceeded. Neither Swedish nor Finnish Sámi Radio had the resources that in the 1990s had been staked out as necessary for the creation of a full service Sámi alternative on radio. Similarly with television, the agreement made in 1998 that the three countries would establish daily Sámi news on television was only followed as planned by Norway. The other two countries were so late in making their final decisions, and Finland de facto joining the project only after the programme had already been on air for some months, that all necessary decisions regarding format and content had to be made by the staff of Norwegian Sámi Radio. Although the staff of the stations managed to work through the early difficulties, the process strengthened the perception of Norway as the central force in Nordic co-operation. As the head of the Norwegian Sámi Radio commented, if the other two countries are not prepared to carry their own weight, then they should be prepared to hand over leadership of the common projects to Norway.

Rather than constituting three equal partners across borders, therefore, the constellation as it developed during the 1990s in particular meant that one of the three increasingly emerged as the leader, with the units in the two other countries trying to keep up as best they can. And if they could not, there was no guarantee of continued co-operation. As the project of the common daily news on television was stalled by both Sweden and Finland, NRK Sámi Radio became increasingly prepared to continue the project alone, with the aim of covering Swedish and Finnish parts of Sámiland through other means. This could of course have had negative effects not only on Sámi co-operation, but also on Sámi media services in Sweden and Finland. One consequence could be that Sámi living in Finland or Sweden would not have access to the material generated in Norway; whilst a second consequence could be that they would not have editorial control of the programming they imported from their Norwegian partners.

Although the Sámi broadcasters have so far managed to address the challenges facing their common goals; and have continued to sustain and develop their co-operation, the example of Sámi broadcast media points to some of the tensions that can arise around the interface of ethnic identities with political economies tied to national interests and priorities. The priorities in multiethnic policies made within individual states here can be seen to be reflected in the division of resources within the media; and this in turn affects the possibilities for the Sámi to develop their transnational linkages across borders. That the Sámi are the citizens of different state powers is a salient factor in determining the development of the Sámi media system within Sápmi.

The present and future

Across Sápmi pressure continues for the continuing development of Sámi media. Now, as in the past, the status of the Sámi as an indigenous people is a reality and a political resource that is deployed in dialogues with State agencies. A recent document from the Finnish Sámi Parliament to the Ministry of Transport and Communication in Finland in April 2006 invoked ILO 169 in arguing for a sufficient state subsidy for Sámi press in Finland. Also in 2006, following Sámi lobbying of Parliament in Helsinki, with Sámi children, participation of YLE television in Sámi programming for children was agreed. And, across the Nordic states the staffing levels of Sámi media have seen a progressive increase over the last few years. The specific media needs of distinct Sámi linguistic and cultural groups may also see positive developments as the project for the development of the Kildin Sámi radio in the Kola Peninsula evolves.

In a necessary, and parallel, development the Sámi media system has experienced a major innovation in recent years with the creation of a professional degree structure for Sámi journalism training at the Sámi University College in Guovdageaidnu (Kautokeino), in Norway. This course recruits students from across Sápmi and provides professional training infused with the specific sensibilities of Sámi identities and the global politics of indigeneity. The students have no difficulty in finding appropriate training placements, and are heavily in demand by the Sámi media system. As in other aspects of the Sámi media world, the distinct Sámi community identities of specific students operate in dynamic relation to the wider claims of a collective Sámi identity, and identification with indigenous peoples and struggles elsewhere.

A brief chapter such as this can only sketch some of the essential ingredients that have shaped, and do shape, the formation of a Sámi media system. Whilst recognising academic concerns with diasporic and hybrid identities this research concretely reveals how in the translation of identity into politics and practice the distinct *national discourses* on the management of ethnic diversity provide a framework within which the routines of national media systems have responded to the demands of the Sámi. At the same time there are different discourses in play between the different realms of the *intra-group politics* of Sámi identity, where *inter alia* linguistic, territorial and generational differences are interactively generating contemporary hybrid Sámi identities; and the *inter-group* engagement between the Sámi communities and state institutions, where common Sámi concerns are predominant. The inclusive political identity of the Sámi as indigenous peoples has been a particular expression of this inter-group dynamic: where in defining themselves as an indigenous people the Sámi have been effective in mobilizing the 'boomerang pattern' of communicative influence (Keck and Sikkink 1998) by invoking international linkages in their argument with the majority ethnic state. As Keck and Sikkink phrase it:

> When channels between the state and its domestic actors are blocked, the boomerang pattern of influence characteristic of transnational networks may occur: domestic NGOs bypass their state and directly search out international allies to try to bring pressure on their states from outside. (ibid, p.12)

Thus in different ways, and at different times, the national political systems of these three Nordic countries have proved susceptible to local expressions of the political claims of the global indigenous movement.

Within the context of the historical-political formation of their current nation state identities, in each country the Sámi have emerged in the last five decades or so as having a necessary presence in the national imagined community. Complacent denial, or assimilation, as strategies to manage Sámi claims upon the state are clearly no longer available options. At the same time the potential implications of the state recognizing Sámi claims to group differentiated rights (Kymlicka, 1995) are politically troubling. In different ways each nation state seeks to maintain a pragmatic calculus that aims to balance a recognition of their indigenous peoples, with a deeply cautious commitment to current expenditure.

Framed by the political relevance of globalised indigenous rights discourses, and the nation state's attempt to recognize their indigenous people, the Sámi communities continue to negotiate the realities and benefits of inclusive Sámi-ness. The concept of Sápmi as the imagined homeland of a collective people, the Sámi, has a comfortable fit with the conceptual language of international indigenous rights discourse. At the same time the territorial, cultural and linguistic priorities of specific Sámi communities provide the basis for a hybrid consciousness that can modify and add richness to this trans-border homogeneity. The fact that the Sámi are citizens of specific states has provided a context in which those seeking to develop a Sámi media system are able to employ these differing constructions of identity when engaging with their state institutions. In this context national identities may become significant for both majority and Sámi actors.

Notes

1. There are, however, different views on the number of separate Sámi languages.
2. However, Sámi programming was broadcast in Russia also before this time.
3. However, in the following text only the Sámi media situation in the Nordic states will be explored, as the situation in Russia was not included in the research.
4. In Finland, however, only the digital broadcasts are subtitled.
5. For example through the so-called *Lapp Codicil*, which has also been called the Sámi Magna Charta, from 1751 (see e.g. NOU 1984:18).
6. For general information on the Sámi society and developments in Sámiland, see for example, Lehtola (2002).
7. There is, however, an ongoing process for a common Nordic Sámi Convention that, if accepted by the three Nordic governments, could provide a more similar framework for Sámi rights in the three countries.
8. It should be noted, however, that both digital radio and web casting provide additional possibilities for Sámi broadcasting today. The analogue broadcasting time of SR Sámi Radio has also increased by one hour per weekday.

Bibliography

Aikio, P. and Scheinin, M. (eds) (2000) *Operationalizing the Right of Indigenous Peoples to Self-Determination* (Turku: Institute for Human Rights, Åbo Akademi University).

Alia, V. (1999) *Un/Covering the North: News, Media and Aboriginal People* (Vancouver: UBC Press).

Anaya, J. S. (2004) *Indigenous Peoples in International Law*, 2nd edn (Oxford: Oxford University Press).

F. Anthias and N. Yuval-Davis (1992) *Racialized Boundaries. Race, Nation, Gender, Colour, Class and the Anti-racist Struggle* (London: Routledge).

Bauman, Z. (1997) *Postmodernity and its Discontents* (Cambridge: Polity Press).

Bauman, Z. (2000) *Liquid Modernity* (Cambridge: Polity Press).

Brantenberg, O. T. (1985) 'The Alta-Kautokeino Conflict, Sami Reindeer-Herding and Ethno-Politics', in J. Brøsted *et al.* (eds), *Native Power*, pp. 23–48, (Oslo: Universitetsforlaget).

M. F. Brown, M. F. (2003) *Who Owns Native Culture?* (Cambridge, Mass.: Harvard University Press).

Browne, D. R. (1996) *Electronic Media and Indigenous Peoples – A Voice of Our Own?* (Ames, Iowa: Iowa State University Press).

Cant, G. Goodall, A. and Inns, J. (eds) (2005) *Discourses and Silences. Indigenous Peoples, Risks and Resistance* (Christchurch, New Zealand: University of Canterbury).

Cunningham, S. and Sinclair J. (2000) *Floating Lives: the Media and Asian Diasporas* (Lanham: Rowman and Littlefield).

Elliott, A. and Lemert, C. (2006) *The New Individualism* (London Routledge).

Hartely, J. and McKee, A. (2000) *The Indigenous Public Sphere. The Reporting and Reception of Indigenous Issues in the Australian Media, 1994–199X* (Oxford: Oxford University Press).

Heckmann, F. and Bosswick, W. (1995) *Migration Policies – A Comparative Perspective* (Stuttgart: Ferdinand Enke Verlag).

Ivison, D. Patton, P. and W. Sanders (eds) (2000) *Political Theory and the Rights of Indigenous Peoples* (Cambridge: Cambridge University Press).

Keck, M. E. and Sikkins, K. (1998) *Activists Beyond Borders* (Ithaca: Cornell University Press).

Koopmans, R. and Statham, P. (eds) (2000) *Challenging Immigration and Ethnic Relations Politics: Comparative European Perspectives* (Oxford: Oxford University Press).

Kymlicka, W. (1995) *Multicultural Citizenship: a Liberal Theory of Minority Rights* (Oxford: Clarendon Press).

Langton, M. (1993) *Well, I Heard It on the Radio and I Saw It on the Television: an Essay for the Australian Film Commission on the Politics and Aesthetics of Filmmaking by and about Aboriginal People and Things* (Sydney: Australian Film Commission).

Lawrence, R. (2005) 'Sámi, citizenship and non-recognition in Sweden and the European Union', in G. Cant, A. Goodall & J. Inns (eds), *Discourses and Silences. Indigenous Peoples, Risks and Resistance*, pp. 103–14 (Christchurch, New Zealand: University of Canterbury).

Lehtola, V. P. (2002) *The Sámi People – Tradition in Transition* (Inari: Kustannus– Puntsi / Fairbanks: University of Alaska Press).

Markelin, L.(2003a) 'Media, Ethnicity and Power. 'A Comparative Analysis of the Nordic Sámi Media Environment in Relation to State Policies', unpublished PhDthesis (Bradford, UK: University of Bradford).

Markelin, L. (2003b) 'En gemensam samisk offentlighet? Om en nordisk samisk infrastruktur', in B. Bjerkli & P. Selle (eds), *Samer, makt og demokrati. Sametinget og den nye samiske offentligheten*, pp. 398–424 (Oslo: Gyldendal Akademisk).

Minde, H. (2005) 'The Alta case: from the local to the global and back again', in G. Cant, A. Goodall & J. Inns (eds), *Discourses and Silences. Indigenous Peoples, Risks and Resistance*, pp. 13–34 (Christchurch, New Zealand: University of Canterbury).

Molnar, H. and Meadows, M. (2001) *Songlines to Satellites. Indigenous Communication in Australia, the South Pacific and Canada* (Annandale/Wellington: Pluto Press Australia/ Huia Publishers).

Myntti, K. (1998) *Minoriteters och urfolks politiska rättigheter. En studie av rätten för små minoriteter och urfolk till politiskt deltagande och självbestämmande*, Juridica Lapponica No. 18 (Rovaniemi: Nordiska Institutet för Miljö- och Minoritetsrätt).

Myntti, K. (2000) 'The Nordic Sami Parliaments', in P. Aikio and M. Scheinin (eds), *Operationalizing the Right of Indigenous Peoples to Self-Determination*, pp. 203–21 (Turku: Institute for Human Rights).

NOU (1984) *18 Om samenes rettsstilling* (Norwegian Ministry of Justice and the Police).

Nils Oskal (ed) (2002) *Samisk selvbestemmelse* (Kautokeino: Sámi Instituhtta).

Solomos, J. and Back, L. (1995) *Race, Politics and Social Change* (London: Routledge).

Svonni, M. (1996) 'Saami Language as Marker of Ethnic Identity among the Saami', in I. Seurujärvi-Kari & U-M. Kulonen (eds), *Essays on Indigenous Identity and Rights*, pp. 105–25 (Helsinki: Helsinki University Press).

Taylor, C. (2003) *Modern Social Imaginaries* (Durham: Duke University Press).

Tuulentie, S. (2001) *Meidän vähemmistömme. Valtaväestön retoriikat saamelaisten oikeuksista käydyissä keskusteluissa* (Helsinki: Suomen Kirjallisuuden Seura).

7
Refugee Communities and the Politics of Cultural Identity[1]

Ramaswami Haridranath

Introduction

The term 'diaspora', which productively engages with the complexities of migration and the formation of cultural identities, has itself come under theoretical scrutiny. In his attempt to build on and refine Safran's (1991) tabulation of features that characterise the diasporic experience, Cohen (1997) distinguishes between types of diaspora and the subtle differences between them. In his book Cohen sets out to delineate the features of what he describes as 'adjectival diasporas' (p. 29), communities whose constitution accommodates circumstances of their dispersal: victim diasporas, labour and imperial diasporas, and trade diasporas. Even more than conceptual clarity, Cohen's qualifications, specifically in terms of 'victim diasporas' enable a particular political stance. As he observes, 'In Chapter 1 I identified the Jewish, Palestinian, Irish, African and Armenian diasporas as the principal ones that can be described with the preceding adjective of "victim". Although this is primarily a scholarly grouping, writers and political leaders representing these peoples reinforce this classification with their constant cross-references and comparisons with one another' (p. 31). He sets out to compare and contrast the various victim diasporas he has identified – what are the common features, and what sets them apart from the others in the group.

Cohen's careful depiction of the histories of dispersal and settlement of 'victim diasporas' clearly portrays such communities as having complex ties with notions of 'home' that are qualitatively different from that of other types of diaspora. In addition to this, his argument includes an attempt to distinguish between the different victim diasporas: the Jewish, Palestinian, Irish, African, and Armenian. Underlying this, and relatively unexplored in the book, is the claim or assumption that the *experience* of their forced migration and of 'victimhood', as well as the *mediation* of them both within and outside the communities themselves, inform the identities of such communities. The present chapter seeks to explore a few of the complex ideas that buttress this important observation, building on Malkki's (1995) ethnographic study of Hutu refugees in Tanzania to engage with the notions of 'experience', subalternity, and the intricate politics of cultural expression and identity. It will be argued that conceiving refugee communities as diaspora includes exploring the validity of the politics of the subaltern's appeal to experience. Intrinsic to this, as we shall see, is the politics of representation and recognition.

On the one hand, 'diaspora' as a concept supplies a necessary epistemological tool with which to negotiate the complex convolutions that contribute to the experiences and identity formations among minority groups. It is a productive concept that allows for conceiving identity as being constantly renewed and constructed, and not fixed in terms of 'race' or community, or religion (Gilroy, 1993; Clifford, 1997). On the other hand however, as Lewellen (2002) observes, 'currently there is considerable controversy about how "diasporas" should be defined in an era of globalization' (p. 160). Until recently, Safran's (1991) identification of the characteristics of diaspora communities was generally accepted as a useful taxonomy. Chief among these was the notion of a common ancestral homeland – 'roots' in Clifford's (1997) formulation – that the community's ancestors were dispersed from, the myths and folklores that form a collective, idealised memory of 'home', and a commitment to homeland as an imagined space encouraged by cultural alienation from the host cultures. As Lewellen points out, later approaches to diaspora that have included a more general understanding of it as ethnicity and group cohesion also underline the importance of a real or imagined homeland, which, as an apparently defining category raises a few conceptual difficulties. 'Many Jews do not view Israel as a homeland in any but a historical sense. And what is one to make of the Black diaspora, which, for most, has no specific homeland, only a sort of generalized Africa? Diasporas may have multiple centres, such as may be found among Jamaicans, Haitians, Dominicans, and many others living in New York or Miami' (p. 161).

These 'multiple centers' reveal the historical trajectories of migration, often marking diverse groups within the same diasporic community depending on whether they are once, twice, or multiple migrated or displaced. In such cases, the notion of homeland presents a problem.

Describing the divergent routes and histories of migration that make up the Indian diaspora for instance, Mishra (1996, 2002) makes a distinction between 'old' and 'new' diasporas, marked respectively by migration as indentured labour and by economic migration – the 'diaspora of plantation labour', and the 'diaspora of late capital'.

As Gilroy (1993, 2000) has brilliantly argued in the case of the 'Black Atlantic', the complexities that such heterogeneous histories of mobility bring to diaspora formation requires a re-thinking of place, geography, and genealogy in terms of hybrid and non-territorial identities: 'As an alternative to the metaphysics of 'race', nation, and bounded culture coded into the body, diaspora is a concept that problematises the cultural and historical mechanics of belonging. It disrupts the fundamental power of territory to define identity by breaking the simple sequence of explanatory links between place, location, and consciousness' (2000: 124). In Clifford's (1997) view, diasporic communities retain a creative tension with national spaces and identities, constructing public spheres and forming collective consciousnesses that transcend national boundaries and form alliances with similar others elsewhere.

Akin to the debates around multiculturalism, disputes on the conceptual validity of 'diaspora' testify to significant aspects of minority politics. As Gilroy (1994) has observed, '[Diaspora is] more than a voguish synonym for peregrination or nomadism.' In terms that recall Doreen Massey's reference to the 'power-geometry' that informs migration, Gilroy declare that '[l]ife itself is at stake in a way the word suggests flight or coerced rather than freely chosen experiences of displacement. Slavery, pogroms, indenture, genocide and other unnameable terrors have all figured in the constitution of diasporas and the reproduction of diaspora-consciousness' (p. 204). Besides the light it throws on the constitution of diasporas, Gilroy's comment is relevant in the context of on-going debates in the media and in the political sphere on the status of refugees, and the recent escalation of fears of terrorism that inform protective measures being adopted in Western countries.

Lived experience and the formation of collective identity

For our present purposes, the principal and most relevant aspect of Malkki's study is her argument concerning the efficacy of the experience of exile in the formation of identities, in particular, the divergence in the experience of Hutu groups who had settled in 'a carefully planned, physically isolated refugee camp' (Mishamo Refugee Settlement) as against the Hutu refugees living in 'the less regimented setting of Kigoma township on Lake Tanganyika' (p. 2). Crucially, her analysis reveals important differences between these two settlements in terms of ideas of home and of exile as a collective, identity-forming experience, and of significance given to national history and identity. The refugees in the Mishamo camp invoked autochthonous origins of Burundi as a "nation" to narrate their history as "a people", a move that simultaneously constructed a historical account of themselves as the natives of Burundi, and identified the Tutsis as the foreign aggressors. The construction of Burundi nationhood underpinned the camp refugees' conception of themselves as a nation in exile, and consequently to the value placed on their refugee status – a celebration of it as temporary exile, which accompanied a refusal to be naturalised as Tanzanian citizens.

While their status as refugees and as displaced citizens of Burundi enabled the camp refugees to construct a form of categorical purity as a nation, and consequently not as an immigrant community in Tanzania, with the notion of 'home' not so much a geographical territory as a moral destination, this was markedly different from the social imaginary of the town refugees. According to Malkki, the latter, negotiating a collective identity within Tanzanian national culture, inhabited identities constructed and 'borrowed' from their experience of life in the township, creating a lively mixture of creolised, changeable identities and a marked cosmopolitanism. Unlike the camp refugees, for those living in Kigoma the notion of 'home' was a distinct territorial entity and not a moral category, which allowed them to challenge notions of purity as well as the authenticity of the Burundi 'nation'.

Malkki's analysis, by problematizing the treatment of ethnicity as a distinct category in the formation of diasporic consciousness and identity, allows us to examine more closely the complex relations between location, experience, and the formation of identities of such refugee communities for whom the notion of 'home' – a defining characteristic of diaspora – is imagined and constructed in distinct ways that relate to their experience in host communities. As she argues, 'the opposition between the historical-national thought of the camp refugees and the cosmopolitan ways of the town refugees made it possible to discern how the social, imaginative processes of constructing nation-ness and identity can come to be influenced by the local, everyday circumstances of life in exile, and how the spatial and social isolation of refugees can figure in these processes' (p. 3). This is a crucial point that carries a particular resonance in terms of the current policies on refugees and asylum seekers in Australia and Europe. Malkki's insight on the township refugees is pertinent in this context, as it alerts us to the politics inherent in the construction and mediation of identities among refugee communities around the globe. While the camp refugees, ironically, utilised their status as exiles to protect the idea of a "nation" by way of negotiating displacement and deterritorialisation, the town refugees, by circumventing the call of authentic nationhood through the creation of a more cosmopolitan forms of identity through everyday practice, can be seen, Malkki argues, as subverting attempts at being categorised as refugees. 'What emerges in this case is a study ... of two quite specific, locally situated liminalities that were intimately related to each other and yet irreconcilably opposed. For camp refugees perpetuated and reified that very categorical order in terms of which they were displaced, while the town refugees' lives seemed to have the effect of challenging and dissolving totalizing, essentializing categories' (p. 4). Later in the book she explores the dialectic relationship between camp and town, the ways in which the Hutu refugees located in these sites imagined and identified themselves in terms of opposition and antagonism to each other (pp. 197–231).

Embedded in Malkki's argument is the claim to constructions of identity that are based on experience and mediation. Two inter-related issues arise from this: the as yet unresolved debate regarding the validity of the appeal to experience, particularly from subaltern communities, that often underpins and provides an ethical-political justification for struggles for recognition; and secondly the continuing contestation over subaltern discursive practice, that is, the question of what forms the subaltern speech can and has to take in order to be heard in their calls for recognition in a climate in which the trope of 'illegal immigration' often informs official positions and policies on asylum seekers and refugee communities. In the current atmosphere in which attitudes to potential refugees are characterised by a politics of suspicion, what forms of communicative practice, informed by an imagined collective identity, can such communities adopt in order to negotiate what Taylor (1994) has called 'the politics of recognition'?

Subaltern agency and its appeal to experience

The question of representation and voice is central to deliberations of subaltern agency. The challenge for us is to extrapolate from Gramsci's original formulation of subalternity the issues of representation and praxis or agency, in other words, locate in his conceptualisation of the subaltern echoes that resonate with our present concerns and our contemporary historical situation. San Juan's (1998) observations on the validity of considering the developing world as subaltern are pertinent here: 'Can we describe what used to be called the "Third World", now renamed the "global South", as subaltern? Only, I think, in a provisional sense. If "subaltern" signifies lack of historical initiative, disintegration, and dependency of recent independent nation-states, yes' (p. 98). A similar question pervades the social position of refugees: can such groups be described as subaltern? The issues of representation and agency coalesce in contemporary manifestations of subalternity, as demonstrated in official proclamations on the status and treatment of refugees, which coincide with the acute lack of an engagement, particularly in official and government discourse, but also in academic research, with the everyday experience of refugee communities. As argued, for instance, in Guedes-Bailey and Harindranath (2005) the infamous 'Tampa incident' demonstrates the climate of fear, reinforced by a form of racism that is manifested in a commonly held vision of national security and sovereignty, that contributes strongly to the depiction of asylum seekers and refugees as undesirable aliens. The subaltern, once again, is denied a voice, and they are ideologically interpellated into a persisting position of subjugation and marginality.

The subaltern in Gramsci formulation suggests the importance of social and political contestation in the realm of culture more than in the economic, merging representation with agency. The complexity intrinsic to this is revealed when we consider the two meanings of the term 'representation', namely political representation (that is, 'who speaks for or on behalf of the subaltern?') and representation as signifying practices, in other words what Hall (1997) identifies as 'meaning producing practices' (p. 28) such as cultural and artistic production, alongside the question of the subaltern's ability toward achieving social transformation. The issues of culture and politics come together in the representation-agency dialectic, in which the potential for emancipation is realised through the subaltern finding a voice that both challenges dominant representation and provides an alternative world-view, Judith Butler's (1990) notion of 'performative contradiction'. As San Juan (1998) argues, the practice of representation and emancipatory politics involves intentionality on the part of the subaltern: 'Of primary importance in this debate on the politics of difference and identity is the salient question of agency, the intentionality of transformative practice, enunciated in concrete historical conjunctures' (p. 9).

With regard to the subaltern, the issue of representation becomes particularly tricky: in essence, if the subalternity is characterised by the denial of a voice, as Gayatri Spivak (1988) famously asked, 'Can the subaltern speak?' If not how justified are intellectuals and cultural producers in their attempts to speak *for* the subaltern? San Juan presents the predicament succinctly: 'the issue of subaltern speech as an artificial construction precipitates the urgent dilemma of whether we can truly speak for others. ... If these others (usually the alien, foreigner, pariah) cannot speak for themselves, dare we speak for them?' (p. 101). It is possible to discuss this difficulty in terms of the intellectual's or artist's responsibility to present the voice of the subaltern transparently, to perform the role of a conduit for subaltern interests and representations. Nevertheless, the danger of denying the agency to the subaltern persists when it is represented by others, a practice that could well extend the process of producing the subaltern. If subalternity is produced through representation, Beverley (1999) asks, 'how can one claim to represent the subaltern from the standpoint of academic knowledge, then, when that knowledge is itself involved in the "othering" of the subaltern?' (p. 2).

Spivak's question needs to be considered in this context, as the speaking subaltern is no longer a subaltern, in her view, and subalternity is in addition defined by it not being *adequately* represented either in academic knowledge production or in artistic practice. Representing the subaltern entails the risk of assuming a vanguard stance in the place of subaltern agency, even in the case of activists acting on behalf of the marginalised. Spivak (1988) is concerned about the precariousness of what she calls 'paradoxical subject privileging', whereby those who 'act and speak' silence those others who 'act and struggle' (p. 275). The question of 'who represents the subaltern?' here merges and confuses the two ideas of representation in the practice of speaking of and for the subaltern. The crucial question for Spivak and those critics in the field of postcolonial studies is about the politics and boundaries of representation – in particular, how one can know and represent the other. Embedded in this is the issue of experience and its role in the formation of subaltern consciousness and the politics of representing such experience as a corrective to dominant depictions of subaltern communities. In the case of refugee groups, this question becomes even more crucial, as mainstream (mis)representations of them reveal and are informed by particular political agendas. As Rotas (2004) notes, 'Like "black", the term "refugee" smoothes over difference within the group it designates at the same time as reifying the boundary that defines its otherness and the notions that constitute that boundary' (p. 52). Challenging such bureaucratic designations involves recourse to the actual experience of refugee communities.

The concept of "experience" has had a chequered history, in particular in relation to how it informs agency, identity, and resistance, which has been debated and has 'has persistently preoccupied certain strands in cultural, subaltern, and aesthetic inquiry. ... Polemical critiques of the subaltern appeal to experience continue to regard such appeals as dubious theoretical warrant for historical populism' (Ireland 2004: xiii). For scholars preoccupied with the notion of subaltern history and agency however, the primary focus is on the validity of the experience of subaltern communities, which remain subaltern precisely due to the neglect of their experience and histories by dominant groups. For them, subordination entails maintaining the invisibility of the subaltern, and the marginalisation of their voices, be it indigenous communities or refugee groups. Counter-hegemonic resistance therefore, requires the impetus arising from authentic subaltern experience, which provides the ethical foundations for such struggles.

The crux of the debate is around the relevance and validity of 'immediate', that is, not mediated experience, whether or not that constitutes the basis for subaltern resistance, or whether, on the contrary, emphasising lived experience portends essentialist constructions of identity, which approximate forms of ethno-nationalism and tribalism. The Thompson–Althusser debate that epitomised and in a sense inaugurated the academic engagement with such concerns has, as Ireland observes, 'spawned a proliferation of academic and para-academic "histories from below" and subaltern cultural enquiries that, in spite of their differences, share the notion that the identities and counter-histories of the voiceless and disenfranchised can be buttressed by the specificity of a group's concrete experiences' (p. 4). Such calls for immediate experience to legitimise the claims of the subaltern result, as he argues, in cases where 'the recourse to immediate experience opens the back door to what was booted out the front door – it inadvertently naturalizes what it initially set out to historicize' (p. 17). And therein lies the dilemma: recourse to allegedly prediscursive, concrete experience, while it provides the vocabulary for cultural and collective identity, is simultaneously susceptible to the vagaries of fundamentalist politics.

As Ireland argues however, Thompson's (1963) conceptualisation of subaltern or working class politics based on experience not only recognises and accommodates the significance of mediation, but also includes the idea of the *unexpected*, which Thompson considers a crucial aspect of subaltern agency and resistance. Significantly, Thompson's insistence on the role of local cultures in the articulation of subaltern experience validates the importance of its mediation, a crucial move in the formation of subaltern consciousness. Moreover, as Ireland rightly observes, Thompson recognises the ideological aspect of mediated experience, an acknowledgement that underpins his insistence on the disjunction between expectations emerging from dominant discourses and ideologies and the immediate experience of the subaltern. 'The appeal to immediate experience actually capitalizes less on the assumed proximity of experience to prediscursive materiality than it capitalizes instead on the *disruption of a congruence* – on the incongruence in other words – between the expectations fostered by dominant ideology and the subaltern's "necessary business of living"' (Ireland: 29).

Subaltern speech and the politics of recognition

Strongly implicated in the attempt to resuscitate subjugated knowledges are the issues of representation and identity formation. Gilroy (2000) among others, has insisted on the discursive and intersubjective aspect of identity formation. The intersubjective element of the formation of individual and collective identity is founded upon interaction with the world. As we saw earlier, the distinction that Malkki makes between the two differently located Hutu communities attest to the ways in which everyday experience contributes to the shaping of collective identity. The crucial question however, is 'how selves – and their identities – are formed through relationships of exteriority, conflict, and exclusion' (p. 109), a process that involves the acceptance of differences both within and between identities. Like Benhabib (2002), Gilroy insists on the feature of dialogue in identity formation and maintenance that at once points to the need for a dialogic Other, allows for the instability of identities. 'The Other, against whose resistance the integrity of identity is to be established, can be recognized as part of the self that is no longer plausibly understood as a unitary identity but appears instead as one fragile moment in the dialogic circuits.' (p. 109). He uses Debbora Battaglia's (1995) useful phrase 'representational economy', part of her argument that 'there is no selfhood apart from the collaborative practice of its figuration. The 'self' is a representational economy: a reification continually defeated by mutable entanglements with other subjects' histories, experiences, self-representations; with their texts, conduct, gestures, objectifications' (p. 2).

Two related points can be raised here. First, as Radhakrishnan (2003) points out in his exploration of what he calls the 'perspectival legitimacy of representation' (p. 33) the issue of representation figures strongly in *multicultural politics*, particularly in relation to the subaltern perspective from which the 'multivalent realities' that constitute a multicultural society are voiced and arbitrated. With regard to refugee communities, the positioning of such groups in dominant discourse – official, governmental, media – on the one hand, and the self-narrativisation of refugees, which is crucial to any counterhegemonic endeavour, become central. Noteworthy here is the absence of dialogue in the configuration of refugee experience from the perspective of dominant (national) culture and discourse. The unequal power relations that are intrinsic to this lack of dialogue and 'mutual narrativization' renders, for Radhakrishnan, the dominant perspective invalid because it is one-sided. His call for subaltern representation stems from this insight.

The other issue relating to Gilroy's point about the *discursive* dimension of identity formation is its links to Charles Taylor's discussion of 'the politics of recognition'. In his influential essay (1994), Taylor presents his argument that 'our identity is partly shaped by recognition or its absence, often by the misrecognition of others, and so a person or a group of people can suffer real damage, real distortion, if the people or the society around them mirror back to them a confining or demeaning or contemptible picture of themselves' (p. 25). In his treatment of the term 'recognition', Taylor combines two different meanings: that of *equal* recognition that is conceived in terms of equal rights and dignity for all citizens, thereby the politics of universalism on the one hand, and the recognition of *difference* that discerns the distinctiveness of cultures. Paradoxically, the recognition of difference is couched in the language of the universal, in that it is declared as a general – that is, universal – rule, thereby universalising the particular. Central to his argument is the validity of *both* meanings, as, while the first sense of the term ensures equal treatment of all citizens within a multicultural democracy and guards against prejudice, the second militates against assimilation. 'Where the politics of universal dignity fought for forms of non-discrimination that were "blind" to the ways in which citizens differ, the politics of difference often redefines non-discrimination as requiring that we make these distinctions the basis of differential treatment' (1994, p. 39).

In terms of formations of identity, Taylor links two elements of his philosophy: the dialogic model of identity as formed and maintained through intersubjective 'webs of interlocution', and his insistence on the dual recognition of equality and difference. In an earlier book (1989), he describes his conception of the 'web of interlocution' in terms of the connection between the self and language, 'I am a self only in relation to certain interlocuters: in one way in relation to those conversation partners which are essential to my achieving self-definition; in another in relation to those who are now crucial to my continuing grasp of languages of self-understanding – and, of course, those classes may overlap. A self exists only within what I call "webs of interlocution" (1989, p. 36). Taylor's insight contributes a specific philosophical and political valence to the exploration of cultural rights and identity of marginalised communities, in particular, refugees. The sameness-difference dialectic, along with his conception of the formation of the self and the centrality of recognition to it, re-asserts the significance of representation, and provides a framework for the analysis of cultural formations and discourses.

Despite the value of Taylor's contribution, however, it has been critiqued for its overemphasis on recognition and a relative disengagement with re-distribution, and for its insufficient attention to inequalities inherent in patterns of cultural recognition. With regard to redistributive justice, Nancy Fraser's (1997) contributions have been regarded (Benhabib, 2002, Radhakrishnan, 2003) as offering a useful corrective to Taylor's neglect of it. In Fraser's conception, two paradigms of justice imbue demands for recognition and redistribution. These constitute the focus on firstly, cultural injustices (the recognition paradigm) that seeks to redress inequalities and problems associated with patterns of representation, communication, and interpretation, and secondly, socio-economic injustices in the form of exploitation, marginalisation and deprivation. The main thrust of Fraser's argument is the relevance of both paradigms in the demand for social and economic equality as well as recognition of cultural difference. Both paradigms together are constitutive of claims for justice in a multicultural society. Four kinds of collective identity formation are mapped on to the two paradigms: 'race', gender, class, and 'despised sexualities'. In effect, what Fraser achieves is a useful analytical distinction between the politics of difference and heterogeneity on the one hand, and the demands for distributive justice that seek to remove economic differentials in the name of equality, while emphasising the interrelationship between both. In other words, while the two paradigms appear contradictory, Fraser insists on a dialectic link between them, conceiving them as analytically distinct but interlinked domains.

In his defence, Taylor does consider briefly the inequalities inherent in the uneasy balance between non-discrimination and difference, in which attempts to accommodate difference within a presumed homogeneous national culture often reveals asymmetries of power whereby the hegemonic subsumes the non-hegemonic, the minority and the subaltern. Radhakrishnan (2003) however, is unconvinced about the adequacy of Taylor's avowal of power differentials. For him 'the politics of recognition has to be articulated with and informed by the politics of subalternity', since 'some cultures have been recognized more than other cultures; some cultures have had recognition as a *fait accompli* while others have had to struggle against heavy odds' (p. 54). Given this context, Radhakrishnan argues, the politics of recognition 'needs to be played out between the utopian and trans-ideological invocation of a relational universalism and an active and critical awareness of the representational failures and injustices of the status-quo' (ibid).

In terms of Taylor's dual modes of 'recognition' of equality and difference, marginal voices lack the enunciative power of the hegemonic bloc, with the result that the dialogue between cultures is unequal. How ideal-typical then, is Taylor's assertion that 'democracy has ushered in a politics of equal recognition' (1994, p. 30)? Radhakrishnan's insistence on *multilateral recognition* is therefore crucial, as it seeks to address the unevenness of the realization of 'cognitive human landscape' that continues to marginalise communities and subjugate knowledges. The call for multilateral recognition however, is 'is not in the name of the authenticity of any one group's self-image, but in the name of a categorical and systemic fairness and openness that rigorously guards against the possibility of "recognition" becoming the exclusive function of any one particular gaze. It is rather like an anti-trust provision against cognitive and epistemic monopoly and control' (p. 55). Extending Spivak's assertion about whether the subaltern can speak, Radhakrishnan argues that subalternity is constructed through unilateral misrecognition that fixes the subaltern in the gaze of the other. Subaltern understanding of its own experience, in other words, is only through the objectification of it by the elite and the mainstream. He makes a crucial distinction between subaltern demands for recognition and Taylor's argument regarding enunciations of 'authenticity' as marking difference.

The issue seems to be one of addressing the non-reciprocal recognition of the subaltern. Subaltern demand is for participation in a dialogue, for mutual and reciprocal recognition. It is 'for permission to narrate a certain story from a certain place and a certain position, so

that the story and "where it came from" can be made sense together'
(ibid.). The politics of representation alluded to here involves the
recognition of subaltern expressions as arising from particular historical and social locations – the 'locus of enunciation' – that contain
within them the various coordinates that constitute subaltern culture,
including racism, and economic and social inequality. More than a
question of an alleged authenticity therefore, the struggle entails
locational or perspectival legitimacy. Moreover, it also involves safe-
guarding the legitimacy subaltern cultural expression, since 'when the
self-image of a dominant culture meets up with the self-image of a subaltern culture on a world historical stage, the former all too easily
destroys all subaltern defence on behalf of itself and prescribes its own
mode of cognition as the answer to the subaltern question' (p. 57).
This is why, according to Radhakrishnan, 'The politics of recognition
has to be articulated with and informed by the politics of subalternity.'
  This raises several epistemological issues. First, with regard to the
status of experience in relation to formations of cultural identity and
representativeness, identity politics has been conceived differently by
different frames of reference that either privilege the notion of inher-
ited essences or the constructivist critique of essentialism. As Mohanty
(1998) points out, 'the essentialist view would be that the identity
common to members of a social group is stable and more or less
unchanging, since it is based on the experiences they share. Opponents
of essentialism often find this view seriously misleading, since it
ignores historical changes and glosses over internal differences within
groups by privileging only the experiences that are common to everyone' (pp. 202–3). Whatever position is adopted, however, the question
of belonging is 'unavoidable as we translate our dreams of diversity
into social visions and agendas' (ibid.). Secondly, the potential for disagreement between dominant and subaltern representations of experience and the consequent incommensurability between them prompts
the subject of relativism that damages mutual recognition. Thirdly,
examining the value of enunciative practice involves, as Frow (1998)
avers, both positionality and the set of 'ethical and political questions:
Who speaks? Who speaks for Whom? Whose voice is listened to,
whose voice is spoken for, who has no voice? Whose claim to be pow-
erless is a ruse of power?' (p. 63). This clearly echoes Spivak's concern
about the representational politics of the subaltern.
  Building on the Alcoff's (1991–92) attempt at suggesting an ethics of
enunciation, Frow (1998) underscores the importance of appraising the
'enunciative modalities' of subaltern representation. Critical in this

context, for him, is Alcoff's concern that the practice of being spoken for compounds the marginalisation of subaltern groups by denying them their own voice. Her linking of 'social position and the semantics of utterance' by way of examining the politics of speaking is for him a way around the complexity of subaltern representation, although he concedes that the relationship between position and meaning is complicated. The essential problem of 'positionality' underlying the ethico-politics of enunciation is that 'whereas the act of speaking for others denies those others the right to be the subjects of their own speech, the refusal to speak on behalf of the oppressed, conversely, assumes that they are in a position to act as such fully empowered subjects' (p. 65).

If the struggle for enunciative authority is one problematic issue with regard to subaltern agency, the other is with regard to the political legitimation of this authority, in particular, questions of essentialism and inclusion. How legitimate is it for the refugee to speak on the basis of an exclusive experience or history that provides the essence of subaltern identity? Likewise, how does refugee representation include or exclude issues such as gender and sexuality? Given that essentialism is anathema to cultural theorists, especially but not only because of its suspect epistemology as well as its potential to lead to political and cultural fundamentalism, these issues are central to the exploration of subaltern agency. Spivak's solution to this dilemma is to call for 'strategic essentialism', an invitation to cultural and academic practitioners repeated by Stuart Hall in the context of ethnic minorities in the West. The 'strategic' element is to be interpreted in political terms, as a pragmatic approach to destabilising dominant, authoritative discourse with the intention of achieving political and social change. Representations by refugee communities of their experience of exile and repression encapsulates this move, as it simultaneously attempts to undermine the inadequacies of being represented in the dominant media, while selectively (how could it be otherwise?) portraying experience that synecdochically stands for exile and 'refugeeness'.

As Malkki has demonstrated, the collective identity of refugee communities as diaspora cannot be assumed simply in terms of places of origin, notions of home, or circumstances of enforced migration. Even in the case of such 'victim diasporas' the experience of every day life plays a significant role in how their lives are managed and in the ways in which collective or cultural identities are imagined and constructed, both in terms of imagining 'home' as well as narrating these identities. Intrinsic to this are three issues that were explored in this essay: the political relevance of the immediacy of experience and its

Thompsonian disjunction to dominant representations that ignore such experience. The politics of collective struggle for recognition and redistribution is predicated upon the second issue, that is, subaltern representation. Refugee communities constitute the subaltern in most host national cultures, in which they are positioned by dominant media and official discourse as at best a 'problem', at worst a threat to national security. This relates to the third issue: if, following Taylor, identity results from the recognition of the self in the other, and of equality and difference, the role of dialogue, of mutual recognition, between generators of dominant discourse and refugee representations becomes crucial.

Note

1. Some of the ideas and arguments presented in this chapter are elaborated in greater detail in Harindranath, R. (2006) *Perspectives on Global Cultures* (Maidenhead and New York: The Open University Press).

References

Ahmad, A. (1992) *In Theory: Classes, Nations, Literatures* (London: Verso).

Alcoff, L. (1991–92) 'The problem of speaking for others', *Cultural Critique*, no. 20.

Alcoff, L. (2003) 'Who's afraid of identity politics?', in P. Moya and M. Hames-Garcia (ed.), *Reclaiming Identity: Realist Theory and the Predicament of Postmodernism* (Berkeley: University of California Press) 312–44.

Battaglia, D. (1995) 'Problematising the self: a thematic introduction', in D. Battaglia (ed.), *Rhetorics of Self-Making* (Berkeley: University of California Press).

Benhabib, S. (2002) *The Claims of Culture: Equality and Diversity in the Global Era* (Princeton: Princeton University Press).

Beverley, J. (1999) *Subalternity and Representation: Arguments in Cultural Theory* (Durham: Duke University Press).

Butler, J. (1990) *Gender Trouble* (New York: Routledge).

Clifford, J. (1997) *Routes: Travel and Translation in the Twentieth Century* (Cambridge: Harvard University Press).

Cohen, R. (1997) *Global Diasporas: An Introduction* (London: UCL Press).

Dirlik, A. (1997) *The Postcolonial Aura* (Boulder, Co.: Westview Press).

Fraser, N. (1997) *Justice Interruptus: Critical Reflections on the 'Post-Socialist' Condition* (New York: Routledge).

Frow, J. (1998) 'Economies of value', in D. Bennett (ed.), *Multicultural States: Rethinking Difference and Identity* (London: Routledge) 53–68.

Gilroy, P. (1993) *The Black Atlantic: Double Consciousness and Modernity* (Cambridge: Harvard University Press).

Gilroy, P. (1994) 'Diaspora', *Paragraph* 17 (1).

Gilroy, P. (2000) *Against Race: Imagining a Political Culture Beyond the Color Line* (Cambridge: Harvard University Press).

Gramsci, A. (1971) *Selections from the Prison Notebooks* (New York: International Publishers).

Guedes-Bailey, O. and Harindranath, R. (2005) 'Racialised "othering": the representation of asylum seekers in the news media', in S. Allan (ed.), *Journalism: Critical Issues*, (Maidenhead and New York: The Open University Press) 274–86.

Hall, S. (1997) 'The work of representation', in S. Hall (ed.), *Representation: Cultural Representations and Signifying Practices* (London: Sage) 13–74.

Ireland, C. (2004) *The Subaltern Appeal to Experience: Self-Identity, Late Modernity, and the Politics of Immediacy* (Montreal: McGill-Queen's University Press).

Lewellen, T. (2002) *The Anthropology of Globalisation: Cultural Anthropology Enters the 21st Century* (Westport: Bergin and Garvey).

Malkki, L. (1995) *Purity and Exile: Violence, Memory, and National Cosmology Among Hutu Refugees in Tanzania* (Chicago: The University of Chicago Press).

Mishra, V. (1996) 'The diasporic imaginary: theorizing the Indian diapora', *Textual Practice*, 10:3.

Mishra, V. (2002) *Bollywood Cinema: Temples of Desire* (New York: Routledge).

Mohanty, S. (1998) *Literary Theory and the Claims of History: Postmodernism, Objectivity, Multicultura l Politics* (New Delhi: Oxford University Press).

Mohanty, S. (2000) 'The epistemic status of cultural identity: on *Beloved* and the postcolonial condition', in P. Moya and M. Hames-Garcia (ed.), *Reclaiming Identity: Realist Theory and the Predicament of Postmodernism* (Berkeley: University of California Press) 30–66.

Moya, P. (2000) 'Introduction: reclaiming identity', in P. Moya and M. Hames-Garcia (ed.), *Reclaiming Identity: Realist Theory and the Predicament of Postmodernism*. (Berkeley: University of California Press) 1–26.

Moya, P. and Hames-Garcia, M. (ed.) (2000) *Reclaiming Identity: Realist Theory and the Predicament of Postmodernism* (Berkeley: University of California Press).

Pickering, M. (1997) *History, Experience and Cultural Studies* (New York: St. Martin's Press).

Radhakrishnan, R. (2003) *Theory in an Uneven World* (Oxford: Blackwell).

Rotas, A. (2004) Is 'refugee art' possible?, *Third Text*, vol. 8, issue 1, 51–60.

Safran, W. (1991) Diasporas in modern societies: myths of homeland and return, *Diaspora* 1 (1), 83–99.

San Juan, E. (1998) *Beyond Postcolonial Theory* (New York: St. Martin's Press).

Spivak, G. (1988) 'Can the subaltern speak?' in Nelson, C. and Grossberg, L. (eds), *Marxism and the Interpretation of Culture* (Urbana: University of Illinois Press).

Taylor, C. (1989) *Sources of the Self* (Cambridge: Harvard University Press).

Taylor, C. (1994) 'The politics of recognition', in A. Guttman (ed.), *Multiculturalism: Examining the Politics of Recognition* (Princeton: Princeton University Press).

Thompson, E. P. (1963) *The Making of the English Working Class* (London: Gollanz).

Thompson, E. P. (1978) *The Poverty of Theory* (London: Merlin).

8
Ethnic Media, Transnational Politics: Turkish Migrant Media in Germany*

Kira Kosnick

Introduction

The past fifteen years have witnessed a veritable explosion of mass media productions that cross the boundaries of nation-states. Whereas the early 20th century saw territorial nation-states as the main container of broadcast media both structurally and politically, the late 20th century witnessed an interlinked de-territorialization and commercialization of electronic mass media. These developments have most prominently been linked to the emergence of global media conglomerates which operate across different continents in their pursuit of profits (McChesney and Schiller, 2003), prompting fears of cultural homogenization and the demise of pluralism. Less noted has been the diversification of broadcasting landscapes through satellite television in parts of the world such as the Middle East, where new communication technologies have helped to subvert different state broadcasting monopolies and censorship regimes (Sakr, 2002). And finally, even less attention has been given to smaller-scale, locally evolving efforts to produce broadcast media by groups who once were the most marginalized of mass media audiences, namely immigrants and diasporic populations. While these groups now have easy access via satellite and the internet to broadcast media from former 'home countries' and elsewhere, new technologies have also led to a proliferation of mass media created by and for migrants themselves.

One of the most evolved landscapes of migrant media has come into existence in Germany's capital city Berlin, with Turkish-language radio and television taking centre stage.

This chapter will provide an overview of Turkish media activism in the city, and link it with German integration debates and multiculturalist policy-making that shape and contain this activism in different forms. Key in such debates is the expectation that migrant media will provide immigrants with a 'voice' in public affairs, and aid integration by competing with satellite imports for the attention and the loyalties of immigrant populations.

'Having a voice' in the media

Berlin is home to the largest Turkish population outside of Turkey, with almost 200,000 of the city's residents carrying or once having carried a Turkish passport. The bulk of Turkish migration to Berlin took place in the early 1960s, when the West German government actively recruited labour migrants from different Mediterranean countries. Over the past four decades, migrants from Turkey have established an extensive infrastructure in the city, an infrastructure which includes a range of Turkish-language radio and television projects targeting local audiences.

Apart from Berlin's long-standing Turkish radio programme now broadcast daily on the public service station Radio MultiKulti, a private radio station has established itself as a successful commercial venture on Berlin's airwaves, offering Turkish-language radio around the clock. With the slogan *'bizim dalga'* (our airwave), *Metropol FM* markets itself explicitly as a local radio station produced by Turkish Berliners for Turkish Berliners. In the realm of television, the cable channel TD-1 (Turkish-German Television) has been broadcasting since 1985, when cable broadcasting was just getting established in Germany. Surviving on advertising revenues from small-scale Turkish businesses in the city, TD-1 has held out with a mostly amateur production crew and staff, mixing local reporting and studio talk shows with downlinks from Turkish satellite channels such as Turkey's news channel, NTV. Metropol FM and TD-1 are complemented by a wide range of smaller broadcasting projects, commercial and non-commercial, which produce Turkish-language programmes for local audiences irregularly but with unfailing enthusiasm.

Whereas until the mid-1980s immigrants from Turkey had to make do with a half-hour radio programme and the occasional five minutes of Turkish television provided by public service broadcasters, the situation nowadays is dramatically different (Kosnick, 2000). Both satellite imports and local developments have been noted by German observers and have prompted some to speak of an 'ethnicization' of the media landscape in Germany, meaning that ethnic minorities are increasingly drawing upon 'their own' media (Becker, 1998a).

Negative consequences of 'ethnicization' in Germany have been particularly feared with regard to satellite television imports, especially those from Turkey. Surveys have shown that Turkish households have been increasingly turning to imported programmes, raising concerns that this might hinder integration by culturally and politically orienting immigrants toward the country of origin (Becker 1998b, 2001; Heitmeyer *et al.*, 1998; Okkan, 1998; but see Hargreaves and Mahdjoub, 1997; King and Wood, 2001, for contrary evidence). Local media produced by and for immigrants, however, have generally been regarded in a much more positive light. They are seen as responding to the specific needs and conditions of immigrant communities where they reside, and as 'speaking for' the community they represent (Busch, 1994; Husband, 1994; Riggins, 1992). Local immigrant media are expected to have a local community focus, addressing their audience not as extensions of a 'homeland' audience as imported programming tends to do, but rather providing them with a mass-mediated forum of self-representation that reflects their needs and interests by virtue of being 'their own'.

The issue of immigrants not only being served by mass media but actually 'having a voice' in them did not emerge in the Federal Republic of Germany until the late 1980s. This decade witnessed not only the crumbling of the public service broadcasting monopoly and the rapid increase in private radio and television channels at local, state and national levels, but also a shift in political discourse that eventually moved toward the recognition of Germany as a multicultural society. With the commercialization of broadcasting and new communication technologies that have multiplied the channels of mass communication (Aksoy and Robins, 2000), new spaces for 'ethnic programming' opened up that were no longer tied to the 'benevolent patriarchism' of 'oh so well-meaning German representatives of integration-oriented media' (Becker, 2001:17).

But the issue of representation has become more prominent in public service broadcasting as well, with increasing calls for the inclusion and promotion of immigrant and ethnic minority journalists in German media institutions. Moreover, as immigrants were apparently beginning to 'do their own thing' (ibid.) in the media, some sectors of the public service establishment came to identify the need for an 'ethnic point of view' as a contribution to public debates in Germany. This trend went hand in hand with an increasing visibility of ethnic minorities in German programmes on private channels – as characters in soap operas, as guests and moderators on afternoon talk shows.[1] These developments marked an important moment for the symbolic construction of German society within the politics of representation: young people of Turkish origin could for the first time appear on television to talk about relationship problems, hairstyles and the like, rather than having to solely comment on their identity as Turks in Germany. Obviously, talk shows construct a very particular voice for their invited guests on television (Livingstone and Lunt, 1994). But by including ethnic minorities as a choreographed voice in staged debates in the studio, private channels have changed their mode of representation from describing or depicting these groups as a topic of discussion – what Gayatri Spivak called 'subject predication' – to their representation as active participants, representing and 'speaking-for' themselves (Spivak, 1988).

While ethnic minorities were increasingly included as participants in mass-mediated public debates, this was accompanied by the more or less unexamined conviction that immigrants or ethnic minorities are nonetheless best served by programmes produced 'by themselves.' Analysts and policy-makers agreed that programmes *for* immigrants should be ideally produced *by* immigrants, thereby ensuring that they reflect the immigrants' real needs and concerns. If an ethnic minority background validates a journalist's statements as 'an ethnic minority point of view' in the German media, the productions of ethnic broadcasters is assumed to be all the more representative in the context of programmes designed for ethnic minorities. Subaltern ethnic groups are assumed to 'speak for themselves' if given the chance, and what is voiced, particularly in the native tongue and to the members of the native group, must consequently be an authentic expression of minority culture. It is this assumption which informs statements such as the following, which describes the emergence of a Turkish media sphere in Germany as an 'ethnicization process':

> Ethnicization of the media means, from a cultural perspective, the primacy of including that which is one's own over that which is not. Ethnicization of the media allows the members of one's own group to see themselves, their own destinies, their own problems, their own bodies. Ethnicization of media enables finding oneself, determining one's own destiny and cultural identity. (Becker, 2001:16)

Media here become a means of self-orientation and self-expression by which the self is linked to the cultural identity of an ethnic group.

In this understanding of ethnic minority media, two basic meanings of the concept of representation are collapsed: representation in the sense of *'darstellen'* or 'subject-predication' by which the ethnic group is invoked, and representation in the sense of *'vertreten'* or 'speaking-for,' as in the political representation of that group. In her influential essay, 'Can the Subaltern Speak?' Gayatri Spivak discusses the deployment of these two meanings of representation in the writings of Karl Marx, and argues for the importance of keeping them conceptually distinct. To collapse them, she argues, means to sustain the illusion of the 'constitutive subject' of the oppressed as unproblematically able to 'know and speak for themselves' (Spivak, 1988: 275–9). If ethnic minority media are equated with collective self-representation, their claim to represent 'the community' in this double sense (of being authorized not just to speak/produce images of it, but to also be its voice) cannot even be questioned.

But what kind of 'voices' do Turkish-language media programmes produced by and for immigrants in Berlin represent? Under what conditions and in what language do they articulate community concerns, and how does this language relate to other dominant discourses of national and multicultural identity?

Radio MultiKulti

Writings on ethnic minority media from a variety of disciplines and theoretical traditions share assumptions regarding the ability of ethnic minorities to 'speak for themselves' and to use mass media as tools for 'cultural preservation' or for the 'defense of identity.' Such assumptions are pervasive not just in academic discourses, but also in the political and institutional environment in which ethnic minority media have developed in Germany and Berlin over the past decade. They have shaped decisions pertaining to the licensing of radio and television projects, the philosophy of public service broadcasting for immigrant groups, the feeding of satellite television into the Berlin cable system, policies on open-access channels, and the political debates on integration that posit Berlin as a multicultural or cosmopolitan city. Despite the increasing emergence of commercial immigrant broadcasting ventures, Turkish-language media production in Berlin still depends to a great extent on public policy and financial support. Reliance on such support is most evident in the case of the Turkish-language programme on Radio MultiKulti, a public-service station that owes its existence to public funding legislated by the state.[2]

In the early 1990s, a surge of racist violence directed at immigrants and asylum-seekers in the newly united Germany spurred intense debates on how public service broadcasting could expand its educational mission. Educating the German majority population about immigrant groups and generally furthering 'intercultural' understanding was identified as an urgent task by public service broadcasters and policy makers alike. It was particularly the racist murders in the cities of Mölln and Solingen that added new urgency to the calls for an anti-racist, multicultural broadcasting strategy. In their wake, Berlin's public service broadcasting corporation SFB received the go-ahead for a new radio station, Radio MultiKulti (Bünger, 1995; Vertovec, 1996, 2000). A station serving as 'a forum of integration and communication among ethnic minorities and Germans in the city' (Holler, 1997: 15) was seen as an appropriate response to increasing anti-immigrant sentiments and racist violence.

Providing a 24-hour programme broadcast on a terrestrial[3] frequency in the city, *MultiKulti* has the double mission of serving different immigrant groups and raising levels of tolerance among the German majority population (Busch, 1994; SFB 4-MultiKulti, 1995). World music featuring music of every style except Anglo-American, late afternoons and evenings devoted to foreign-language programmes in about 18 different languages, and daytime programmes in German reporting on 'multicultural' life in the city, are the major elements through which the idea of 'integrationist' broadcasting is put into practice.

Radio Multi-Kulti's ambitious effort to create programming both for and about immigrants has been widely regarded as a success. Conceived as a three-year experiment in 1993, the station was finally assured permanent funding in 1997. Apart from the positive audience response that the station claims for itself (Mohr, 1996), it has won acclaim as a unique and innovative approach to 'intercultural' broadcasting and has received numerous awards both nationally and internationally. On *MultiKulti*, immigrants are to present their own views on all kinds of topics instead of just being a topic of discussion themselves. The director of the station, Dr Friedrich Voß, has highlighted this aim as a central aspect of MultiKulti's broadcasting philosophy:

> The magazine parts in the German lingua franca are dedicated to comprehensive information but also to the idea of integration. The programme wants to let primarily foreign moderators and commentators have the word, in order to render the programmatic stance of a 'different viewing angle' audible as well (Voß, 1996: 6).

MultiKulti thus aims to not only reflect multicultural diversity in the city, but also to serve as a forum for intercultural dialogue. The 'different viewing angle' suggests that the issues presented are matters of common and public concern, not so different from those of other radio stations, except that they are now viewed and discussed from a 'foreign' perspective.[4] It is the afternoon and evening programming which comes closer to ethnic programming as defined above, programmes produced by and for different immigrant groups in their native languages. With programme space alotted according to the relative size of the immigrant population, there is an hour-long Turkish programme broadcast every weekday, and additional Turkish-language and/or Turkish music programmes on weekends. But recently, Radio MultiKulti has received fierce competition.

Metropol FM

Berlin's radio landscape is one of the largest and most competitive in Europe, with 26 terrestrial radio stations competing for listeners in the city, and some in the neighbouring federal state of Brandenburg. The commercial, private stations are licensed, monitored, and regulated by a Media Council whose members are appointed by the parliaments of the federal states of Berlin and Brandenburg. Even though its criteria for licensing are primarily economic, the MABB (*Medienanstalt Berlin-Brandenburg*) also aims to ensure 'diversity' (*Vielfalt*) in the form of a wide range of formats and programme contents. In the fall of 1998, the MABB announced its decision to grant a license to the Makaria GmbH, a group of young second-generation Turkish radio enthusiasts backed by German investors, who were organizing the first Turkish-language commercial radio station outside of Turkey. Just eight months later the radio station went on the air under the name Metropol FM, and has since then become a household name for Turkish-speaking Berliners.

It was the group's second attempt to obtain a license from the Media Council, after the first one had faltered because of problems with the original investor, a media conglomerate from Turkey. The Uzan Group (*Uzan Grubu*) had wanted to import most of the programme content for the new station from its own broadcasting ventures in Turkey, but the group in Berlin insisted that the programmes be produced locally, with a focus on Berlin affairs, and found new German investors. This orientation proved to be a major factor in the Media Council's decision. The press-release announcing the licensing decision made explicit reference to the local character the station should have:

The programme is to be produced entirely in Berlin. The Media Council therefore expects that, contrary to television programmes that are by and large imported from Turkey, it will focus especially on the Turkish-speaking population of Berlin and its environs (MABB, 1998).

In its application material submitted to the Media Council, Makaria GmbH stressed the importance of filling an alleged 'information vacuum' resulting from the reliance of immigrants on media imports from Turkey, which rarely cover German issues. Makaria promised that by producing programmes with a local focus, they would further the integration of the Turkish-speaking population in Germany as well as promote intercultural understanding (Makaria GmbH, 1998). This was to be realized through a staff recruitment policy based on the criteria of bilingualism, migration background, and familiarity with life in Berlin (Duyar and Çalağan, 2001: 91).

The actual recruitment process, however, presented the management with a number of problems. Firstly, it turned out that most of the applicants born and raised in Berlin could not fulfill the criteria for bilingualism. Their spoken Turkish was not close enough to *öztürkçe*, Turkey's official linguistic standard,[5] which the management considered essential as part of their vision for a 'serious' Turkish radio station in Berlin. Secondly, the management took pains to eliminate all candidates who could be seen as associated with a particular political position on Turkish affairs, be it nationalist, Islamist or Kurdish. In order to appeal to the largest possible number of Turkish-speaking Berliners, the station felt it needed to circumvent the great potential for political conflicts that divide the immigrant population as much as they divide the population in Turkey. Beyond avoiding the hiring of controversial staff members, broadcast programmes similarly avoid all reference to divisive issues such as, for example, the capture of PKK leader Abdullah Öcalan, alleged human rights abuses in Turkey, the *Imam Hatip* (religious school) debate, and so on.

Open channel programmes

Such controversial issues are more often discussed on Berlin's open-access television channel, *Offener Kanal Berlin* (OKB), which represents the third institutional arena of broadcasting in Germany (after commercial and public service). Unique in the world for its infrastructural support and lack of interference in programme content, Open Channels were instituted in Germany as a kind of 'grassroots' balance to the increasing commercialization of the mass media landscape in the 1980s (Kosnick, forthcoming). Open Channels are intended to make radio and television accessible to every citizen, regardless of economic or educational background, and to contribute to a healthy democracy, as its initiators have argued: 'The democratic process cannot function without the exchange of arguments, continuous public debate, and the contest of opinions in the public sphere' (BOK, 2000). Open Channels are, additionally, envisioned as turning passive consumers of mass media productions into active producers, and as giving a voice to those who do not find their interests, opinions, and identities reflected in the dominant structures of broadcasting (Jarren *et al.*, 1994).

In order for these target groups to become active participants at Open Channels, access barriers are kept as low as possible. At the Open Channel Berlin (OKB), for example, no fee is charged for the use of technical equipment; programme makers, or 'users', as they are called, receive technical assistance and training; the broadcasting schedule is based on a 'first come, first served' policy; and channel administrators do not interfere with programme content. The OKB is proud of the strong immigrant presence among its programme creators, which have at times produced up to 40% of broadcasts for its television channel. In a self-description included in a brochure published by the working group on Open Channels in Germany, the OKB claims that:

> It is precisely in the great interest that foreign groups have in broad-casting in their native language that the concept of Open Channels is most impressively realized: all those who do not have a voice in the other media can express themselves here (Arbeitskreis Offene Kanäle, 1996, p.21).

Turkish-language programmes are produced at the OKB in great numbers: in the first half of 1998, their share of the overall broadcasting time was as high as 26 per cent. The majority of Turkish-language programmes have a focus on Islam. While most of them represent Sunni-Hanafite Islam, the dominant orientation of Islam in Turkey, there is also a variety of Alevi programmes, which are viewed by producers as more cultural or political than religious in nature.

The Islamic groups broadcasting on the Open Channel form part of a religious spectrum that is situated outside and in opposition to Turkey's state-condoned Islam. Whereas representatives of the Turkish Directorate of Religious Affairs (*Diyanet İşleri Başkanlığı*) have regular programme hours on Berlin's commercial Turkish cable channel TD-1, the groups that make use of the Open Channel have no access to other radio and television venues in the city.[6] They include several mystical Sufi groups,[7] Alevis, and different Nakşibendi-derived organizations quite powerful in Turkey today, such as the Nurcu, Süleymancı and Millî Görüş sympathizers.[8]

Additionally, a range of nationalist programmes are produced at the OKB, with a focus on either right-wing Turkish nationalism or Kurdish nationalism. Moreover, there is a small number of programmes produced by groups and individuals ranging from youth initiatives and soccer clubs to a retired journalist. It is the first two groups of programmes (religious and nationalist) which constitute a major problem for the Open Channel. Intended as a medium for local 'grassroots' concerns of citizens that otherwise do not have easy access to the public sphere, the involvement of allegedly extremist groups whose political roots originate in Turkey or elsewhere seems to contradict the democratizing intentions of Open Channels. The Berlin parliament has therefore repeatedly debated the closure of the OKB, and Islamic producers have faced special restrictions after the September 11th attacks in the United States.

Speaking in 'one's own voice'

Examples from all three institutional arenas of broadcasting in Germany – public service, commercial, and open access – have shown that political support for the idea of 'immigrants broadcasting in their own voice' can be mobilized in every realm. While this concept explicitly informs broadcasting at the public service station *Radio MultiKulti*, it also influences licensing decisions in the commercial realm, and forms part of a general 'grassroots' broadcasting philosophy at Berlin's Open Channel. However, the examples above have also shown that the particular Turkish voices emerging from these institutional arenas differ quite dramatically from each other. So will the 'real' Turkish Voice please stand up?

The evidence presented above points to the problematic nature of minority media in Western and Central Europe, and to the difficulties with assuming that they represent the 'voice' of their constituencies, be they defined as ethnic, indigenous, immigrant or otherwise. The groups represented in these media are subaltern – minorities not just in the sense of their numerical size, but also their relative lack of power and subordinate position on the scale of ethnic, cultural, and sometimes racial hierarchies within their respective nation-states. Subaltern groups usually lack the financial capital to establish their own broadcasting ventures in the commercial broadcasting sector, and their audiences tend to be weak in terms of both size and consumer power. In public service or state-controlled broadcasting arenas they rely on the benevolent (though not disinterested) attention of state or public bodies to be recognized as legitimate participants in and recipients of programming.

It thus comes as no surprise that institutional structures, policies, and financial constraints significantly shape the kinds of 'voices' that claim to represent and speak for immigrant minorities. Approaches to minority media production that regard it as a direct expression of the concerns of its respective constituency not only fail to take the power of these determinants into account, these approaches also form part of a discourse that actively informs multicultural policy-making and thus minority 'voices' such as they are heard in Germany. In this discourse and its one-dimensional contrast between ethnic minority and majority society, any potential heterogeneity within the ethnic minority population as well as the institutional constraints of broadcasting are rendered invisible. Media produced by immigrants for immigrants appear to directly and obviously reflect that 'which is one's own' (*das Eigene*) and to represent those groups 'themselves' (Becker, 2001, p.16) 'Finding oneself' in media representations transforms these representations into authoritative subject-predications which, because they are authoritative (the immigrants are predicating themselves), can also represent in the second sense, that is, in 'speaking for.'

However, it is only from a perspective of cultural reification that ethnic minority culture can be approached in these terms. Obliged to legitimate their own productions within a framework of German multiculturalism that tends to reduce culture to a marker of ethnic group identity, many immigrant producers take recourse to arguments of ethno-cultural membership to authorize their work. It is not necessarily Turkish culture as such that is posited as the context of membership, but often 'German-Turkishness' as the cultural and ethnic territory to which producers claim organic links. Thus, Metropol FM producers claim that having grown up German-Turkish in Berlin constitutes proof of sharing the same *Lebenswirklichkeit*, the same lifeworld, as that of the audience that they are both addressing and representing, in the double sense of 'speaking to' and 'speaking for' (Duyar and Çalağan, 2001, p.89).

For another interpretation of this representative function, the anthropologist Ayhan Kaya uses Gramsci's concept of the 'organic intellectual' to describe German-Turkish Hip Hop musicians who claim to articulate the experience of young German-Turks in Berlin (Kaya, 2002). Gramsci has stated that what characterises organic intellectuals is their having been brought forth by social groups as those groups' own intellectuals (Gramsci, 1971). Moreover, the relationship between intellectuals and their respective group should be the same as that between theory and practice, with intellectuals providing the social group with 'an awareness of its own function' (ibid., p.5). However, in Gramsci's analysis an intellectual's background does not *guarantee* that she or he will in fact theorize that function and bring the group to awareness, whereas in the context of ethno-cultural essentialism, claiming membership to a social group is sufficient evidence of the capability to authoritatively articulate that group's practices and function.[9] However, even a cursory look at Turkish-language broadcasts produced by and for immigrants in Berlin reveals a conflicting heterogeneity of positions articulated as authoritative representations of immigrant life. A closer investigation shows that this heterogeneity is systematically related to the institutional contexts in which immigrant broadcasting must operate.

The public service domain

Along a spectrum of positions ranging from the integration agenda's insistence on Berlin as the only legitimate reference point for identities, to the assertion of a Kurdish diaspora or the nostalgia of the *gurbetçi*,[10] it comes as no surprise that the first position is mostly reflected in the public service domain of German broadcasting while the latter two are mostly found on the Open Channel's programmes. Interestingly, the public service context, although committed to ideals of objective reporting and inclusiveness, nevertheless institutes the tightest controls over who and what will represent a local Turkish voice on Berlin's airwaves. Radio MultiKulti's 'objective reporting' in Turkish includes a focus on Berlin combined with a secularist stance, a marked hesitation to address the 'Kurdish question,' a commitment to human rights, a willingness to criticize the Turkish state, and a tendency toward didacticism that is also reflected in its high-brow Turkish. Many Turkish Berliners regard the station's Turkish programme as being mainly for an intellectual audience despite the many years it served as the only Turkish-language broadcast available in Berlin. The insistence on *öztürkçe* as spoken on Turkey's state radio and television channels has meant that despite its local orientation, the

Turkish programme at Radio MultiKulti has had to recruit staff members who have received at least part of their education in Turkey. Some of them had even worked for Turkey's TRT (*Türkiye Radyo ve Televizyon Kurumu*), the state radio and television agency which operates a channel designed for Turks abroad with the mission of strengthening their identification with Turkey.[11] Up until the mid-1990s, the *öztürkçe* language policy of the Turkish programme extended even to interview material. Young people of Turkish origin often mix German into their Turkish, and these instances would be cut out in the editing process – evidence both of the educative mission of the programme and of a gap between a changing immigrant lifeworld and its representation on the air.

The current editors of the programme claim to be much more in tune with the realities of Turkish life in the city. However, they are nevertheless selective in regard to the audience they seek to reach, as one of the younger Turkish editors of the programme described:

> We want listeners who identify with Berlin, with the life here. Who think of themselves as Berlin Turks. ... We want to reach people who understand themselves as part of this society, not as part of the society in Turkey. Either you live here, we think, or in Turkey (interview with Cem Dalaman).

For this editor, to see oneself as a member of society means to identify as a Berlin Turk, not as a Turk from Turkey. Different from other Turkish-language broadcasts available to immigrants, MultiKulti is for those who identify with life in Berlin. For the editor, this is a question of either-or, and he calls other Turkish programmes in the city which report on Turkey 'backward-facing.' In this view, maintaining ties with Turkey and identifying as a Turk from Turkey appear as a residue, something that characterized the early period of immigration but should no longer dominate people's identifications. Life in Turkey should no longer be a major focus of interest for Turks in Berlin.

The Open Channel

The Turkish-speaking producers at Berlin's open-access television channel OKB take a different view on the matter. For most, it is not life in a multicultural society that is the central political issue, but rather the conflicts that divide political opinion in Turkey today. Questions of religious freedom are addressed by Sunni and Alevi producers alike, with heated discussions on dress prohibitions and religious *Imam Hatip* Schools, and images of the Sivas[12] murders flashing regularly over the screen. Kurdish nationalists attack Turkish state policies in the South-eastern regions, and Turkish nationalists give lessons on the historic roots of the Turkish nation and stress the importance of national unity. The State Media Council which supervises OKB programmes regularly receives complaints by Turkish viewers objecting to programme content, but does not intervene unless a programme espouses violence, contains commercial advertising, or violates the German constitution.

The freedom and ease with which immigrant producers may create and broadcast programmes on the Open Channel has allowed them to establish something akin to public spheres in exile, and many producers are convinced that they would be imprisoned or at least banned from broadcasting in Turkey since their political agenda contravenes the politics of the Turkish state. While Open Channel programmes have provoked official protests from the Turkish embassy in Berlin, German authorities have seen little cause to intervene. However, the events of September 11, 2001 in the United States have led the channel management to a re-evaluation of its guidelines for Islamic programming. For some months they required that producers provide a German translation of their programme ahead of time, and be limited to a 'religious broadcasting track' aired on weekends. The number of programmes has dropped significantly as a result.

Turkish-language programmes on the OKB reflect neither the socio-political mission of the Open Channel as a broadcasting institution nor the cultural and political orientations of the majority of immigrants from Turkey living in Berlin, as both the Turkish embassy and umbrella organizations such as the *Türkische Gemeinde* (Turkish Community, TG) or the *Türkischer Bund Berlin-Brandenburg* (Turkish Union Berlin-Brandenburg, TBB) frequently complain. While the TG and the TBB differ in terms of their political and religious leanings, they are united in their rejection of most OKB Turkish-language programmes. The OKB is a place for those agendas and positions that cannot find representation within the other two institutional spheres of broadcasting. As those within the public service domain would see it, those positions fall outside the realm of integration-oriented broadcasting and lack both objectivity and professionalism. Regarding the commercial domain, Open Channel producers lack the financial means to invest in a private venture, as well as the 'mainstream' qualities that would win them wide audience appeal without alienating a substantial part of the immigrant population.

The commercial domain

Not alienating segments of their target audience is a central concern of Turkish broadcasters in the commercial domain. In recent years, Turkish immigrants have been identified as a functional consumer group in Germany, amenable to ethnic marketing strategies (Çağlar 2002, IPA Plus 1994). Despite their relatively low socio-economic level, immigrants have increasingly focused their spending activities on Germany, moving away from the 'save up and return' orientation of 'guestworkers' during the early period of labor migration. Large companies such as the German Telekom or the car producer Mercedes Benz have been among the first to seek to profit from immigrants' telecommunications needs and car preferences, placing Turkish-language advertising in both German and Turkish media. The recognition of Turkish Germans as a group possessing significant buying power constitutes the basis for commercially viable Turkish broadcasting ventures.

Berlin's commercial Turkish television station TD-1 has been able to survive financially by exploiting the advertising market offered by small-scale Turkish businesses such as in auto repair, apparel, dining and specialty foods, all of which contribute to the Turkish commercial presence in the city. Advertising in larger media outlets is financially out of reach for most of these small businesses, and TD-1 provides an opportunity to reach their target group at relatively low cost. TD-1 keeps costs down by operating with a mostly amateur staff and by taking much of its programming from channels in Turkey. The station owner is pessimistic regarding prospects for professionalization and expansion since TD-1's advertising niche is not likely to grow significantly, meaning that higher professional standards and more self-produced programming would not translate into an expanded revenue base.[13]

Radio, however, is a different matter. Programme production costs are lower, and for a station like Metropol FM there is little competition in the area of Turkish music on a terrestrial frequency in Berlin, especially during radio 'prime time' in the early hours of the day. Despite fierce competition among the city's 25 radio stations, Metropol FM offers a format that attracts a formerly untapped target group, thus making it interesting to advertisers. By limiting themselves to a Turkish-speaking local audience, however, both Metropol FM and TD-1 have to take care not to alienate segments of an already limited target group marked by deep political, ethnic, and religious divisions.

As stated above, the founders and administrators of Metropol FM have taken great care to eliminate politically divisive applicants in their staff recruitment. This sensitivity toward the controversial is also reflected in the programme content, which avoids any explicit political statements that could be expressed through music choices or in news and information programmes. The focus is on entertainment, of the kind that constitutes a non-controversial common denominator for all but a few fringe groups of the target audience. TD-1 has taken a somewhat different path, aligning more explicitly with the more conservative elements of the Sunni majority, as exemplified in regular religious broadcasts by members of DİTİB (*Diyanet İşleri Türk-Islam Birliği*), which represent Turkey's Directorate of Religious Affairs abroad, and in political talk shows that favour conservative positions. However, the station maintains a sufficiently non-partisan image for representatives of the more liberal and left-leaning Turkish immigrant umbrella organization TBB (*Türkischer Bund Berlin-Brandenburg*) to participate in programmes as well.

Given the extent of political and religious cleavages in the immigrant population from Turkey, even an explicitly *apolitical* broadcasting orientation might lead to problems, since the refusal to side with a particular 'camp' or to address a divisive issue becomes a political statement in itself. Metropol FM, like TD-1, had to seek police protection after the capture of PKK leader Abdullah Öcalan, having received credible threats of violence from Kurdish nationalist groups. Nevertheless, Metropol FM's broadcasting strategy seems to have paid off, with no serious public contestations of its slogan '*bizim dalga*' (our airwave) having emerged since it started broadcasting in 1999.

Prospects

In sum, within Turkish-language immigrant media in Berlin a long-standing presence in the public service domain has been complemented over the past fifteen years by Open Channel and commercial programmes. Despite commercialization, politically motivated projects of minority representation and the education of audiences according to an integrationist agenda still play important roles. This holds true for broadcasting ventures such as Radio MultiKulti that derive their *raison d'être* from the politics of integration, and also for those whose political agenda originates in and mostly relates to Turkey – as in the case of many Open Channel programmes and the television station TFD, which represents the views of the Islamist Milli Görüş organization in Berlin.

However, the trend toward commercial broadcasting in Germany is an important dimension of the larger media environment within which such projects are situated. Commercial reasoning has also begun to affect the public service domain. Radio MultiKulti, for example, must now justify its existence by high ratings, not just its political–representational role. Since its success is measured against commercial channels, the station has been forced to adopt the entertainment logic that prevails in the commercial domain at least to some extent, by reducing the percentage of word content in favour of music and by addressing a 'niche' population not served by other stations.

The emergence of successful commercial Turkish-language channels and stations also threatens to undermine the political mission of representation that has bolstered integration-oriented programming in publicly supported media. The idea had been that immigrants needed radio and television in their own language as part of a general right to be serviced by public service broadcasting. The success of Turkish-language commercial enterprises such as Berlin's Metropol FM and cable TV station TD-1 can however be interpreted as evidence that commercial projects suffice to fulfill this function. Acceptance among their target audience, expressed in ratings, can be taken as proof that they are sufficiently representative, thus putting into question the need for programming that derives its rationale from a political-representational logic. Projects such as Radio MultiKulti are thus at risk of being deemed superfluous, particularly as commercial projects attempt to be 'inclusive' of a range of political positions. In practice, this often means the *exclusion* of divisive political issues, as shown above. But the 'consensus' suggested by high ratings – a general acceptance of the programme among its target audience – can easily be mistaken for a consensus in the political sense of the term, the programme responding to its audiences needs and representing its views.[14] However, the question of just what and whom a particular station or programme in fact (re-)presents cannot be asked once the ethnicization thesis has reduced immigrant broadcasting to the contrast between ethno-cultural minority and majority society, positing that the station or programme allows immigrants to find and represent 'themselves.'

Conclusion

The assumption that any kind of minority mass media production is a good thing, that it gives minorities access to the public sphere and enables them to voice their interests, puts on hold crucial questions regarding the relationship between cultural production, categorical identities, and power. There is no question of ideology, then, only issues of material access for groups which are seemingly constituted outside the realm of discourse. 'Resource mobilization' becomes the center of concerns, and subordination mainly a matter of being denied the resources that would allow the subordinated group to enter the realm of public representation. If the categorical identity of ethnic groups is unproblematic and it is only access that is at stake (that is, groups possess a 'voice' which simply needs to be heard) then commercial programming can indeed be viewed as a realization of minority representation. Thus programming can point to ratings as an apparent kind of 'plebiscite' of minority will: people are watching or listening. In commercial broadcasting today, ratings authorise representation at the same time that they package audiences for sale to advertisers (Heath, 1990).

But what are the factors that render some representations of immigrant life more authoritative than others, and for whom? This is not simply a question of particular audiences differing in terms of how they engage with such representations – interpreting, contesting, or accepting them. It is also a question of the wider social and cultural fields that these audiences and programme producers are situated in, fields which shape the frames of reference they employ and the material means at their disposal. As shown above, the German institutional environment and its multicultural agendas exercise considerable influence upon immigrant 'voices' and where they can be heard.

Furthermore, the authority of a media 'voice' depends on the extent to which it builds upon meanings accepted as common sense by its audience, aligning itself with hegemonic articulations in the process. Media representations of immigrant culture are always caught up in the 'ideological,' since representation can in fact never be the mere presentation of objective facts. What is taken for granted or accepted as common sense is not something that is 'naturally' evident, but has been historically established as evident (Bourdieu, 1977; Hall, 1982).

Dominant multiculturalist discourse in Germany today takes immigrant minority media as authoritative on the sole basis of their minority origin. The heterodoxy of positions articulated in contexts like the Open Channel constitutes a somewhat baffling fact that cannot easily be accommodated in this discourse, and is thus often attributed by German politicians and analysts to an illegitimate transfer of political conflicts from Turkey to Germany. In such dismissive attributions that aim to exclude positions which implicitly undermine the premises of multiculturalism, another important fact is forgotten: even those Turkish voices legitimated by multiculturalist discourse because they seem entirely 'rooted' in Berlin and/or Germany cannot be entirely divorced from political conflicts and hegemonic discourses in Turkey. The research presented above has revealed some of the aspects through which broadcasters remain implicated in such conflicts and discourses, whether they must avoid certain divisive issues in their programmes, try to enforce a standard of language that is associated with secularist modernization in Turkey, or attempt to remain close to 'mainstream' religious positions of Sunni Islam. Asked to comment on their perceptions of locally produced Turkish-language programmes, broadcasters as well as members of their audience almost always referred to Turkey's religious, ethnic, and political conflicts in their attempts to 'locate' programmes vis-à-vis each other.[15] While this was not the exclusive frame of reference, it was certainly a significant one, and one that was employed also by people who explicitly subscribed to the multiculturalist integration agenda. The point is not to argue that Turkish-language media in Berlin simply reproduce Turkey's conflicts abroad. But in trying to understand what 'voices' these media actually represent, it is as important to account for the German context of policy and institutions that shapes these voices' existence as it is to analyse the multiple frames of reference that they employ and are themselves judged by.

Turkish-language broadcasting in Berlin operates with signs and functions as signs, as does all human communication. What renders this case of broadcasting so interesting is the multiplicity of ways in which the signs that it operates with can actually signify, and to whom. The Russian linguist Voloshinov insisted that 'The sign may not be divorced from the concrete forms of social intercourse' (Voloshinov, 1973, p. 21) and, as a consequence of the conflictual character of this communicative process, the ideological sign is 'multiaccentual.' It carries within it the refractions of social conflict within a sign community, most often the nation-state. Rendered in Marxist terms of class struggle, Voloshinov has suggested:

'Class does not coincide with the sign community, i.e., with the community which is the totality of users of the same set of signs for ideological communication. Thus various classes will use one and the same language. As a result, differently oriented accents intersect in every ideological sign. Sign [sic] becomes an arena of the class struggle. ... The ruling class strives ... to make the sign uniaccentual' (Voloshinov, 1973, p. 23).

Human communication, whether mass-mediated or not, is thus not simply about mutual understanding, but also about the political effort to make others understand a sign in one particular way and not others (Hall, 1982). It is not necessary to employ a Marxist perspective and regard 'class' as the central category of socio-cultural analysis to see the production of meaning as a conflictual process (Laclau and Mouffe, 1985). Making the sign 'uniaccentual': this political project becomes all the more problematic when the different accents that intersect in the sign originate from within *different* sign communities of which immigrants simultaneously form a part. While the nation-state continues to be a crucial political entity that shapes and contains the boundaries of sign communities, cross-border migration as well as communication has encouraged the transnational formation of such communities, and has also enabled immigrants to participate in more than one such community at a time. 'Multi-accentuality' acquires a greater complexity when thought of not just in terms of the politics of cultural struggle within one social formation (ibid.), but when the articulatory practices of immigrants draw upon and intervene in different fields of what Voloshinov has called 'ideological communication'. Thus, while immigrant media productions might signify the public emergence of authentic immigrant voices to German multiculturalist experts, they can simultaneously be understood as an intervention in the politics of cultural struggle in Turkey. The actual complexity of Turkish-language broadcasting in Germany can be made sense of only by paying close attention to the multiple frames of reference that media programme creators employ, and to the financial and institutional constraints that shape their work.

Notes

* A previous version of this chapter has been published by the author in *New Perspectives on Turkey*, Spring–autumn 2003, nos. 28–9: 107–31.
1. Representatives of private channels have claimed that it was in fact them who have started this trend, at a ZDF (*Zweites Deutsches Fernsehen*, public service television channel) conference in Mainz, 1998.
2. All radio and television users in Germany have to register their receiving sets and pay monthly fees to cover the operating costs of public service broadcasting in the country.
3. As opposed to cable or satellite radio stations which are commercially irrelevant due to their tiny audience shares.
4. The choice of words here indicates the slowness with which even 'progressive' proponents of multicultural positions move away from the '*Ausländer*' terminology, still using the label of foreigner for people whose presence in Germany they seek to normalize (Mandel, 1995).

5. Not only do young people have a habit of mixing Turkish and German words and sentences, their Turkish is often learnt from parents who themselves speak dialects or forms of Turkish that do not qualify as *öztürkçe*.

6. Supporters of Millî Görüş (National View) form an exception. The organization, which is the foreign branch of Turkey's former Welfare Party, operates the television station TFD (*Türkisches Fernsehen Deutschland*) in Berlin, broadcasting a few hours each week on commercial cable.

7. Of the Mevlevi, Kadiriye, and Nakşibendi orientation (see Jonker, 2000).

8. The latter three all have mass media networks in Turkey that include newspapers, television channels, and radio stations, leading Seufert to claim that Islamic communities have 'veiled' themselves as modern institutions to enter and restructure Turkey's public space (Seufert, 1997).

9. This is not to deny that sharing experiences related to one's position in a hierarchical scheme of ethnic or racial classification is without consequence for representation, merely to criticize the inside-outside distinction that disregards differences 'within' ethnic minority groups and turns every statement of an 'ethnic' into an ethnic statement.

10. A Turkish term for someone living far from his or her homeland, also denoting guest worker (*Gastarbeiter*).

11. The channel TRT-International has its own studio and correspondents in Berlin, and thus presents an interesting case of a satellite channel that does not exclusively export its programs but produces a small part of them where its migrant audience abroad is located. Its productions nevertheless focus on the ongoing ties and affinities of Turkish immigrants with Turkey.

12. In 1993, a hotel in the Turkish town of Sivas where Alevi left-wing intellectuals held a conference was burnt down by angry Sunni extremists, killing many people and igniting a wave of Alevi activism both in Turkey and Europe in response.

13. Personal interview with the owner and director Atalay Özçakır.

14. For a discussion of the interplay between market forces and and state policies with regard to ethnic media in Germany, see Çağlar (2002).

15. This is all the more significant in light of the fact that the researcher presented herself as a German with no Turkish immigration background, and tended to be seen as an 'outsider' with little or no knowledge of these conflicts.

References

Aksoy, A. and K. Robins (2000) 'Thinking Across Spaces: Transnational Television from Turkey', *European Journal of Cultural Studies,* vol.3 no.3, 343–65.

Arbeitskreis Offene Kanäle (1996) *Offene Kanäle und Bürgerfunk in Deutschland – Rundfunk der Dritten Art* (Kiel: Arbeitskreis Offene Kanäle und Bürgerrundfunk).

Becker, J. (1998a) 'Die Ethnisierung der Deutschen Medienlandschaft – Türkische Medienkultur zwischen Assoziation und Dissoziation', in S. Quandt and W. Gast (eds), *Deutschland Im Dialog der Kulturen: Medien, Images, Verständigung* (Konstanz: UKV Medien) pp. 295–302.

Becker, J. (1998b) 'Multiculturalism in German Broadcasting', *Media Development*, no.3, 8–12.

Becker, J. (2001) 'Zwischen Integration und Abgrenzung: Anmerkungen zur Ethnisierung der Türkischen Medienkultur', in J. Becker and R. Benisch (eds), *Zwischen Abgrenzung und Integration: Türkische Medienkultur in Deutschland* (Loccum: Evangelische Akademie Loccum) pp. 9–24.

BOK (2000) *Was sind Offene Kanäle?*, http://www.bok.de/was.html (Bundesverband Offene Kanäle Deutschland).

Bourdieu, P. (1997) *Outline of a Theory of Practice* (Cambridge, New York: Cambridge University Press).

Bünger, R. (1995) 'Offen für Neues', *Agenda*, no. 18, 46–7.

Busch, J. (1994) *Radio Multikulti: Möglichkeiten für lokalen Ethnofunk Berlin – Deutschland – Großbritannien* (Berlin: Vistas).

Çağlar, A. (2002) 'Mediascapes, Advertisement Industries and Cosmopolitan Transformations: Turkish Immigrants in Germany', paper presented at the Third Workshop on Contemporary European Migration History, http://www.network-migration.org/workshop2002/papers/AyseCaglar.pdf., visited.

Duyar, A. and N. Çalağan (2001) '94,8 Metropol FM – Das erste Türkischsprachige Radio in Deutschland', in J. Becker and R. Behnisch (eds), *Zwischen Abgrenzung und Integration: Türkische Medienkultur in Deutschland* (Loccum: Evangelische Akademie Loccum) pp. 85–98.

Gramsci, A. (1971) *Selections From the Prison Notebooks* (New York: International Publishers).

Hall, S. (1982) 'The Rediscovery of 'Ideology': Return of the Repressed in Media Studies', in M. Gurevitch *et al.* (eds), *Culture, Society and the Media* (London and New York: Routledge) pp. 56–90.

Hargreaves A. G. and D. Mahdjoub (1997) 'Satellite Television Viewing among Ethnic Minorities in France', *European Journal of Communication*, vol.12, no.4, 459–77.

Heath, S. (1990) 'Representing Television', in P. Mellencamp (ed.), *Logics of Television: Essays in Cultural Criticism* (Bloomington and Indianapolis: Indiana University Press) pp. 269–302.

Heitmeyer, W. J. Müller and H. Schröder (1998) 'Islamistische Expansionspropaganda: Mediennutzung und religiös begründete Machtansprüche bei Türkischen Jugendlichen', in H. Bielefeldt and W. Heitmeyer (eds), *Politisierte Religion* (Frankfurt a.M.: Suhrkamp Verlag) pp. 256–79.

Holler, W. (1997) 'Radio MultiKulti gefährdet?', *UNESCO Heute*, I–II, 15–16.

Husband C. (ed.) (1994) *A Richer Vision: The Development of Ethnic Minority Media in Western Democracies* (Paris: UNESCO).

IPA-Plus (1994) *Türken in Deutschland 1994: Markt-Media-Studie* (Frankfurt a.M.: IPA).

Jarren, O., T. Grothe and R.Müller (1994) *Bürgermedium Offener Kanal* (Berlin: Vistas Verlag).

Jonker, G. (2000) 'Islamic Television "Made in Berlin"', in F. Dassetto (ed.), *Paroles d'Islam: Des nouveaux Discourses Islamiques en Europe* (Strasbourg: Gallimard), pp. 267–80.

Kaya, A. (2002) *'Sicher in Kreuzberg': Constructing Diasporas: Turkish Hip-Hop Youth in Berlin* (Bielefeld: Transcript Verlag).

King R. and N. Wood (eds) (2001) *Media and Migration: Constructions of Mobility and Difference* (London: Routledge).

Kosnick, K. (2000) 'Building Bridges – Media for Migrants and the Public-Service Mission in Germany', *European Journal of Cultural Studies*, vol.3 no.3, 321–44.

Kosnick, K. (forthcoming) *Migrant Media: Turkish Broadcasting of and Multicultural Politics in Berlin* (Bloomington: Indiana University Press).

Laclau E. and C. Mouffe (1985) *Hegemony and Socialist Strategy: Towards A Radical Democratic Politics* (London: Verso).

Livingstone, S. and P. Lunt (1994) *Talk on Television: Audience Participation and Public Debate* (London and New York: Routledge).

MABB (1998) *'Radio Makaria für die UKW-Hörkfunkfrequenz 94,8 MHz ausgewählt'*, press release (Berlin: Landesmedienanstalt Berlin-Brandenburg).

Makaria GmbH (1998) *Das Erste Türkische Radio in Berlin – Präsentation* (Berlin: Makaria GmbH).

Mandel, R. (1995) 'Second-Generation Non-Citizens: Children of the Turkish Migrant Diaspora in Germany', in S. Stephens (ed.), *Children and the Politics of Culture* (Princeton: Princeton University Press) pp. 265–81.

McChesney, R. W. and D. Schiller (2003) 'The Political Economy of International Communication: Foundations for the Emerging Global Debate About Media Ownership and Regulation,' Technology, Business and Society Programme, (Geneva: UN Research Institute for Social Development), Oct. Paper no. 11.

Mohr, I. (1996) 'SFB 4 MultiKulti: Öffentlich-Rechtliches Hörfunkangebot nicht nur für Ausländer', *Media Perspektiven*, no. 8, 466–72.

Okkan, O. (1998) 'Anmerkungen zum Projekt "Europäisches Migranten-TV"', in Adolf-Grimme-Institut (ed.), *Migration und Medien* (Marl: Adolf-Grimme-Institut) pp. 14–16.

Riggins, St. H. and Stephen Harold (1992) 'The Media Imperative: Ethnic Minority Survival in the Age of Mass Communication', in St. H. Riggins (ed.), *Ethnic Minority Media: an International Perspective* (Newbury Park: Sage Publications) pp. 1–20.

Sakr, N. (2002) *Satellite Realms: Transnational and Television, Globalization and the Middle East* (Lodon: I.B. Tauris).

Seufert, G. (1997) *Politischer Islam in der Türkei: Islamismus als symbolische Repräsentation einer sich modernisierenden Muslimischen Gesellschaft* (Istanbul: Franz Steiner Verlag).

SFB 4–MultiKulti (1995) *Project Description* (Berlin: Sender Freies Berlin).

Spivak, G. Ch. (1998) 'Can the Subaltern Speak?' in L. Grossberg and C. Nelson (eds), *Marxism and the Interpretation of Culture* (Urbana: University of Illinois Press), pp. 271–313.

Vertovec, S. (1996a) 'Berlin Multikulti: Germany, "Foreigners" and "World-Openness"', *New Community*, vol.22, no.3, 381–99.

Vertovec, S. (1996) 'Multiculturalism, Culturalism and Public Incorporation', *Ethnic and Racial Studies*, vol.19, 49–69.

Vertovec, S. (2000) 'Fostering Cosmopolitanisms: A Conceptual Survey and a Media Experiment in Berlin', *Transnational Communities Working Paper Series*, http://www.transcomm.ox.ac.uk, 1–31.

Voloshinov, V. N. (1973) *Marxism and the Philosophy of Language* (New York: Seminar Press).

Voß, F. (1995) 'Radio MultiKulti: Babylon auf dem Äther', *FU:N*, no.8/9, 23.

Part III

Transnational Lives and the Media

9
Diasporic Mediated Spaces

Sonja de Leeuw and Ingegerd Rydin

Introduction

Within the context of migration and globalisation of media, questions concerning the transformation of culture have become manifest among communication scholars. Due to alterations in the global political and economic order, such as deregulation of the media market, the media landscape has undergone extensive transformations during last decades of the twentieth century. Moreover, processes of decolonisation and post-colonisation, the opening of borders in Europe and the outbreak of wars, have led to increased migration movements and generated a flood of people, who for different reasons are looking for new places and new homes. Cultural communities are no longer fixed in particular geographical spaces. As a result we are facing what Hall has called 'the global post-modern' (1996), involving the possible shifts of power relations and cultural hierarchies that in particular apply to diaspora, people connected to a cultural community, now living dispersed. What interests us here are the processes of cultural transformation that are taking place within 'the global post-modern' where increasing numbers of people are negotiating their identities between continuity and change, between similarity and difference. In the new place, senses of homely belonging are necessarily being constructed with references to both the new place and to what has been left behind.

Media and communication technologies seem to play a determining role in the processes of cultural transformation that involves the re-invention and redefinition of cultural identity. The media create spaces of identity (Morley & Robins, 1995) in the sense that identity processes are formed and reformed in a process of cultural transformation.

In this chapter we will explore media practices among young people in diaspora communities to see what *functions* various media have in processes of identity formation (e.g. social, ethnic, national, cultural). We are referring here in particular to media use as a means of sustaining bonds with the home country (bonding) or engaging with the new country (bridging), that is to say media use by people who are in a continuous process of cultural change (Rydin & Sjöberg, 2005). In particular, we address how diaspora communities engage with the television medium, both global, mainstream (local and national) and transnational (satellite) diasporic television. We believe they all are of importance, but they have different functions in diasporic life. Gillespie's pioneer research (Gillespie, 1995) along with recent studies (Karim, 2003; De Block *et al.*, 2004; Christopoulou & De Leeuw, 2005; Rydin & Sjöberg, 2005) indicate that media use among diasporic communities seems to play a fundamental role in the construction of everyday spaces in which experiences and identities (eg. cultural, ethnic, social) are constructed and negotiated.

Following up on recent ethnographic research[1] in which we ourselves were involved, we will present in a more explorative way the study of diasporas as *mediated spaces*. For this paper we will mainly focus on the common practices in media use and address different levels of media consumption. It is precisely the extent to which global, transnational and local media practices intersect in diasporic communities that is central here.

Research methodology

We consider ethnography an appropriate and instrumental methodology in yielding in-depth information about a process of cultural change that is very complex and that involves the equally complex concept of identity. Diaspora follows naturally from transnationalism in terms of the exchange of resources, including people, across the border of nation states (Vertovec, 2002). We want to emphasize in particular the central role of the family: in a migratory context families, mediating between past and present, become a site of negotiating identities as different generations each in their own way struggle with the obvious tensions between the 'old' and the 'new' world (Christopoulou & De Leeuw, 2005).

For this analysis we will rely on three sets of data, collected between the years 2001–2005. In the European CHICAM project (2001–2004), in which the present authors participated, we collected case study data through observations and interviews about media practices from more than 60 children (in the ages of 10–14) and their families in six European countries. These children also participated in practical media production projects in the form of a media club. An analysis of these data is presented in a summary report by De Block, *et al.* (2004). Furthermore, we rely on an ongoing project of migrant and refugee families (parents and children in the ages of 10–14) in Sweden (Rydin & Sjöberg, 2005) as well as data on media use among migrant adolescents in the Netherlands (de Leeuw, 2006). The children and their families represent a range of different ethnicities. The common denominator between them is that these children and their parents have a migration history; a journey from one culture to another, i.e. a western European culture, for various reasons, often due to escape of war and conflicts in their home countries. What is significant here, is the process of cultural change, among other things, and the shift of language. These sets of data will be considered in relation to the theoretical issues discussed in this paper.

Negotiating identities and media use

We are in particular interested in such media practices that attempt to overcome cultural exclusion and construct senses of home and belonging, based on the presupposition that there is a strong relationship between media use and identity construction. However, identity is a very complex concept. It refers to both a conception of self and a conception of self in relation to a social context of belonging such as a 'nation', a 'community', a 'diaspora'; also identity can be defined in terms of gender and age which can be interconnected with ethnicity again. Having said this, we acknowledge the construction of identity as a continuous process, in which past and present, difference and similarity are mutually inclusive. 'Identity are the names we give to different ways we are positioned by and position ourselves within the narratives of the past' (Hall, 1990, p. 225). This means that our identity changes when our history will be told in a different way. In this respect, as Hall argues, identity not only becomes an understanding of being, but also of becoming, which in particular applies to Diaspora communities. However the narratives of the past in our view are directly related to narratives that are beginning to be told and constructed in the new world. References to a common history and traditions that were celebrated in the homeland are being negotiated in the new places where new alliances are being made both with people of the same origin and with the native inhabitants of the new country. It is the process of negotiation that we find crucial in the lives of people who are in a situation of cultural change and which we seek to capture in ethnographic research.

As diaspora is a state of consciousness about the characteristics of the community one feels to belong to, it could be described as an 'imagined community' (Anderson, 1983); a community hold together by stories, images and symbols that represent shared meanings about itself. As identities are constructed and found in representations, in narratives, in the same way they can be seen as 'imagined' identities. In the age of electronic media these narratives were and are increasingly constructed through and in media, which may justify the notion of 'mediated' identities. It goes without saying that in the age of digital media the possibilities of constructing imagined and even virtual identities have become multiple. In 'the global post-modern' loyalties have become as diverse as the different social groups that people are invited to relate to.

First of all the notion of national identity has become blurred. In the 19th century in Europe so called nation states were founded. The basic idea of national identity was articulated in the concept of the nation state that tried and built people's loyalty based upon a common history, language and ethnicity that was capable of producing a shared meaning about nationhood. The national narrative emphasized the continuity of the nation in terms of a testified loyalty to the president or king. In the media age these notions of national identity were strengthened by national media and were also exported and reproduced in narratives about the glorious days of history as not only many American films may illustrate, but also the representation of royal families in the media as symbols of the nation, the true bearers of continuity. For example, one could indeed easily say that the media provide the image of 'Americanness' for 'us as Europeans'. On the other hand, the increased output of global and transnational satellite media during the last decades may blur (or weaken) such concepts of national identities.

Speaking of diaspora communities we see different ways in which people who are involved in processes of cultural change may relate themselves to the 'here' and 'there'. As to the 'here', the new country, the place where people try to build new loyalties, we have to keep in mind that the 'imagined identity' of the host country is being created through the media as well. Social exclusion, particularly among elderly and unemployed migrants /refugees, may imply that people adopt the images about the host country supplied by television. In trying to remain loyal to the 'there', the old country, people's 'imagined identity', based upon a common narrative that is being reproduced in e.g. transnational media, may become blurred with the images of media images in the host country. In such cases one could eventually speak about a 'mediated identity'. The post-modern notion of hybridity is obvious here, in its reference to a multi-layered identity that is continuously being negotiated. Though this is considered the dominant discursive practice in post-traditional global societies (Barker, 1997), it is too loose a concept to describe the construction of identity in diaspora communities. The notion of hybridity does not consider the need to keep old certainties and the efforts of people of perceiving themselves as constant and stable persons.

Globalisation also provides many a source available for the production of identities, incorporating the local into the global. Barker (1997, 205) adopts the concept of 'glocalization' in order to describe this process, referring to the global production of the local, and the localization of the global. This is an unequal process that involves people in different ways. However there is evidence that people are very conscious about cultural differences in everyday life, but also when it comes to differences in media policy, programming, formats, and genres (De Block *et al.*, 2004; Rydin and Sjöberg, 2005). This reflexivity reveals an awareness of media spaces and of the production of meaning within these spaces. Reflexivity in this sense opens up the possibility of creating new cultural ('mediated') spaces, in consumption and eventually in production practices as in the CHICAM research project that will be discussed below.[2]

In this respect, concepts such as exile, space and time are relevant to further explore. Werbner (2002) emphasizes the positive dimensions of transnational existence and cosmopolitan consciousness, discussing the construction of diaspora in time through its scattered and dispersed communities. The notion of diaspora as the result of an active intervention, a communicative construction is one of the observations of Vilem Flusser (1920–91), a Czech philosopher who fled via London to Brazil in 1940, built a career in Sao Paulo and returned to Europe in 1972. Flusser (2003) describes the relationship between migration and homely belonging, and the role of communication in this relationship. His writings reflect the notion of space as the result of creation that he sees as 'the freedom of the migrant', the very title of his book. Flusser emphasizes the positive value of seeing oneself as different and to use this difference to create something new, which we think can be empowering.

In his view exile can be seen as a challenge to creativity (Flusser, 2003, p. 81). As is discussed in the introduction to his book (Flusser, 2003, pp. xii–xv), the overarching principle for him is the principle of dialogue. Nomad, migrant, homeland, and exile are notions that Flusser interweaves with his principle of dialogue. In thinking about place Flusser distinguishes homeland from home: 'People think of heimat as being a relatively permanent place; a home, as temporary and interchangeable. Actually, the opposite is true: one can exchange heimats – or have none at all – but one must always live somewhere, regardless of where' (Flusser, 2003, p. 12). So home and homeland should not be confused. Actually, the concept of 'home' is a metaphor, which is often used to describe the immigrant's special life situation both among media scholars e.g. Morley (2000) and anthropologists, e.g. Salih (2001). 'Home' can according to Salih (2001, p. 51) be understood both as the physical space and the symbolic conceptualization of where one belongs. The latter definition ties in with Flusser's. And here we address the role of the media and various communication networks. The idea is that this actual place to live is built upon communication networks that come into being in dialogical confrontation of the expellee and the settled inhabitants. Flusser sees this as 'togetherness', yet polemical because the expellee threatens the singularity of the settled inhabitants, putting it in question by his own foreignness. But according to Flusser, even such polemical dialogue is creative, because it, too, leads to a synthesis of new information (Flusser, 2003, p. 87).

Settling somewhere involves building new spaces and engaging in dialogical communication both with the native inhabitants and with people belonging to the same group inside and outside the new country. The role of the media in this respect is apparently strong, especially in those cases where the old contingencies are not rejected. As Dayan (1999) argues, media reorganize separated geographical spaces into a continuum. They enable a shared experience of time for people living in different time zones. He points to the fact that diaspora groups are no longer exceptional. Studies should not be bound to geographic areas, but rather analyse communication models that diaspora groups keep alive by linking the margin to the centre and the present to past. By the same token one could argue there are different shared experiences, ones already built and reinvented, ones to be constructed (in the new country with the native inhabitants), ones with people belonging to the same minority group. These experiences are being articulated and constructed in diverse media productions that cut across private and public spaces (Dayan, 1999, p. 22). These could range from conventional media such as television to private media such as pictures, home videos (an example of the creative dimension). Thus diaspora communities to a certain extent have developed into semi-autonomous communication spaces within modern societies that involves processes of 'glocalization'. These micro public spheres are embedded in bigger (mediated) public spheres and interact. That is why in the following we will address these different levels of media use finding out about the dialogical interaction between bonding and bridging that is inherent in the situation of cultural change in Diaspora communities. We will mainly limit our focus to examples related to television, as this medium seems to be the most dominant, if in a diversity of manifestations such as diasporic, national (meaning television in the new country) and global television. Because the notion of a diasporic network of communication is central here, we will to some extent also discuss other media that help building this network, and Internet in particular.

Diasporic television viewing

The introduction of transnational satellite television in the eighties in many European countries and somewhat later in the Scandinavian countries has had a great impact on the viewing habits among immigrant and refugee families in Europe. Access to cable (including pay-TV) and satellite television seemed to be standard among the families in the CHICAM project. One common denominator across the countries was that satellite viewing played both the role of maintaining continuity with the past and of keeping in contact with the present. Keeping in contact with the country of origin took different forms such as watching news programmes or watching familiar series or movies that they used to watch before they moved. Satellite television also offers a multicultural output of global series above all. One of the main roles that television played for the parents was to maintain continuity with their past lives and their countries of origin, that is for bonding and keeping ties. This need was often combined with the need to reinforce and preserve the mother language. A variety of reasons for watching television illustrates the *functions of the media* in diasporic family life.

As many migrants are refugees coming from politically unstable conditions, one important function of transnational television was to be informed about the *political situation* in the former home country. For example, Greece is a transit country for refugees coming from the

Middle East and Balkan. A family (from Turkey) in the Greek project had a strong affiliation to a political party and their children were very much exposed to media from their country of origin. However, it was not only parents who exerted influence over television viewing but also the wider community within which the child and immediate family lived, such as the political situation of the diaspora at hand. As the family's social life revolved mainly around the party office, the children's viewing patterns were those of the adults there, who constantly watched news reports and discussions about events in their country. They also spent hours watching taped documentaries about the revolt of their party comrades in Turkish prisons, as well as about some of them declaring their credo before embarking on fatal food-strikes. All these contained violent scenes, as well as a lot of propaganda. Television for these families was a source of information (and teaching) and not of entertainment. As a result, the children often did not take part in informal discussions about popular series on Greek TV along with the other kids in the club. One of the boys in the Greek project, in particular, although he was fascinated by the technical abilities of working with media equipment such as camera editing and the potential to produce the things he was interested in, was quite snobbish about entertainment TV and claimed he never watched anything other than what interested him for information reasons. His attitude was very much influenced by the adult attitudes in his social environment, and by what was deemed acceptable and 'serious enough' by them (De Block *et al.*, 2004).

Other parents were worried about the political content in the media and that their children could get wrong images of their home country. A Kurdish father[3] who had settled in Sweden reported on the Kurds' political situation and how it influenced the family's media use. He complained about the Kurdsat and its frequent broadcasts on violent scenes showing Saddam Hussein's massacre on the Kurds in North Iraq and that these pictures once accidentally had hit his little daughter of four. The father stated that he preferred to tell the daughter *his* version of the story, not the media's. This example shows how the media are supplying narratives about the past, which eventually become the 'grand narratives' of a nation or a people. At present, the general stereotypical public picture of the Kurds, is related to the massacre instigated by Saddam Hussein. Films about these violent events have been cabled out in the world and repeated over and over again creating a 'mediated identity' of the Kurds. This image opposes the father's private interest to present an alternative story of the Kurds, which perhaps avoids the political issues and provides a more optimistic view and which does not put off the daughter to return some day. One can here see how national identity is negotiated by means of the media and how the public media sphere with its pictures of 'homeland' is in contrast to the micro public sphere of the family's conception of 'homeland'.

We also found that in refugee families, the role of television was different from that in migrant families. The satellite often was the only link between asylum seekers and their home countries, where many of them left family and friends. Depending on their specific situations, some of the refugee families had no contact with their family and friends for many years. News and live reports served as evidence of the places they left behind, and as a search tool for finding family members. During the war in Iraq, TV was very important to many of the children. In the Netherlands, refugee children were discussing the political situation and stressed the importance of news viewing:

One girl, Rana watched for example a Syrian network on satellite, and related it to how the Iraqi government had been deposed. Another girl, Masja added that two palaces have been captured. In Iraqi refugee families in the Netherlands nostalgia too was openly expressed while watching news reports. There is a strongly felt need to check that everything is in order, as it used to be, which was apparently not the case. As other means of communication were too dangerous and thus almost impossible, watching satellite TV increasingly turned the alliances to the home country into a mediated experience. Thus keeping in touch with *current events* and *cultural changes* back home was important.

In other cases it was not so much connection with the country of origin itself that was important but the continuation of activities that the family used to enjoy before their migration, that is *nostalgic pleasures*. Turkish children in several clubs were heavy consumers of feature films from the Turkish video shop and Moroccan boys in the Dutch club watched action series and action movies broadcast on Moroccan television. And children in UK watched Hindi films, for example. In family conversations about such nostalgic pleasures, the situation of being in cultural change or transition also revealed generational gaps between parents and children, which were played out over TV programmes, thus emphasizing how complex the process of negotiation of national/cultural identities can be. For the children, especially soaps offered an easy way of moving between different cultures. An Albanian refugee family from Kosovo, living in Sweden, talked about an

Albanian soap opera (De Block *et al.*, 2004). Here is also a comparison of morals and standards between the homeland and the host country, and therefore an illustration of cultural differences. On Sunday nights, Albanian families often gathered around the set to watch the everyday life of *Familie Modern*, broadcasted on Albanian satellite television. Reported glimpses of episodes indicate that it has a humorous touch and that it mirrors generational differences and illuminates how life used to be in Albania as compared to how it is now. Elderly people represent the old days and they joke about it in the series, whereas the younger family members strive towards a modern life.

Extract from interview with Hana:

Hana: It is really funny. It is about a family, who tries to be as modern as possible.

And actually they have modern stuff in their house too. You know, in Albanian families, girls are not allowed to go to disco and stuff, but the girls in this series they go to disco and they are sleeping with guys. They can do anything they like. They can colour their hair everyday, and the son in the family, he brings Danish, Swedish and English girls every night. Strange! They are like a Swedish family (in an ironic tone).

Int: What do your parents think about the series?

Hana: They really think it is fun. The father is working, the mother is working, and then they have a grandmother, who is not modern. She is old-fashioned, as Albanians are in reality. She says: "You cannot do that and that. And what are you doing?" (voice affected). She is saying this all the time and nobody listens to her. "Mind your own business and go to bed", they say. Then they do whatever they like, anyway.

An older sister of Hana, who had memories from the time the family lived in Kosovo, spoke about the series with a smile and ironic tone commenting that this series and television in general is much better now than it used to be. Albania has opened up towards the West, with less regulations and control of the media. From the interview with Hana, it comes out that modern life in the series is more progressive or secularised than the Albanian way of upbringing in Sweden is. Once again, television gives rise to discussions about national identity. Albanians seem to keep an image of themselves as more strict and moralistic than Swedes who are considered more liberal, and this picture is challenged by the series *Familie Modern*.

At last, diasporic television has the function of *language maintenance*. Diasporic television offers great possibilities for both adults and children to keep in touch with their mother languages and parents generally encouraged this whilst also encouraging the use of television to acquire the new language. Some children complained, however, that they had difficulties understanding their mother language on television, whereas the parents tried to encourage them to follow programs in their mother language to strengthen it. So once again, generational gaps are revealed and we have a situation where the parents look back to 'there' and children are more directed to the future and life 'here' (Rydin & Sjöberg, 2005).

National television viewing

Several families actively encouraged their children to watch national television to assist their *acquisition of the new language* (De Block *et al.*, 2004). In one example from the German partner this intervention had consequences for a boy's communication with his mother who is living outside Germany, in the home country (Turkey): the Turkish father liked his son to watch programmes in German and not in Turkish so as not to hinder the development of the son's competence in the German language. The boy himself told the researchers that he sometimes got into language difficulties when speaking to his mother in Turkish over the phone:

'I speak bit German because I have forget Turkish. I speak to my mother. I think always "what I say, what I say?"' I think German but I say to my mother German my mother say "what is that'" I think "what is that, what is that in Turkish" like that.'

In the Netherlands, migrant and refugee children watched the Dutch Youth News:

Kambooye (a refugee from Somalia) states that he watches news: 'So that you know what is happening in the world.'

Confirming other studies of youth audiences it was clear that what you say about what you watch on television defines your identity in terms of age and gender but also in terms of ethnicity and cultural origin. This means that there were also some programmes that were not accepted to watching. Young people use television both to negotiate their new identities in their new locations and to negotiate a shared space with their peers across culture. There were specific programmes (and films) that were very popular that highlighted relationships across cultural differences and distance that seemed to hold some *emotional resonance* for the children. These programmes appeared to touch a very important chord for these children, as this extract from the Greek study reveals:

> Their (two children) favourites are two Greek series. One of these is a romantic comedy about a love affair across the continents ('You are my match'). The other is a series about the love story between a Greek woman, married to a wealthy land-owner who falls in love with the Albanian worker who works in their fields ('Love came from faraway'). In both of those, there is the element of distance, physical or otherwise, which both girls found exciting as it intensified the drama. Both series were very popular during the club year, and as such, they were often the subjects of conversation at school, in the neighbourhood or in the club. (De Block *et al.*, 2004)

For some families (De Block *et al.*, 2004; Rydin and Sjöberg, 2005) television and other media are felt *to threaten their family and/or religious values* and parents wanted to protect their children. This applied mainly, but not exclusively, to the national television stations of the new countries of residence and to the global American based satellite broadcasts. A mother with Muslim faith complained about too much nudity in Swedish television (Rydin and Sjöberg, 2005). And some parents control and restrict their children's viewing on national television. While television plays an important role in maintaining information and emotional ties with the place the children had come from, it is also important in helping children (and their families) settle in the new country. One of the Greek case studies highlights the importance of television in finding out about the new place of residence (Christopoulou and Rydin, 2004):

> Balkys, a 13-year-old girl who did not attend school, filtered most of her social activity in her neighbourhood and her community through TV. Lacking other shared ground with her peers (due to not going to school) Balkys had developed a pattern of watching TV for many hours every day. She became familiar with the plots of most series, soaps and dramas, and followed them in such detail that the people around her started recognising her as an authority on the

subject. As this was a current subject in most social interactions, Balkys became popular in her circle also in relation to this, and thus used TV as a means of social acceptance and socialisation.

Global television viewing

Under this heading we discuss programs that have a global format or are broadcasted from global cable networks such as CNN, Al Jazeera or MTV. There are a number of programs having a global format that are broadcast through national television and it was found that the children in the CHICAM project (De Block *et al.*, 2004) followed the most up-to-date soaps, such as *Big Brother* as well as programs like the Eurovision Song Contest, especially to see the performers of their home country, which reflects specific loyalties carried out through music.

When it comes to global broadcasting, it appeared that the news was important to many families. Children, especially refugee children from politically turbulent areas, seemed to be well informed about world events. They watched the news from Al Jazeera or from CNN and they wanted to constantly keep up with the events in the country they fled from. Adolescents in the Netherlands were very keen on getting all the relevant news channels as they considered CNN too dominant while at the same time too negative about 'the others' (de Leeuw, 2006).

Moreover, music television in general turns out to be a very important instrument in creating a common cultural ground across borders. The different music channels, MTV, TMF and The Box, also lead to some identification. Among the boys, the Hip Hop-artists are especially popular, because they are drawn to the 'tough-guy' image of these artists (De Block & Rydin, 2006). Rap is a global language and emphasizes the contours of a global youth community, indifferent to origin. From the Dutch study (De Block *et al.*, 2004):

Najib (NL) likes the music of the black rapper Tupac. He writes in his media collage: 'I am a rapper, too'. He goes by the name of 'Abdel' when he raps. He performs break dances and writes rap lyrics. Together with Beaugarçon, who provides the beatbox, he performs a rap on camera. Just like Najib, Beaugarçon likes the American rappers, and he flashes hand signals during the rap on camera. One of these is the 'W' for 'Westside' (thumb extended, ring-and middle finger crossed), a symbol that stands for the American West Coast. Beaugarçon: 'I learned this on television'. He is from West-Roosendaal, which is his reason for imitating this particular sign. He does not use it often; because he is afraid he might get into fights with other boys from Roosendaal who may be supporting other rappers.

In addition, many families, as we discussed above in the section on diasporic television watch programmes, particularly soap operas originating from regions other than their own, often in a third language. What was important in these cases was the emotional connections that the families felt to the programme as with an Armenian family who lived as refugees in the Netherlands. They watched a Brazilian Telenovela through a Russian satellite channel, which was dubbed in Russian. Children also reported on how global formats, such as quiz shows were adapted to different languages so that they could watch the same show in different settings and in different languages (De Block *et al.*, 2004).

Internet and computer use: keeping in touch

In Western Europe, access to Internet has increased rapidly during the last five years (Livingstone and Bovill, 1999; De Block *et al.*, 2004). Internet has a special role in the process of cultural change. Miller and Slater (2002) emphasizes the role of Internet to such an extent that they rather talk about an Internet family than a Diaspora family in their study of Trinidadian families who live abroad. They also stress that all Internet use (and media use in general) must be contextualized for each specific family. This interplay between real life and virtual life has been widely discussed among scholars with an interest in cyberspace (Kitchin, 1998; Jones, 1999). During the last years, focus has also turned to how the online life and the offline life are connected. Thus, they should not be perceived as opposite poles but rather as being parts in a mutual interplay. Bakardjieva (2003) has studied online forums and found that Internet does not solely create a kind of virtual togetherness, but actions and interactions going on there are also closely intertwined with participants' projects and pursuits in their offline lives. In her study on ICT use among Turkish, Moroccan and Surinamese youth in the Netherlands, d'Haenens (2003) also stresses the importance of contextualization of media use, i.e. research within this area should consider the societal context of the new country, where the children often are born and raised in, as well as the country of origin.

It is also important to keep in mind that the opportunities offered by media such as Internet has different meanings and implications for various social groups within Western societies. Far from all people in the world have access to their own telephone or own computer. This lack of access was also mentioned by migrant families in living in Europe, which makes it difficult for them to, for example, chat with family and friends in the homeland (De Block *et al.*, 2004; Rydin and Sjöberg, 2005). Access to Internet is not equally distributed in the European community; migrant families in the northern part of Europe are wired-up to a higher extent than countries in the southern part of Europe (De Block *et al.*, 2004).

Internet is a means to be kept informed about current political and social events, which in many cases has replaced ordinary newspapers that earlier were read at the library. Other common uses were listening to radio or downloading music from the home country (Rydin and Sjöberg, 2005). Concerning MSN Messenger and email, it appears that these means of communication have become important complements to the traditional telephone, both by adults and children (Hagen, 2003; Rydin and Sjöberg, 2005). It is not a matter of new technology replacing old ones but rather a combination of these. This different function and purpose of use is also stressed in the study by Miller and Slater (2002), where Internet communication has replaced the telephone for casual information of economical reasons. The telephone is now mainly used for exchanging important news, on special occasions and lifetime events such as births, marriages or deaths. However, in some cases the telephone is the only option as friends or relatives have no access to Internet. In comparison to the telephone, the service of MSN and email offers a regular, day-to-day contact with other family members and friends.

The other side of this, is when media (or the lack or loss of) are seen as means of forgetting: Elcin in the Greek project had kept all the phone-numbers of his friends in Istanbul in the SIM card of his mobile. After the journey, he forgot his PIN code. He possibly chose to forget it. This way, his own past could no longer be accessed. The dislocation brought about a selection out of choice or out of necessity, or, even as a coincidence (Christopoulou and de Leenw 2004). Frequent communication, was common among children who have not been so long in the new country, and who might suffer from homesickness (Rydin and Sjöberg, 2005). In her study on 12–19 year-old Turkish, Moroccans and Surinamese youth in the Netherlands, d'Haenens (2003) found a strong connection between the need to search for information about the country of origin and to maintain contact with other youngsters with the same ethnic background and the extent they identified with their homeland. It is of course necessary that family and friends in the homeland also have access to Internet. Here, there are differences between various countries and depending on whether ones relatives live in a city or on the countryside or not. A main difference between the adult and the young person, who often is born in the new country, is Internet as a part of local youth culture and therefore closely linked to the young person's life in the new country rather than being in contact with the parents' homeland. Internet is used to chat with peers from school, to play online games (among the boys), listen to music (usually mainstream pop music or RnB and hiphop), read sites about a specific interest such as bicycling, cars (mentioned by boys) and for searching information for schoolwork. Also gender differences are to be found. Boys play games on the net and visit, on a regular basis, specific sites about a certain topic, which is in line with previous research on young people, in general. Thus, the youth shares an online culture, an extension of playground gossip and interaction (Rydin and Sjöberg, 2005). Miller and Slater (2002) also note the importance of Internet among young Trinidadians and found that this medium replaced the telephone for continuing school conversations after school.

Other media

European studies also indicate that watching films on *video* is popular among migrant children, either on DVD or VHS. The choices reflect both cultural origins and the need to build new peer relations. The repertoire seems to be a mixture of Hollywood productions and movies from the home country. Adolescents state to watch channels that complement each other: 'Arabic movie, Dutch movie, American movie, it does not matter. They all show few things that you experience yourself in daily life, or that you have ever experienced in your life.' (de Leeuw, 2006). Some children also watch home videos such as family events, for example, weddings and other celebrations related to their cultural origins. These videos are also exchanged among communities of the same origin (De Block *et al.*, 2004: Rydin and Sjöberg, 2005).

The same pattern is seen when it comes to *music*, although music is a more private enterprise as compared to the video. Music is very much used as a symbolic space. This needs more discussion as does other media use, such as *print media* and *radio broadcasts* that lies beyond this paper.

Mediated spaces of identity

On the whole, television offered a platform for experiencing different identities, both global and sub-cultural, both related to youth culture and adult culture (Christopoulou and de Leeuw, 2004). Television also was a platform to negotiate the identity of being different, that is being both a migrant or 'foreigner' and a new citizen. As migrants or refugees, children devoted their viewing to media productions made in the home country about the home country and this they shared with their *parents*; media consumption in this respect reflects both a discourse of nostalgia focussing on the there and then, and a discourse of desire, focussing on the there and now (Dayan, 1999; Christopoulou and de Leeuw, 2004). Within this discourse the children apparently perceive the function of media as providing them with feelings of belonging. But the opposite could also be the case, as when the culture of the home country was perceived as foreign and remote to the children, which could happen to those children, who have been in the new country for almost their entire lives.

Other media followed a similar pattern, as they seemed to have both the function of bonding, i.e. chatting with relatives or talk on the phone, and the function of building new friendships and giving a sense of participation in the new country. The importance of Internet and mobile phones was of special importance to the children, in order to make and maintain local contacts and as well as to create a more private zone away from their parents. Chatting with friends on the net and using the mobile phone were of importance for making and keeping friendships and keeping in touch with the peer group. A mobile phone and a chat room on Internet also offer greater privacy than for example television or a fixed telephone line, and it is more difficult for parents to control it. In this way, they both can be thought of as a part of the global youth culture.

Taking in all types of media studied, it appears as if migrant children's cultural identity is created in negotiation with and by inspiration from cultural goods stemming from the global market, from their homeland or ethnic origin as well as from the new country. However, even if young people have a wide media repertoire, they still have a preference for global output, such as mainstream light entertainment on television. From a historical perspective, national media, for example television and radio with a public service mission are supposed to strengthen national identity and bring the people together. But commercialisation of media works in the opposite direction, particularly as young people seem to avoid the public service output in favour of commercial media culture. Also both public and commercial television only very seldom addresses experiences of diaspora communities. Besides, new media technology has opened up a wide range of potential cultural connections. Internet has for example the potential to overcome social and cultural exclusion, because of its flexibility as it offers a range of ethnic web sites aimed for diaspora groups. Television, on the other hand, as it is used by migrant children, only in a very limited way functions as bridging to the local national culture (e.g. to learn the new language), while it does not to minority cultures which are underrepresented. Rather television functions as an instrument of cultural inclusion in connecting children to the international global youth culture.

If comparing children and parents, it appeared that transnational diasporic media had a central role as a mediator for bonding, however less so for children than for the parents. For the parents the media are used to extend the notion of 'home', i.e.' the symbolic conceptualization of where one belongs' (Salih, 200, p. 51). Or in Flusser's conceptual framework: 'home' is where you are, regardless of physical and geographical space. And transnational media as well as Internet reinforce the creation of this symbolic conceptualization of 'home'. Depending on living conditions, such as isolation and segregation, transnational media and other mediated experiences directed to the homeland may reinforce feelings of alienation in relation to the new country, thus being counter-productive to the process of integration.

In the process of identity construction and reconstruction all media seem to be used, both to keep up with the past and to connect to a new future where new narratives are developing consisting of different stories told through different media. The national and transnational media are tied to global media. Global media use in turn is cross cutting with national and transnational media preferences. These preferences are informed by migratory experiences both among the parents and the children, if in different ways. Media use thus reflects a continuous dialogical negotiation of identities within and outside the family; within the family context, in the micro public sphere of the living room between parents and children (as e.g. the example with the Albanian soap opera), and in relation to the macro public sphere of the new country (e.g. watching national news programs or soap operas). The media, may thus construct dialogical spaces, mediated spaces. The media may even facilitate a sense of 'togetherness' as Flusser puts it. However, we believe that the media are embedded in social contexts and that the migrant's socio-cultural situation plays a role. Favourable and safe conditions have to be created in order to attain such sense of 'togetherness' in the new homeland.

Notes

1. We are referring to the CHICAM (Children in Communication about Migration) project, a European project funded by the European Commission, Framework Five. The project was co-ordinated by the Institute of Education, London University.
2. See note 2.
3. Unpublished data from Rydin and Sjöberg, ongoing project. Only parts of the project are published so far.

References

Anderson, B. (1983) *Imagined Communities: Reflections on the Origin and Spread of Nationalism* (London: Verso).

Bakardjieva, M. (2003) 'Virtual Togetherness: An Everyday-Life Perspective', *Media, Culture & Society* 25: 291–313.

Barker, C. (1997) *Global Television. An Introduction* (Oxford: Blackwell).

Christopoulou, N. and de Leeuw, S. (eds) (2004) *Home Is Where the Heart Is! Family Relations of Migrant Children in Media Clubs in Six European Countries* (The European Commission, Community Research). Available on http://www.chicam.net.

Christopoulou, N. and Rydin, I. (eds) (2004) *Children's Social Relations in Peer Groups: Inclusion, Exclusion and Friendship* (The European Commission, Community Research). Available on http://www.chicam.net.

Christopoulou, N. and de Leeuw, S. (2005) 'Children Making Media: Constructions of Home and Belonging', J. Knörr (ed.), *Childhood and Migration. From Experience to Agency* (Bielefeld: transcript Verlag) 113–35.

Dayan, D., 'Media and Diasporas', J. Gripsrud (ed.) (1999) *Television and Common Knowledge* (London: Routledge) 18–33.

De Block, L., Buckingham, D, Holzwarth, P. and Niesyto, H. (eds) (2004) *Visions Across Cultures: Migrant Children Using Visual Images to Communicate* (The European Commission. Community Research). Available on http://www.chicam.net.

De Block, L. & Rydin, I. (2006) 'Digital Rapping in Media Productions: Intercultural Communication Through Youth Culture', D. Buckingham and R. Willett (eds), *Digital Generations. Children, Young People, and New Media* (Mahwah, N.J: Lawrence Erlbaum) 295–313.

Flusser, V. (2003) *The Freedom of the Migrant, Objections to Nationalism* (Urbana/ Chicago: University of Illinois Press), ed. and introduced by Anke K. Finger.

Gillespie, M. (1995/2000) *Television, Ethnicity and Cultural Change* (London: Routledge).

d´Haenens, L. (2003) 'ICT in Multicultural Society'. The Netherlands: A Context for Sound Multiform Media Policy?', *Gazette: The international journal for communication studies*, 65(4–5), 401–21.

Hagen, I. (2003) 'Being a Computer User'. What Does That Mean? A Discussion about Young People's Talk about Computers and Themselves', in T. Tufte (ed.), *Medierne, minoriteterne og det multikulturelle samfund. Skandinaviske perspektiver* (Gothenburg: Nordicom) 197–224.

Hall, S. (1990) 'Cultural Identity and Diaspora', in J. Rutherford (ed.), *Identity, Community, Culture, Difference* (London: Lawrence and Wishart) 222–37.
Hall, S. (1996) 'What Is Black in Black Popular Culture?', in D. Morley and C. Kuan-Hsing (eds), *Critical Dialogues in Cultural Studies* (London: Routledge) 465–75.
Hargreaves, A. and Mahjoub, D. (1997) 'Satellite Viewing among Ethnic Minorities in France', *European Journal of Communication*, 12(4), 459–77.
Jones, S. (ed.) (1999) *Doing Internet research. Critical Issues and Methods for Examining the Net*, (Thousand Oaks, CA: Sage Publications Inc).
Karim, K. H. (ed.) (2003) *The Media of Diaspora* (London: Routledge).
Kitchin, R. (1998) *Cyberspace The World in the Wires* (West Sussex: John Wiley).
de Leeuw, S. (2006) 'Television Fiction and Cultural Diversity: Strategies for Cultural Change', in L. Højberg and H. Sønderga (eds), *European Film and Media Culture (Northern Lights 2006)* (Copenhagen: Museum Tusculanum Press/University of Copenhagen) 91–110.
Livingstone, S. & Bovill, M. (1999) *Young people – new media. Report of the research project 'Children, young people and the changing media environment'* (London: School of Economics and Political Science).
Miller, D., & Slater, D. (2002) 'Relationships', in K. Askew & R. R. Wilk (eds.), *The Anthropology of Media: A Reader* (Oxford: Blackwell Publishers Ltd) 187–209.
Morley, D. (2000) *Home Territories: Media, Mobility and Identity* (London: Routledge).
Rydin, I. and Sjöberg, U. (2005) *Identity, Cultural Change and Generation. Talk About Television and Internet among migrant families in Sweden*, paper presented at the international conference Childhoods, Oslo, Norway. Available on http://www.hh.se/hos.
Salih, R. (2001) 'Shifting Meanings of Home'. Consumption and Identity in Moroccan Women's Transitional Practices Between Italy and Morocco', in N. Al-Ali (ed.), *New Approaches to Migration?: Transnational Communities and the Transformation of Home* (London: Routledge) 51–67.
Sjöberg, U. (2003) 'Making Sense of Screen-based Media.' The Uses and Readings of Television, Computer Games, and Internet among Swedish Young People, in I. Rydin (ed.), *Media Fascinations: Perspectives on Young People's Meaning Making* (Gothenburg: Nordicom) 147–64.
Vertovec, S. (2002) *Religion in Migration, Diasporas and Transnationalism* (Vancouver Centre of Excellence, Research on Immigration and Integration in the Metropolis, Working paper Series 2.7).
Werbner, P. (2002) 'The Place Which Is Diaspora: Citizenship, Religion and Gender in the Making of Chaordic Transnationalism', *Journal of Ethnic and Migration Studies*, 28(1) 119–33.

10
Diaspora: An Urban Communication Paradigm

Gary Gumpert and Susan J. Drucker

Diaspora (dĭăs'pərə) [Gr.,=dispersion], term used today to denote the Jewish communities living outside the Holy Land.

It was originally used to designate the dispersal of the Jews at the time of the destruction of the first Temple (586 BC) and the forced exile [Heb.,=Galut] to Babylonia. The diaspora became a permanent feature of Jewish life; by AD 70 Jewish communities existed in Babylonia, Syria, Egypt, Cyrene, Asia Minor, Greece, and Rome. Jews followed the Romans into Europe and from Persia and Babylonia spread as far east as China. In modern times, Jews have migrated to the Americas, South Africa, and Australia. The Jewish population of Central and Eastern Europe, until World War II the largest in the world, was decimated in the Holocaust. Despite the creation of the state of Israel in 1948, the vast majority of the Jewish people remains in the diaspora, notably in North America, Russia, and Ukraine. The term diaspora has also been applied to other peoples with large numbers living outside their traditional homelands. (*The Columbia Electronic Encyclopedia, 2003*)

Introduction

Diaspora has come to mean many things to many people. But overall it involves mass migration and the separation of a group of people from what might be called their 'homeland'. That sense of migration implies scattering, sometimes unwillingness, coercion, and wrenching resettlement surrounded by an inherent sense of melancholia. At best migration may be bittersweet. Until relatively recently this sense of separation and relocation was permanent with little hope provided for return or even contact. This chapter attempts to redefine diaspora on the basis of communication technology that initially mediates between immigrant and homeland and increasingly mediates between immigrant and urban enclave so important upon arrival in a new land. Further, urban communication patterns are offered as an appropriate approach for the study of diasporic progression. A case study of a Greek community in New York is provided as illustration.

In the past 50 years the meaning of diaspora and its emotional impact has, for some, been radically altered by the revolution in communication that has ameliorated separation and emphasized connection. Globalization has, to a great extent, reduced the anxiety of diaspora and redefined for some, the meaning of diaspora. The finality of diaspora has been transformed into a less permanent and more ambiguous sense of separation. The return to 'home' is facilitated by numerous means. What had been an occasional letter or sometimes an expensive and strained transmission flawed telephone call has been replaced by clear and relatively cheap telephone and mobile phone connection, internet connection with local radio and television stations abroad, instant messaging, voice over Internet Protocol, webcam links, web based newspapers, downloadable programs of news, information, and entertainment, plus satellite transmitted radio and television programming. While there are still regions of the world with which communication is problematic the gap between of those connectable and those not connectable is quickly narrowing.

Diaspora and urban communication

The meaning of diaspora has evolved into the movement of relatively large masses of people, the relocation of people bound together by ethnic ties. Historically, communities in diaspora materialize in cities. While there are exceptions, immigrants are funneled into a nation's primary portals where they have traditionally remained for at times a lengthy transitionary period. Ethnicity and race, immigration and movement, language and culture, contribute to the environment of the urban landscape and become part of the fabric of urban life becoming a observable form of urban communication.

Immigrants, refugees, exiles, guest workers, and others have long made their mark on cities but increasingly, these mobile groups have become a feature of urban environments around the world. But the nature of communication which characterizes their social, economic and political movement is radically different as a result of low cost, high speed communication and transportation technologies. 'The new scholarship stresses diversity, hybridity, flow and flux. 'Here' and 'there' are no longer opposites (Heller, 1992, p. A 9).' Concepts like long-distance nationalism have become increasingly noteworthy in exploring how advances in communication technologies enable migrants to not only remain connected with homeland but involved with political events there as well (Anderson, 1998). Much has been written about "imagined homelands" and the radical changes brought by communication technologies, especially the internet (Anderson, 1991; Chan, 2005). In an age of transnational identity and global ethnoscapes the challenges for cities are enormous.

Diaspora is frequently associated with a radical relocation – the shifting of those groups over large distances – from 'homeland' to 'newland.' That perception refers to the initial movement and misses the nuances of the shifting flow and repositioning once the initial move to the new environment has occurred. The traditional pattern for many immigrants generally begins with their arrival into a transitionary geographical area functioning as a reception and processing center. The immigrant experience changes, reflects and reveals significant lessons with regard to *public social environments* often contrasting significantly with mainstream indigenous attitudes and values attributed to the physical environment. We are suggesting a more complex conceptualization of a process that, over time, involves a series of steps of *diasporic progression*.

1. *Primary phase* – Migration from a long term relationship (several generations) with a homeland to a permanent relationship with a new (and alien) nation and culture. The initial settlement or point of entry is generally in an urban distribution location. Such migration is to an urban enclave where language and custom is similar to that which has been left behind. This location is a place of accommodation and adjustment for some permanent and for future generations a location of transition.
2. *Secondary phase* – Refers to the movement of relatively large groups of former immigrants from the original urban enclaves to suburban settlements in an upward mobile and integrated pattern, but maintain communication connection with both original "homeland" and point of entry or enclave.
3. *Directed functional migration phase* – This form of diapora does not fit into the above Primary-Secondary categories and involves the movement of large masses of workers from abroad to the US Thus for

example, thousands of Chinese were hired as laborers in 1862 to help construct the transcontinental railroad. Similarly, today, Hispanic migrants (both legal and illegal) settle in rural and suburban areas where they serve as a needed work force.

4. *The secondary phase of direct functional migration* is more complex and is dependent upon immigration policy and the shifting requirements for manual labor. Thus a large proportion of this group might be considered as 'sojourners' – long term temporary residents who support the families they have left behind and those who after several decades intend to return to their homeland. To some extent such migration becomes basis for establishing newer enclaves outside their traditional urban venues.

These phases can be understood within the more general framework of urban communication. The study of urban communication is based on the principle that cities are inherently *places of* and *products of* communication. The UN Report on the State of the World's Cities, noted that for the first time in history the majority of the world's population lives in cities (UN Report, 2005). Paul Goldberger, the former architectural critic of the *New York Times* has described the urban impulse as 'an impulse toward community – an impulse toward being together, and toward accepting the idea that however different we may be, something unites us' (Goldberger, 2001, p. 3). The need for community is certainly an important dynamic of the diasporic but the urban manifestation of that impulse is complicated by serious challenges facing cities in general which include the impact of suburbanization, gentrification; and communication technologies.

The concept of urban communication emerges out of a conviction that the physical and social structures of the city are intimately intertwined. The link between the city, identity, communication patterns and media technologies has a long tradition. Urban communication has emerged from diverse disciplines including urban studies, public policy, environmental design and research, planning, geography, sociology and above all human communication and media studies.

The urban landscape must be understood in relation to suburbia and exurbia which are all shaped by an intimate relationship with technology. Increased mobility, whether through human contact or mediated presence, facilitates the redirection of the community impulse transcending the traditional urban impulse. Communication technology alters the relationship between the city, the individual and the sprawling suburb (Gumpert & Drucker, forthcoming). The city is being refor-

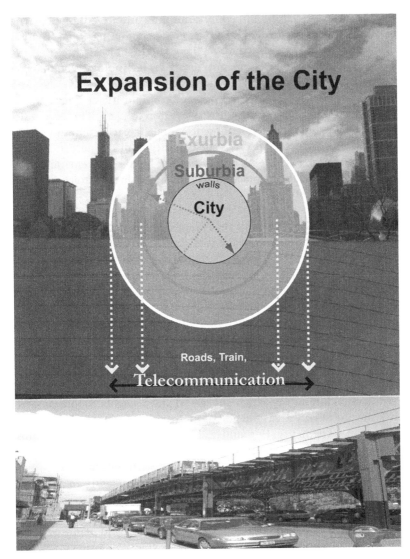

Figure 10.1 Urban diaspora

mulated by technologies that permit and encourage communication through connection. The suburb, edge city, and exurb are all outgrowths of economics, communication technology, and transportation, offering a technologically based social alternatives. Community once tied to geography has been repositioned as an aspatial concept in opposition to social life linked by communication technologies. The relationship of non-mediated and mediated communication activity is recombinant in the sense that William Mitchell (1995) has used the term to describe the phenomenon of digital technology recomposing homes, office, communities, and cities. Each medium alters and changes the nature of self, the basis of community, and results in a multifaceted and often contradictory relation to place. This contradiction is based upon the phenomenon that as each communication innovation connects it also has the capacity to disconnect individual from physical proximate place and people. Media offer emancipation from the limitations of place providing individuals' choice in interactions and affiliations.

In *Urban Ethnicity in the United States* Jose Hernandez fashioned a typology of five community types representing ecological situations most commonly found in residential concentrations. The five distinct community types include 1. the ghetto or barrio marked by the predominance of a single nationality or group or in which several nationality groups with cultural affinities co-exist, 2. the multi-ethnic and multi-racial neighborhood reflecting the new immigrant character of the population in appearance of buildings, shopping and services; 3. gentrification characterized by the succession by white middle-class settlement of immigrant communities, particularly by young urban professional and in some instances, gayification in which the gay presence in stores, churches, places of entertainment is felt; 4. the new immigrant community which appears in older neighborhoods of satellite sites in nearby areas outside of metropolitan centers; 5. scattered suburban settlements (Hernandez, 1985, pp. 108–14). These community types mirror the phases in the *diasporic progression*. The Hernandez typology places in the foreground of analysis the state of the urban environment whereas the diasporic progression suggests an approach placing a given immigrant population in foreground with impact on location of resettlement in the background. The phases of diasporic progression yield challenges for urban governance and planning while suggesting politically sensitive (perhaps explosive) issues of public policy.

The case study of the Greek diaspora in New York

The authors have been studying the Greek diaspora in the New York metropolitan area for 18 years. While many communities would serve to illustrate the diasporic progression we return to the Greek community precisely because it is more settled and less politically and socially volatile a case study.

The primary phase in the modern Greek diaspora in New York began in early 20th century with Greeks congregating in Hells Kitchen area of Manhattan, an area soon superseded by Astoria (Little Athens) which became, at one time, the largest Hellenic city in the world outside of Athens (Shepard, 1991). Located in northwest Queens, separated from Manhattan by a 15 minute subway ride and the East River, it is an area serving successive waves of immigrant communities. Astoria has been home for concentrations of Asian, Irish, Italian, Slavic, South American, and above all Greek immigrants. The Greek community in Astoria dates back to 1927 when it was settled by immigrants in the first wave of urban flight, leaving the west side of Manhattan in the Chelsea area (HANAC, 1973; Leeds, 1991, p. 221). In the 1920s the Greek families migrated to Astoria (Leeds, 1991).

In Astoria it is possible to attend the Greek church, sit in the waiting room of Greek doctors and dentists (read Greek newspapers and magazines while waiting), eat in Greek restaurants, sit over a dark cup of Greek coffee in a café or attend Greek elementary and high school, play on a Greek soccer team, play cards with friends in a Greek club, shop in Greek stores, buy Greek audio and videotapes, be buried by a Greek undertaker, and never speak English unless an emergency presents itself or one wanders outside into an alien world in which English is a required linguistic skill.

The Greeks came to Astoria which was, at the time, a barrio or ghetto for entering immigrants including Italian and Irish immigrants. Although not solely occupied by one group, each co-existed alongside one another leading into what Hernandez would characterize as a multi-ethnic stage two. Diversity was tolerated as pre-existing groups competed for space with newcomers. This is what has become known as contested space. In contested spaces, competing culture groups, like the nationalists and loyalists, strengthen and legitimize themselves and their efforts through the development of adaptive spatial practices (McCann, 1999).

In Astoria, a place where 'Greeks were Greeks,' was changing by the late 1990s with Greeks increasingly and ironically expressing a feeling of being 'foreign' sharing their streets with people from Bangladesh, Brazil, China, the Czech Republic, India, Pakistan and the states of the former Yugoslavia and Arab countries (Siotis, 1995). Astoria came to represent type two of the Hernandez typology. Tensions of co-existence and nature of inter-cultural communication patterns were evident. Add to this mix a type three community of white middle class professionals, particularly the young moving into the area lured by the close proximity to Manhattan and lower rents. Within easy commute to the center city the economic value of residential properties is skyrocketing. The open space currently utilized for the Socrates Sculpture Park (approximately ½ mile from Athens Square Park) has greatly increased in potential value. A real estate developer has proposed investing to build 300 upscale apartments with balconies, a catering hall and a marina. In exchange the developer promises to offer public pools and to offer the public 'more usable, and ... more elegantly landscaped, parkland than Socrates provides' (Martin, 1997, p. B1). The resulting controversy is interesting because it is a case study in the clash of ethnicity and gentrification–and the social and economic roles of space.

The ebb and flow of enclaves

The Greek community of Astoria is presently moving to the fourth and fifth types of communities Hernandez describes. Nearby communities on a direct line out of Astoria further into more suburban Queens county have emerged over the past decade bringing a large Greek Orthodox Church and school, a café, a few restaurants and food stores to Bayside and Whitestone, still within the New York City limits. More recently, the move to the suburbs, reflecting Hernandez's fifth community type, has seen more scattered settlement in which regional churches on Long Island and New Jersey form the basis for Greek community life, supplemented by regular visits back to Astoria, the old neighborhood or new homeland.

Many ethnic enclaves exhibit a life cycle characterized by sites to which successive waves of immigrants are initially drawn, but which become interesting examples of multi-cultural environments char-acterized by some degree of social segregation but which results in an environment in which inter-cultural communication is commonplace.

What remains of Greek Astoria are the public places of the community. Shops, churches, social clubs, cafes, restaurants, night clubs, and Athens Square Park. This park is symbolic of the evolution of the population of the nature of contested urban spaced. Athens Square Park is a small park (0.9 of an acre in size.) celebrating the presence of the Greek community (Delis, personal communication, 1998). The Greek community raised funds for the project which took over twenty years to move from proposal to reality. There is a monument area, a play area and a perimeter area filled with benches. The monument area consists of a series of columns alongside statues of Socrates, with a statue of

Athena, a gift from the city of Athens placed near the entrance to the park welcoming visitors. By the time the park assumed its present shape, the constituents of Astoria and the park have changed and the Greek presence diminished. Children climb atop Socrates's head to drop a water-balloon on a passerby (disregarding the 'keep off' sign), skateboarders take flight above the steps of the amphitheater and the grafitteed chess tables are transformed into seats from which the passing parade can be watched. The steps leading into the sunken amphitheater are used by roller-bladers and bicycle riders seeking an urban challenge. Skaters provide entertainment to onlookers as they take flight ignoring the signs declaring the prohibition of skateboarding. Currently, aside from specially designated and programmed theme nights, the Greek identity resides in the background and not in its intended foreground. The Greek past, rather than the Greek presence remains.

Today the Greek community has moved into the second phase of diasporic progression, a diaspora *from* the ethnic enclave into either satellite communities or assimilated into suburban communities. This *secondary phase* is reflected in a pattern of upward mobility and connection to 'homeland' as well as 'home enclave.' The relationship maintained with homeland and/or ethnic enclave is intimately linked to the technologies of communication. Where once communication to 'home' left behind was a difficult, rare and expensive task, mediated connection has become relatively inexpensive, expected and commonplace. Separation has been ameliorated by communication. This applies to initial movement and subsequent movement away from original enclaves.

Astoria exemplifies a pattern of urban diaspora marked by assimilation into the suburbs, but with connection to the former enclave for social opportunity as that area is developed into a theme park and or is gentrified. With economic success and assimilation, immigrants (and second generation ethnics) leave the enclave. The enclave may be abandoned or ultimately serve a different economic and social function for the departing community as it is transformed into a surrogate homeland and base for those in the suburbs who return to visit, to interact and to shop, to communicate and reaffirm their ethnic identity. Those who used Astoria as a portal to their home may return from increasingly further flung suburbia for social events and shopping. Their children, born in the 'newland' visit for clubs, cafes and the occasional infusion of cultural identity. Community leaders note Astoria has become the 'in' place for second and third generation Greek-

Americans (Papanicolaou, 2006). The result of such movement on the enclave left behind is enormous, with some groups vacating an area to be replaced by a new population, sometimes with little vestige left on the landscape. Or, the enclave may change character in another way by losing its *residential* function but maintaining its *commercial* function. In this case, shops, businesses, social clubs remain and serve as a magnet for the ethnic community itself as well as those outsiders wishing to taste the 'exotic.' The enclave serves as a public space for those living a more private life, particularly those suburbanites, perhaps socially detached from the community to which they have moved. Ethnic restaurants and nightclubs or cafes remain or perhaps proliferate in the wake of 'being discovered' by mainstream restaurant critics or good write-ups in guidebooks. This is the state of evolution of Astoria in which the community finds itself.

The flight for the Greeks of Astoria have taken the form of individuals moving into another diaspora of sorts, moving into heterogeneous communities removed from their ethnic roots, or into the creation of a suburb with a distinct ethnic concentration forming ethnic clusters in an area interspersed among other groups in the neighborhood (Sowell, 1996). They have moved to increasingly suburban areas of Queens in neighborhoods like Whitestone, Flushing and Bayside, Queens. On Long Island suburban flight takes Greeks further and further from central Astoria to Bayville, Hicksville, Merrick, Brookville and Mattituck Long Island. To the north Yonkers, New Rochelle, and across the river to New Jersey suburbs of Paramus, Clifton, and Tenafly and in Connecticut in communities like Stamford. Some of the amenities of the enclave including church, food stores and some variation on the social and familial patterns are perpetuated in the enclave itself. Community leaders note the swift growth rate of these communities in the past ten years (Papanicolaou, 2006).

In recreating community in the new diaspora the church follows the population. The church certifies community and neighborhood. It creates a site of communication as it publicly and institutionally marks location of this community. The church also supports both common faith and common language for the Greek community. When a critical mass settled in Bayside, Queens, St. Nicholas Shrine Church rose on Northern Blvd., the main artery moving from Astoria outward forming the northern spine of increasingly suburban Long Island. Clustered around the church are Greek cafes, food stores, restaurants, banks and professional services. This neighborhood has become the last outpost within the jurisdiction of New York City. Glen Cove, a nearby Long

Island suburb had a vibrant Greek population and church but the church closed as the increasingly affluent Greek community took one step further out into the suburbs as the obstacles of mobility and money were overcome. A new church in Brookville opened in May 2005 marking another easterly migration further away from Astoria, figuratively closer to mainland Greece.

The specific media habits of members of ethnic communities is of importance to the maintenance of cultural identity and heritage. The media landscape of an ethnic community functions on several levels: 1. as a bridge between country of origin and new settlement area; 2. as a means of connecting the group within the new settlement or country; and 3. as a link between those who leave the urban enclave for the suburbs.

The demographic changes in Astoria and the movement of Greeks and Greek-Americans into ever more distant and diverse suburban environments represents a second step in diaspora living. The process of immigrant mobility is part of a two-step diaspora in which not only are ties maintained with the country of origin but with the enclave of origin as well. Community in the modern diaspora is increasingly maintained through media connections, de-emphasizing or eliminating the need for face to face contact. There is a constant tension and antagonism between face-to-face and non-proprinquitous interaction in the mediated contemporary world. Interpersonal media provide alternative interactional opportunities along with mass media which fulfill other informational and entertainment needs. These mediated connections may be perceived as adequate substitution for face-to-face interaction.

The mediated diaspora

The relationship between distance, time and money is changing and with it, the relationship between 'home' and 'away'; between 'here' and 'there'; and between connection and disconnection. The cost of a 3-minute transatlantic phone call 'remained steady for 6 decades'. In 1927 a transatlantic call cost $39.00, in 1956, $12.00 but between 1990 and 1996 the cost of a 3-minute transatlantic call from New York fell from about $3.50 to $0.30. Mobile phones, deregulation, and the rise of the Internet have well-and-truly shattered the old pricing paradigm ('Globalization', 2006). Internet telephony reduces pricing even further. As of 2006 internet telephony plans in the New York region offer 500 minutes or over 8 hours of talk time worldwide for fees as low as $19.95 per month (Optimum Voice, 2006). Online teleconferencing and videoconferencing at no additional cost establishes high quality video through such programs as Skype. The severity of separation ameliorated through media access before has been transformed in the current media environment.

The media of diaspora have been transformed through digitalization and convergence. The traditional diasporic media include the availability of mass media (e.g. books, newspapers and magazines, radio and television, videotape, videocassettes, CDs, DVDs); and micro media (e.g. written letters, telephone, facsimile, text messages, emails). For the Greek American living in the Greater New York the daily newspaper the *National Herald* is available along with the weeklies and bi-weeklies (*Greek News, The Greek Star, Hellas News, The Hellenic Times*), the monthlies (e.g. Eseis, Ellopia Press Magazine, Neo Magazine) and radio and television including Hellas FM, Hellenic Radio, Diaspora FM, Aktina FM radio, Cosmos FM, Hellenic Public Radio, Antenna Satellite TV, National Greek TV, Ellopia TV USA, Hellenic Voice TV Channel 57. The role of ethnic media in shaping community and the experience of diasporic living has been well documented.[1] But diasporic media is being influenced by global media. Access on demand to online publications from the 'newland' and 'homeland' revolutionizes the potential importance of media for those living in away from 'home.' Streaming audio, streaming video, archives and blogs can transform the media experience of Greeks living in the New York area, particularly given ready access to high speed broadband internet access.

The role of the church in these secondary phase diasporic communities cannot be overstated. Interviews support the assertion that they become social community centers, perhaps replacing the market, street, social clubs and kafenion prevalent in the portal enclave. There has historically been an ambiguous relationship between the institution of the church and media development dating back to the 15th century with the introduction of moveable type that altered the way knowledge was communicated thus effecting worship. One is reminded of The *Hunchback of Notre Dame* which we have long regarded as a treatise on communication theory. Beyond the almost immediate image of Charles Laughton playing the role of Quasimodo or even the Disney animated version, the novel contains Victor Hugo's brilliant analysis of the impact of technology upon social reality. Written in 1831 the novel relates events of the 16th century but serves as a paradigm of communication technology impact upon both technology itself and upon social structure in the 21st century. In Book V the Archdeacon proclaims that: 'This will kill that. The book will kill the edifice.'

As we see it, this thought has two facets. Firstly, it was the thought of a priest. It was the alarm felt by the priesthood before a new agent: the printing press. It was the terror and bewilderment felt by a man of the sanctuary before the luminous press of Gutenberg. It was the pulpit and the manuscript, the spoken and the written word, taking fright at the printed word ... it meant the press will kill the church (Hugo, 1978, p. 188).

This passage alludes to the power of Gutenberg's invention upon the church itself with redistribution of prayer from the mouth of the priest to the hand-held text of the worshipper. But Hugo also understood that Gutenberg's letter of lead would also collide with the physical structure of the church itself, that the dominating edifice of power would be weakened by the power of the text.

But beneath this first and no doubt simpler thought, there was in our opinion, a second, newer one, a corollary of the first less easily perceived, but more easily challenged, an equally philosophical notion, no longer that of the priest alone but of the scientist and the artist too. This was the presentment that as human ideas changed their form they would change their mode of expression, that the crucial idea of each generation would no longer be written in the same material or in the same way, that the book of stone, so solid and durable, would give way to the book of paper, which was more solid and durable still. Seen thus, the archdeacon's vague formula had a second meaning: it meant that one art was going to dethrone another art. It meant, printing will kill architecture (Hugo, p. 189).

The passage alludes to the powerful nature of communication technology upon communication technology itself. The 'book of stone' is transformed into the 'book of paper.' The obsolescence of one is necessary for the existence of the other. The power of the church remains but not untouched by the secondary phase and subsequent phases of diaspora. Where once it could be argued the communities in diaspora followed the church, today, the case of the New York metropolitan area reveals the church follows subsequent phases of migration from urban enclave to suburban and exurban havens. Perhaps Hugo was correct. The dominant role of the church has been redefined by the presence of communication technology. Nevertheless, the Greek church continues to serve an important social function for the Greek community.

The Greek American community in New York today clearly illustrates phases one and two of the diasporic progression. The Greek community however does not illustrate phases three and four (*Directed Functional Migration Phase* marked by *the* movement of large masses of workers from abroad since as members of the European Union the educational and employment opportunities of Europe has reduced migration to the US to a trickle).

These phases can be understood within the more general framework of urban communication. Because of the role immigrants serve in their new home countries, there is little doubt that nations require immigrants. There is a well established pattern in which migrant populations move to areas where labor is needed, particularly manual labor we identify as 'rough hands labor.' These locations are increasingly outside the central city in suburbia and exurbia. A new pattern of immigration has been identified in which the urban portal has been bypassed for the suburban neighborhood. The suburban location of the immigrant population relegated outside central French cities drew worldwide attention during the Fall of 2005 when violence erupted in areas of large predominantly African and Arab immigrant populations. In the United States, the rising population of immigrants in suburban communities has come under increased scrutiny recently (Vitello, 2005; Farzad, 2005). Some monied immigrants including a small population from China and South Korea are arriving in suburbs directly from homeland seeking the best school districts for their children and isolating those towns known for producing Ivy League-bound graduates (Vitello, 2006). The suburbanization of legal and illegal immigrations has become a major issue of not only international and national proportions, but of local government as well.

Conclusions

Cities have long been the traditional portals for migrating populations offering intercultural contacts, excitement, and economic energy, but changing patterns of housing, transportation and communication have and are redefining traditional patterns and expectations of the urban realm. The shift is more than a change in physical accommodation and convenience. The transformation involves the radical modification of social and economic values. How and where we communicate with each other has had to adjust and accommodate the communication technology that facilitates interaction. Bringing an urban communication perspective to the study of the phenomenon of diaspora underscores the significance of the correlation between place and media environment. As we gain the ability to communicate over broader and broader areas, local has become regional or local has been removed from place, and some local has gone global. Now we speak of things 'glocal'. The *diasporic progression* provides a methodological device for exploring the dynamics of these media created perceptual changes and diasporic movements. Application of the *diasporic progression* can provide a procedural approach to the study of maturation of diasporic communities. While this approach does not specify procedure for future study, it does articulate significant assumptions underlying the study of the modern diasporic experience.

The communicative functions of ethnic enclaves have not been immune from the transformative power of media changes. Because communication technology is not reversible, one cannot un-discover the technology or eradicate the awareness of that invention from human consciousness, media must be understood and considered as a force with potential transformational influence.

There is a powerful symbiotic relationship between disaporic communities and the urban condition. The shifting demographics, balkanization, ascendancy of suburbia and impact of communication technologies shaping diasporic communities, in turn, reshape the urban landscape. Communication of and to diasporic communities not only transform the diasporic experience, it alters the urban communication landscape itself.

Note

1. See: R. Cohen (ed.), 'Diasporas and Transnational Communities: a Bibliographical and Study Guide,' Transnational Communities Programme, Economic and Social Resource Council: Retrieved 12 May 2006 from the World Wide Web: http://www.transcomm.ox.ac.uk/wwwroot/bibliogr.htm.

References

Anderson, B. (1991) *Imagined Communities; Reflections on the Origin and Spread of Nationalism* 2nd edn. (London; Verso).

Anderson, B. (1998) *The Spectre of Comparisons: Nationalism, Southeast Asia and the World* (London; Verso).

Chan, B. (2005) 'Imagining the Homeland: The Internet and Diasporic discourse of Nationalism,' *Journal of Communication Inquiry* 29: 4 (October) 336–68.

Cohen, R. (2006) (ed.) 'Diasporas and Transnational Communities:a Bibliographical and Study Guide,' Transnational Communities Programme, Economic and Social Resource Council: Retrieved 12 May from the World Wide Web: http://www.transcomm.ox.ac.uk/wwwroot/bibliogr.htm.

Delis, G. (1998) 'District Leader.'

Farzad, R. (2005) 'The Urban Migrants; A Housing Boom Brings Jobs and, Sometimes, Abuse,' *The New York Times*, 20 July, Section C, p. 1.

'Globalization,' Retrieved 2 May 2006 from the World Wide Web: http://www.virtualtravelog.net/entries/2003/12/visualizing_the_shrinking_world.html).

Goldberger, P. (2001) 'Cities, Place and Cyberspace,' Speeches, (February 1). Retrieved 30 May 2005 from the World Wide Web: www.paulgodlberger.com/speeches.php?speech=berkeley.

Gumpert, G. and S. Drucker (forthcoming) (eds), 'The City and the Two Sides of Reciprocity,' in the *Urban Communication Reader* (Cresskill, N.J.: Hampton Press).

HANAC, staff (1973). *The Needs of the Growing Greek–American Community in the City of New York.* (New York: HANAC).

Heller, S. (1992) 'Worldwide "Diaspora" of Peoples Poses New Challenges for Scholars: Researchers seek to explain dramatic new patterns of migration and cultural identity,' *The Chronicle of Higher Education*, 3 June, pp. A7–9.

Hernandez, J. (1985) 'Improving the Data: A research Strategy for New Immigrants,' In L. Maldonado and J. Moore (eds.), *Urban Ethnicity in the United States: New Immigrants and Old Minorities* (Beverly Hills: Sage Publications) 101–19.

Hugo, V. (1978) *Notre-Dame of Paris* (translated by John Turrock) (New York: Penguin Books).

Leeds, M. (1991) *Passport's Guide to Ethnic New York* (Lincolnwood, Illinois: Passport Books, a division of NTC Publishing Group).

Martin, D. (1997) 'Philosophies Differ on Future of Socrates Sculpture Park,' *The New York Times*, 10 August pp. B1–2.

McCann, E. (1999) 'Race, Protest, and Public Space: Contextualizing Lefebvre in the US City,' *Antipode* 31, 163–184.

Mitchell, W. J. (1995) *City of Bits: Space, Place, and the Infobahn* (Cambridge, MA: MIT Press).

Optimum Voice, Retrieved, 12 May 2006 from the World Wide Web: http://www.optimumvoice.com/index.jhtml2006).

Papanicolaou, P. (2006) President, Cyprus Federation of America.

Shephad, R. F. (1991) '*Astoria Greek isle in the New York City sea*', *The New York Times*, pp. C1, C6, November.

Siotis, D. (1995) 'Tales from the big (and golden) apple,' *Odyssey: The World of Greece*, March/April pp. 72–7.

Sowell, T. (1996) *Migrations and Cultures: A World View*, New York: Basic Books.

The Columbia Electronic Encyclopedia, Sixth Edition, Columbia University Press. Retrieved 4 April 2006 from the World Wide Web: www.cc.columbia.edu/cu/cup.

'UN Report: State of the World's Cities Report 2004/5 Globalization and World culture,' Retrieved 14 July 2005 from the World Wide Web: http://www.unhabitat.org/mediacentre/sowckit.asp.

Vitello, P. (2006) 'Seeking Less Stress, and Finding Great Neck,' *The New York Times,* 21 February, Section B, p. 1.

Vitello, P. (2005) 'As Illegal Workers Hit Suburbs, Politicians Scramble to Respond,' *The New York Times*, 6 October 2005, Section A, p. 1.

11
Transnational Identities and the Media

Olga Guedes Bailey

Introduction

This chapter came out of my own experience as a 'foreigner' and my interest in finding out about a Latin American diaspora in Liverpool, where I lived for few years. The order of that experience could be translated into two points: first, on the issue of ethnic identity and diaspora, particularly in relation to the Latin American women, and second, on the role of the 'diasporic' media in shaping a transnational identity. This is not to suggest that the diasporic and mainstream media define identities but rather that they might play a part in creating communicative spaces of inclusion and belongingness or/and segregation. In this sense, mediation is a political process as mainstream media mostly define the representation of ethnic minorities' identities in the public sphere while diasporic media allow for resistance, appropriation, and counter representation as well as identity assertion. In fact, the role of the diasporic media is particularly important in mediating the experience of hybridity and migration of diasporic groups as it works as a third cultural space where diasporas are creating sites for representation and where different forms of resistance and syncretism are valued. (Naficy and Gabriel, 1993)

I have a personal investment in asking about what constitutes 'Latinidade' abroad. I never thought of myself as a 'Latin American' before, but a Brazilian. Hence, I had to register a new meaning to what meant to be a Brazilian abroad and a new signifier to my own identity. Living in Britain I become also a Latin American, which is a definition imposed from outside as a given ethnic category. In British official discourses, as for example in questionnaires about 'ethnicity', Latinos/as are included as the 'other' ethnicities, invisible and homogenised in their differences, history, culture, and experiences. The claim to be autobiographical here, i.e. the narrating of life as lived, is in order to rescue notions of emotion and experience for my intellectual exercise, and to avoid the tendency of grand narratives that generalize the singular experience of the 'other' which only serves to de-contextualize and homogenize 'difference' (Ang, 2001).

The research was concerned with the making of Latin American cultural identities in Liverpool and the significance of transnational media for Latin America 'diasporic' identity. The methodology was centred on conversational individual interviews and visits to the home of Latin families. We interviewed thirty-five individuals and visited six families for a period of six months during 2004. The interviewees included recently arrived immigrants, older immigrants (now British citizens) and British-born of immigrant parents. Their legal status varied between asylum seekers, refugees, permanent visa, and British citizenship. In addition, we mapped the cultural practices of Latinos/as in Liverpool, visiting restaurants, bars, salsa and samba classes, and interviewing people involved in these activities as I understood these places not only as the setting for Latin American events but related to the formation of cultural identities.

Latinos/as in Liverpool

Latin American migration from any particular Latin American country seems to follow a hierarchically ordered global pathway, i.e. routes along which people, goods, places and ideas travel, as in the case of Latin American migration to the United States (cf. Webner, 1999). The first choice of many 'Latinos/as' is there because of historical and political reasons, which established a first generation of Latinos/as or Hispanics who have created opportunities to others to join them in a new 'home'. In the 1970s, Britain became a new pathway[1] for Latin Americans, and the migration has been particularly complex. It has included Latinos/as originating from a wide range of class backgrounds, from professionals and an urban bourgeoisie, to villagers from the least developed areas of Latin America. This flow of people was caused mainly by political and economic turmoil in the region, which resulted in a great number of people applying for asylum. Along side these there are political refugees, women and men in cross marriages, and economic migrants. They come from many different countries in Latin American and have different reasons for immigrating to Britain, which make them a very diverse diaspora that are constituted as much in difference and division as it is in commonality and solidarity.

The group of Latin Americans in Liverpool is a transnational relatively small community,[2] in the sense of strategic alliances rather than origin and stratified by class, education, occupation, religious affiliation, cultural interests, urban or rural background, and so forth. They have a Latin American association, which has a philanthropic rather than political agenda; it aims to help Latinos/as to adjust to a new life in Britain by providing legal advice and informational resources – employment opportunities, language courses and so on – and promoting social events. Social events play a significant function for them as an interactional social network, with families socializing on weekends for leisure or special celebrations. These events are an attempt to reaffirm cohesion and continuity and to hold firm processes of disintegration and change in the community. Nevertheless the group is full of division and dissent, caused among other things, by their internal disagreement on how a political project should be developed, discrepancies of viewpoints regarding their own perception of themselves as 'diasporic', and internal tensions regarding their own social, economic, and gender positions. The bound, if or when it happens, is not based on difficulties of immigration[3] (cf. Cohen, 1997) but constructed through a common political and social project, alliances which might include Latinos/as and non Latin Americans. Thus, as a diasporic community or "complex and segmented diaspora",[4] the Latin Americans create spaces for celebration and debate and as an organized group they are a "cultural, economic, political and social formation in process, i.e. they are culturally and politically reflexive and experimental (cf. Werbner, 2004).

While studying the cultural and media practices of Latin Americans it is important to locate the cultural identity of 'Latin Americans' as an ethnic category socially defined which can be the product of self-identification or placed by others. For instance, in the United States, someone might self-identify as Mexican American or Porto Rican, but institutional bodies such as governmental organizations and universities might define that person as Hispanic or Latin American.

The signifier 'Latin American' refers to a multitude of identities since Latin American encompasses a large and diverse geographical region, with different histories, languages, cultures, and political systems. In this vein then a Latin American identity is typified by cultural diversity which makes problematic to attempt to fit a particular group in a homogeneous category such as 'Latin American' that hides the complexity of its people. The designation 'Latino/a' for example, hides from view the large number of Afro-Latin Americans in Brazil,

Colombia, Cuba, Haiti, Guadalupe, and Martinique. Cleary then, the 'Latino/a' label responds to and is a legacy of colonial processes and other legacies resulting from the making and classification of the non-colonized world (cf. Alcoff, 2000).

In this chapter, 'Latinidade' is not viewed as a category with a fixed content – be it racial, ethnic, cultural or geographical – but one that function as an open and indeterminate signifier whose meanings are constantly renegotiated and rearticulated in different sections of the 'Latin' 'diaspora'. Being 'Latino/a' outside Latin American cannot mean the same thing inside. It varies from place to place, shaped by the local circumstances in different locales where Latin people live, by choice or force. This proposition suggests that it is not possible to think of Latin American identities as fixed and essentialised but rather as engaged in a dynamic and constant process of negotiation of identities in-making.

As it happens in other multicultural countries, Britain is redefining itself out anew. In this process of cultural redefinition, ethnicity and culture have become important to characterize the British identity, while differences based on class and political association become less prominent. It is in this context that the analysis of how Latinos/as are negotiating their 'diasporic' identity and the influence, if any, the local, national and transnational diasporic media have on the ways Latinos/as perceive themselves will be discussed. To understand the tensions of the empirical findings, I draw on the framework of media studies, cultural studies and postcolonial studies. The next part considers the meaning of Latin American identities 'abroad' and the strategies of negotiation between the old and the new, predominantly by Latin women, in what Hall calls the development of the 'cultures of hybridity' (1992).

Negotiating 'Latin' identities

> When my family moved to this country (England) over thirty years ago, we use to see ourselves as part of two cultures, we had our home country and were adjusting to our new home (Chilean woman).

It seems that times have changed. Today people move across the world and interact with distinct cultures to reach various sites of connection among them. This movement has led to a change of paradigm, i.e. from a 'by-cultural' to a hybrid identity (cf. Schutte, 2000). Hybrid Latin identities are slowly gaining space in the imagination of Latinos/as in Liverpool. There is a sense that they can 'shop around' and become whoever they want to be as they chose from the multitude of cultural possibilities that, in turn might help to their inclusion in multicultural Britain without losing their 'Latinidade'. This postmodern approach to the identity of nomads and hybrids (Bhabha, 1994; Bradiotti, 1994; Clifford, 1994) suggests that the bonds of ethnic ties and the fixity of boundaries have been replaced by shifting and fluid identities. This paradigm change however, may not be universally applicable to the experiences of each and every Latino/a because of their different attachments – religion, ethnicity, gender, age and class. As Anthias points out: 'the perception of diasporas as breaking the 'ethnic spectacles' with which the world was previously viewed, may vastly underestimate the continuing attachment to the idea of ethnic and therefore particularist bonds, to a new reconstructed form of ethnic absolutism' (1998: 561). The tensions of Latin American identities negotiation seem to support this concern. As while there is a shift in the way cultural identity is perceived it is too easy to interpret this as the dismantling of the ethnic imperatives across a range of identity, and to treat the new agents of 'diasporic space' as unproblematic throwing out their investments in the resources of ethnicity politics (Brah, 1996).

The celebration of hybrid identities should not overlook the material reality of the Latin American community being doubly marginal: in one respect, it is marginal in relation to the country and culture of origin, and in relation to the mainstream identity of the British culture. Moreover, the Latin American as a 'pick and mix' identity still can work as a marker of difference and has created tension for women. A Bolivian woman suggested that instead of presenting herself as Bolivian, which in her view causes people to see her as 'different' she often says to people that she is from Spain 'because people start talking if you say that you are Spanish because British people go on holiday there'.

Several of my informants raised the issue of the commodification of 'Latinidade' and were quite sceptical of the promotion of 'Latin' identity, given the susceptibility of these 'identities' regarding their commercialization by multinational companies, particularly the media, which is a similar phenomenon in the USA. (cf. Schutte, 2000). The topic was especially upsetting for women, who suggested that a stereotype of 'Latin women' is in place, represented as 'exotic' and 'sensual' as, for example, in adverts (tourism), film, and music. The signifier 'Latin' and its mainstream representations have been marking them and, ultimately potentialising their perception of 'otherness' and displacement in the new 'home'. It could also be argued, that these stereotypes work as a form of 'rituals of exclusion' of alterity (cf. Sibley, 1995) which can be expressed by 'their' consumption as 'exotic' in various commodified forms. However, this is only one side of an ambivalent story, in so far as alterity can also be a focus of desire. Where this leaves Latin Americans politically is with the awareness that with respect to ethnicity, as with respect to gender or national origin, they must constantly negotiate their identification in relation to the representation and political forces that mark them (cf. Schutte, 2000: 67).

The conflict of ethnic boundaries (Barth, 1969) between one's homeland heritage and one's diaspora or 'minority' condition in the 'translocal' environment does not end here, especially for women. Overall, women brought up in patriarchal societies have their bodies defined and represented by a masculine orientation in social symbolism. That is, the 'Latina' body has a double signifier; it is free but also signifies a reproductive body working for the patria, the fatherland. Conversely, while subordinated to British values, the Latina's body becomes an exotic, racialized body or an impoverished, health-risk body. As Latin women, we have to negotiate our identity constantly among a series of stereotypes produce by the patriarchal culture and reproduced by mainstream media, which impose definitions of what a woman should do with her body and her professional aspirations (Alcoff, 2000). This might happen because some women may be empowered by retaining home traditions but they may also be quick to dump them when they are no longer strategies of survival. The Latin American women in Liverpool might be a case of that, since to survive in Britain most of them had to re-construct themselves as independent and 'bread winners' somehow breaking some of the rules of patriarchalism brought from home. Compared to their position as working-class wives in their countries of origins, Latino American women's social world increased in Britain, as they gained a wider range of roles, including participation in the economic and other public spheres. Employment, even if in underpaid jobs, brought not only certain economic freedom but also an occupational identity coupled with greater self-esteem. In their new position Latin women were capable, though not without tension, to reconcile their new roles with the traditional expectations and concerns held of them and by them as mothers and wives. In contrast, men's world shrank as most of them have rudimentary understanding of the English language and felt that working in low paid jobs weren't fulfilling enough to provide them with their 'men's dignity'. Their lives became more private and disconnected from the public sphere as they knew at home.

> There are problems in the community; economic and psychological, especially among men because they feel they don't have the power they use to have back home. Some of them had good jobs and they come here to low paid jobs (Venezuelan woman).

In any case, men and women had to be experimental in creating new meanings and identities out of the contradictions between past and present. While these contradictions seem to be an expected mark of the migration experience, the Latin Americans in Liverpool demonstrate a case in which migrant women have been relatively successful in integrating their past into a meaningful present. In doing so, they have managed to reconcile traditional role expectations with the demands of the new society, and collective concerns with personal experience and aspirations. Perhaps their media practices have played a role in facilitating this process as the British media have provided them with new 'ways of life' which question and encourage them to rethink those traditional roles brought from 'home'.

However, these relatively successful female stories conceal another problematic issue for the Latin women; that of her body as signifier of ethnicity, the racialized body, the body of 'women of colour', which does not reflect our multicultural configuration. The label lies on a binary opposition between white and non-white, in which it is assumed that unless a woman is white, she is a woman of colour. The maintenance of this binary reproduces the superiority of 'whiteness' and brown, yellow, red, black, and mixed race become the marks of difference. This way of thinking, which 'reproduces the vestiges of racism, and is in turn reproduced by mainstream media, limits the Latina's voice to the demand for inclusion in an order of representation marking her as "other"' (Schutte, 2000:71). Instead, the meaning of 'women of colour' needs to assume a "political significance with respect to the agency of women in racially and ethnically marginalized groups who actively oppose racism, sexism, cultural imperialism, and heterosexism' (Schutte, 2000: 73).

In order to move beyond the problems raised by these identities in tension, unresolved identities, the contradictions and complexities in subject position presented here will be perhaps better understood if we recognize Latin American identities as constructed not exclusively in notions of 'ethnicity' and 'homeland – 'either/or' – but on identification as 'and/and'. That is, focusing on the difference and sameness of the connective culture across different Latin groups i.e. in the 'sense of both fit and non-fit, belonging and longing that seems to exemplify the diasporic experience, as well as the multiple identifications and third-or-more spaces in which diaspora is conducted' (Sreberny, 2000).

The media of Latinos/as

I shall move on to consider the specificities of the Latin American's patterns of media consumption and their relation to the process of negotiation of 'identities in tension'. But first – because it provides an important point of reference for my line of reasoning – I want briefly to consider few arguments on media and diaspora raised in the literature.

Seeking to understand the effects of transnational flows on local populations, commentators have conceptualised and interpreted these new transnational forms and processes from different perspectives (Vertovec, 1999). Appadurai (1996) points particularly to the power of transnational media to produce transnational imaginaries capable of creating and sustaining new forms of transnational publics. Comparing these new transnational media forms to the powers of print capitalism in creating the imagined communities of the nation-state (Anderson, 1983) Appadurai suggests a similar development of alternative types of modern identities that connect individual and social groups to new types of transnational cultural formations. Moreover, in relation to diasporic symbolic communicative spaces media academics have made important suggestions on ways to define them. For example, Schlesinger proposes the idea of the 'audio-visual space' in relation to European identity and argues that to understand these spaces it is necessary to combine them with an analysis of cultural identities as they are not oppositional terms (cf. Schlesinger, 2000). Morley and Robins, (1995) propose that in the context of globalization a new 'electronic space' has been created which is a 'placeless geography of image and simulation'. How these spaces of media diaspora – national and transnational – influence the cultural identities of diasporic Latin groups and facilitate inclusion and/or exclusion is a concern of this discussion. The literature on media and diaspora (Naficy, 1993; Gillespie, 2000; Sinclair and Cunningham, 2000, Sreberny, 2000; Christiansen, 2004) seems to suggest that hybrid cultural expression is part of a struggle for survival, identity, and assertion, in which the 'diasporic media' maintain new kinds of long-distance imagined communities, and consequently sustaining identities and culture. This approach has been contested by Aksoy and Robins who have argued that this assumption is based on a 'national mentality' with its categories of community, identity and belonging which overlooks new possibilities of transnationalism. Based on their research on Turkish-speaking groups in London, they point out that media consumption is determined socially rather than by ethnicity. For them, the television experience of Turkish audiences is related to its ordinariness, familiarity, and everydayness. More important to our discussion, is their point about Turkish television as an agent of 'cultural de-mythologisation', i.e. the ordinariness of Turkish television, of bringing the everyday of Turkish life so close to them works to demystify ideas of the homeland (Robins, 2000; Robins and Aksoy, 2001, 2005; Aksoy and Robins, 2003). This in turn leads to the argument of 'de-Ethnicization' developed by Milikowski. Her analyse is centred on how the Turkish satellite television could further ethnicization or de-ethnicization of Turkish immigrants in the Netherlands, and argues that Turkish television 'de-ethnicizes' rather than 'ethnicizes' viewers' perception of cultural difference. While 'ethnicization refers to the formation of social boundaries created to protect ethnic–cultural heritages, de-ethnicization refers to the "undoing" of such boundaries' (Milikowski, 2000: 444). In this construct, the concept of ethnic-cultural boundaries related to pos-immigration ethnicity is paramount to clarify how different groups establish their own subjectivity and dynamics (cf. Milikowski, 2000). I shall now examine the consumption of diasporic media and music by Latin Americans living in Liverpool drawing upon the arguments raised here.

The diasporic media landscape available to Latin Americans in Liverpool is very limited, in sharp contrast to what is offered in London. This could suggest the lack of institutional recognition of the group as an ethnic minority as well as the low level of economic affluence – though some people in the group are economically comfortable.

For those people who do not have the financial means to access the internet or satellite television, the main medium of communication with their countries is by the use of phone cards for cheap calls ringing once or twice a week, some women still write letters but it is not a practice for the rest of the group. Again, this is different from the experiences of Latin Americans in London who have access to most transnational Latin American channels and radio in Spanish and Portuguese. According to one informant, in London 'people do not miss anything from their countries because they find things – media, music, food, clothes, and films – everywhere, as long as you can pay for it' (Columbian woman). In that context, they have access to consume goods and the world of Latin American consumer culture, being 'Latino' in London (cf. Robins and Aksoy, 2005).

The common average practice in Liverpool regarding media consumption, bearing in mind their social economic differences, is to read newspapers and magazines such as the weekly newspapers 'Latin American News', 'International Extra' and 'Noticias – Latin America' in Spanish, and monthly magazines such as 'Leros' and 'Br@sil.net' in Portuguese. Some of those media have an online version but their printed version are accessed when in London, Manchester or Leeds where they are widely distributed because of the larger groups of Latin Americans, by subscription or when friends send them. They also consume Spanish newspapers such as *El Pais* or Brazilian newspapers such as *O Globo* and *Journal do Brasil* or weekly magazines such as the Brazilian *Veja* though not very often as they are considered to be expensive by some Latinos/as. Nevertheless, as one Argentinean woman suggested:

> the newspapers/magazines help us to keep an 'eye' on what is going on at home, even though sometimes it is not good to know that things there are not stable as we would like to hear, especially with the economic crisis.

This expression of mixed feelings relates to the process of 'de-mythologisation' suggested by Aksoy and Robins (2003) i.e. to read the news about home is informative but also disturbing as the reality presented does not correspond to the imagined, nostalgic image of their home country.

The female group – older women – were very strong in presenting a wish to use the newspapers and magazines produced in their countries to maintain the link to 'home'. The responses to this need were not centred on a nostalgic wish to go back home but as a way of keeping their cultural background alive in what Brah suggested as a 'homing desire, as distinct from a desire for a homeland' (Brah, 1996:16).

Some of my informants expressed disappointment with the political role of the diasporic media produced in Britain. These media indeed provided information and entertainment about 'home' and Britain but did not seem to function as a voice to articulate their political needs and concerns as a 'community'.

> I feel we are missing the opportunity to use the newspapers/ magazines to express our problems of disconnection with British

society. Latin American journalists should think of our problems and bring them to the front page of their newspapers (Brazilian woman).

Nevertheless, while their position in relation to the local/national diasporic newspapers suggests a look inward towards Britain as it is more about local and national news, the 'here' and 'now'. One could suggest that these diasporic media also provide a potential 'third space' in the experience of hybridity and diaspora, speaking to the troublesome but also exciting spaces of the postcolonial subject.

The cultural boundaries in terms of exclusion from the mainstream British culture and strengthening of Latin ethnicity (difference) appear at times to be reinforced when reading diasporic newspapers and magazines coming from outside Latin America. As part of the reason to read these diasporic media, a first generation migrant Peruvian male mention the 'feeling of being visible' as well as a sense of inclusion, of reading about a place that has resonance to him, where he understands the political issues, the humour and public figures discussed, which encourages a look back to the past.

By contrast, the young Latin Americans though being by-lingual showed no interest in reading about 'home' as they do not feel connected to their parent's country of origin enough to engage with what is happening 'there', for them it sounds too far away, a place which they associate to holiday and visits to the extended family, not as their 'home'. This is not to suggest that they have no emotional links with Latin America but that their interest lies elsewhere, for example in exploring their Latinidade through other cultural expressions such as in Latin music and dance.

There is a strong movement among the young people regarding the consumption of music, which gives them an important space for expression. Thus, Latin music is part of what constitute their identities as British-Latinos, be it through down-loading music on the internet, buying Latin music, attending concerts of Latin American musicians in London or wherever they are being held and attending 'samba school' and salsa classes.

Additionally, the 'dancing' scenario of Latin music is very much alive in Liverpool, with clubs and bars offering special 'Latino' nights as well as salsa classes as a form of attracting new comers. One could argue that it is a 'commodification' of Latin culture but it also brings the 'Latinidade' to the public eye and invites an interaction of different people through the Latin music/dance. As one Chilean-British young man puts it: 'To be part of these 'nights' makes me feel at home and proud of being Latino as I can see people enjoying our music and dance.'

This space of celebration of Latin culture becomes the means for different generations of Latin Americans to establish a sense of identification through the process of transforming and using these places to express a Latin American cultural identity. That is to say, music and dance contribute towards the (re) construction of a collective identity, based on an 'imagined community'. However, the generational and gender difference seems to indicate a distinct look regarding their sense of belonging. For the older generation, going dancing is part of a process of 'recovering' some of their forgotten 'roots', a look 'backwards' towards their idealized homeland. For the youngsters is a way of immersing further in their British 'home', it is a look 'forward' in their British-Latin subjectivity.

In the continuum of media uses by Latin Americans, let me first mention their views on British mainstream media. There is a feeling of strangeness to British media translated by complaints that these media do not recognise their existence, especially in the news programmes. Here the issue of representation is important as they feel invisible – underrepresented and/or represented in negative ways thus excluded from the public sphere. One could argue that there is a dynamic of withdrawal and separation of Latin Americans from the British media, though it is important to qualify that patterns of British media consumption varies among them as for example, young Latinos/as view those media as part of their daily lives. Nevertheless, some claim that there are few connections between what they watch on television and their own experiences. A Brazilian woman suggested that

> The media here only remember us when we are bad news, as in drug traffic from Colombia to the wealthy countries, political problems in Bolivia or in the 'favelas' of Brazil.

If broadcasting has a role in the construction of a sense of national identity, of connectivity that bind people together and create an invisible and imagined community of audience, the aspirations of inclusion of Latinos/as are not voiced in the British media. A Peruvian woman suggested 'my voice is not heard, what I hear is a strange talking to me in a posh accent'. As Morley points out in relation to Scannell's (1996) celebration of national forms of broadcasting as a 'public good', providing a culture in common, is that British broadcasting fails to embrace

the cultural diversity of people living in Britain, as it invites to participate only white, middle-class, English ethnic culture. 'We see that not
everyone can feel at home in this public sphere – as opposed to feeling
particularized and (at best) tolerated, as 'others' within it' (Morley,
2001: 437). Yet, watching British television is still part of Latin Americans' media experience. They watch entertainment and news programmes which provide them an understanding of British culture and
works particularly for the female audience as a way of comparing them
to their own culture. For example, looking at fashion trends, how
women perform different and more liberating roles than the traditional
ones the Latinas are used to, which in turn become topics of conversation among them. Perhaps we could link this to what Robins and Aksoy
call the 'ordinariness' of media consumption among immigrants (cf.
Robins and Aksoy, 2005) which disrupts their media use from a strict
diet of diasporic media and helps in the process of 'de-ethnicization'.

The consumption of transnational television is based on those who
can afford to access satellite and cable broadcast, and on what channels are available. Brazilians tend to watch the Brazilian channel now
accessible on Sky *Record International* along with other English,
Portuguese and Spanish channels, while Spanish watch the Spanish
channel *TVEi* or English channels depending on their interests.
Although these channels do not address particularly the migrant and
diaspora audience, they still a resourceful font for Latin Americans to
remain 'in touch' with trends in 'the other side of the world', as posed
by a Bolivian woman. The types of programmes that people most often
watched on television and their viewing preferences varied widely.
Latino/a's favourite programmes are comedies, variety shows, sport
events, science fiction, Brazilian soap operas, and news formats. The
viewing of transnational television is a social practice that congregates
families and friends particularly to watch especial programmes about
their countries. In those occasions, their sense of belonging to a distant
culture is highlighted but, at the same time, it is an activity in which
the sameness of television is perceived for example, in the programme
formats – global standard – and types of programmes such as Big
Brother and Who Wants to be a Millionaire, with the difference only
in the language. The appeal of those programmes thus is because not
only it is about 'home' but also it is part of a search for gratification
and pleasure on what is familiar.

Beyond the set of programmes offered on television, video rental and
cinema attendance provided expanded choices for Latino/a viewers.
Here once more, however, their choices were circumscribed by what

was available. Different types of video rental outlets offered various combination of movies, especially of Brazilian, Argentinean, and Mexican films.

The technologies that appear to collapse space and time such as the internet had a great use among the Latinos/as. The inferential reading suggests that the place-transcending of the internet facilitates the creation of ties through space and reduce the separation between here and there, negating place which can strengthen a sense of ethnic and diasporic identity. The Latinos make use of a great range of web pages, mainly produced for Latin people in the US but also the ones produced elsewhere. These websites are for the purpose of not only cultural preservation and the maintenance of diasporic identities, but to support cosmopolitan, intercontinental lifestyles, consumption habits as well as political engagement. Linked to these sites are a great number of sites on Latin America: online versions of different Latin American newspapers, business, and cultural sites. The internet appears to provide the central means of access to news and Latin culture for the educated and middle class living overseas.

The vast, international complex of interlinked websites used by the 'Latin diasporas' and residents in Latin America is part of a more variegated space of international and multicultural communication which incorporate the internet and other media such as music CDs and films, radio and television forming what Froehling calls 'a number of overlapping communicative links in different media spaces' (1999: 170).

What, then, can I concluded about the influence of transnational and diasporic media on Latin identities? The core point is that Latinos/as appreciate the opportunity to access a wide variety of Latin and non-Latin media from various places. There is little indication that transnational media are currently promoting or encouraging any unified sense of transnational Latin American identity as these media continue to present specific historic, economic, and cultural conditions tied to their place of production and audience reactions reflect their own responses to these specificities.

Furthermore, it can be suggested that the consumption of transnational/diasporic media by Latin Americans is part of our lives in Europe, which suggest that tensions and conflicts in the process of identity negotiation is resolved according to the material reality of our specific circumstances and internal cultural practices. The issue here is perhaps to emphasise the strategy of multiple gaze used by Latin Americans to the media. Sometimes is a look to the past which reinforces our ethnic identity, in others is a look to the present which strength a sense of belonging to our new home. As Madianou suggests on her study of the media among Turkish speakers in Greece, 'shifts in viewing patterns do not necessarily relate to strategies about belonging, but are often contingent and pragmatic decisions' (Madianou, 2005: 536).

The gender, social class, and generational gaps were visible in terms of preferences and patterns of consumption. Young people are more attracted to 'Latin pop' while older men are more likely to enjoy programmes that reinforce their traditions and beliefs, and women are more inclined to negotiate their views according to their interests and experience of new subjectivities. One could suggest that the use of these media provides a way for cultural adaptiveness to the host culture as well as cultural connectiveness to the Latin culture while allowing us to compare the different cultural worlds offered by these diverse media.

Concluding remarks

This chapter has presented the complexities of the diasporic movement of Latin Americans in searching of a meaning to the signifier of 'Latin American' outside our country of origin as the term has different referents in different contexts, depending on very particular historical, geographical and demographic factors. What is clear is that 'diasporic Latin identities' have been constructed not grounded in an essentialised past, but refers to the different positions in which we locate ourselves within discourses of history and culture in the present. Our cultural identity is formed out of similarities and continuity, difference and rupture. The first is established through continuity with the past, the second through a shared experience of discontinuity by the process of migration (Hall, 1990). The politics of cultural diaspora in the case of Latin Americans seems to follow the logic put forward by Ang, i.e. it does not 'privilege neither host country nor (real or imaginary) homeland, but precisely keep a creative tension between 'where you are from' and "where you're at"' (Ang, 2001: 35).

The media and social practices of Latin Americans in Liverpool show that we are open to the diversity of media cultures available to us and that there are several dynamics working when defining our media and social practices choices, which are related to language, individual interests, ethnicity, gender, and age.

The Latinos/as have an ambivalent relationship with British mainstream media and I see a dialectical process at work. On the one hand, there is resentment caused by a sense of exclusion, in terms of under-representation and misrepresentation as in the case of stereotypes and negative news. At the same time, British media is viewed as a positive space for cultural comparison and a learning experience about the host culture.

The music and the diasporic and transnational media have an impact in establishing a sense of belonging and inclusion yet they can also disturb idealized notions of the homeland culture as well as in altering their identity positioning. Whether the media impact is 'de-ethnicization' or 'ethnicization' is more likely to be determined by the ways Lationos/as are interpellated by the different media and how they position themselves in relation to those media discourses. It is possible to suggest that our media practices, be it the consumption of music, film, diasporic, national or transnational media – are embedded in a sense of ordinariness, as an element of our daily lives influenced perhaps by our own experience of multiple belonging and awareness of the ambivalence of our diasporic existence. Moreover, it is not obvious if our media practices impact on our feelings of inclusion or exclusion except in the instance of Latin representation in British mainstream media. Concerning transnational media, it is possible to suggest that rather than generating a process of guettoization of Latin Americans it has rather provided opportunities for Latin Americans to engage with other cultures and the wider British society.

Overall, the media experience of Latin Americans in Liverpool has created the possibility for questioning and renegotiating of our identities, which in turn has provided opportunities for transformative experiences where one fights one's way through the many trappings of 'race' and 'ethnicity'. My own learning from the experience of my contact with other Latin Americans is that we have to distance ourselves from what Schutte calls the 'essentialized locations' of being Latin American. Through my encounter with fantastic women of different ethnic and religious backgrounds and different ages, I have learned to look at and respect the differences within Latin American groups. Without losing sight of our different cultural history and language, I have come to value the significance of being 'Latina' in the multicultural and multiethnic British society. This experience has showed me the political dangers of essentialism, the need to be doubtful of orthodoxy and to consider the full political implications – as well as opportunities for personal fulfilment – associated with the 'identities-in-the-making' we ascribe to ourselves (Schutte, 2000).

Notes

1. The reasons for their immigration to Britain can be attributed, among other factors, to the immigration laws in the earlier 1970s – Immigration Act of 1971 – which granted work permits and later permanent visa to people from countries which were not former British colonies. That Act has since been replaced by more draconian rules to enter Britain. (cf. Juss, 1993)
2. The concept of 'community' is used here cautiously as it is a problematic category in terms of homogenizing group differences. (cf. Cohen, 1997)
3. For Cohen, 'diaspora' forms a transnational community, which is a natural and unproblematic social formation without division or difference, having the same political project (s). Diaspora is viewed as existing primarily through 'bounding' created by the difficulties and anxieties faced by diasporic groups in another country.
4. Webner uses this idea of diaspora to differ from the traditional sense of people sharing a place of origin, religion and history. Late modern diasporas come from immense cultural and geographical regions with different religions, nationalities and languages. They are segmented because 'members of such diasporas may unite together in some contexts and oppose each other in other contexts'. Their members' identities are not fixed but circumstantially determined. (Webner, 2004: 900)

References

Aksoy, A. (2003) and K. Robins 'Banal Transnationalism: The Difference that Television Makes' in: K. H. Karim (eds), *The Media of Diaspora* (London: Routledge) pp. 89–104.

Alcoff, L. M. (2000) 'Is Latina/o Identity a Racial Identity?' in J. J. E. Gracia and P. De Greiff (eds), *Hispanics/Latinos in the United States: Ethnicity, race and Rights* (New York: Routledge) pp. 23–44.

Anderson, B. (1983) *Imagined Communities: Reflections on the Origins and Spread of Nationalism* (London: Verso).

Ang, I. (2001) *On Not Speaking Chinese* (London:Routledge).

Anthias, F. (1998) Evaluating '"Diaspora": Beyond Ethnicity?', *Sociology*, 32(3): 557–80.

Appadurai, A. (1996) *Modernity at Large: Cultural dimensions of globalization* (Minneapolis, MN: University of Minnesota Press).

Barth, F. (ed.) (1969) *Ethnic Groups and Boundaries: The Social Organization of Culture Difference* (London: Allen and Unwin).

Bauman, M. (1995) 'Conceptualising Diaspora: The Preservation of Religious Identity in Foreign Parts, Exemplified by Hindu Communities Outside India,' *Temenos*, 31: 19–35.

Brah, A. (1996) *Cartographies of Diaspora* (London: Routledge).

Bhabha, H. *The Location of Culture* (London: Routledge).

Buijs, G. (ed.) (1993) *Migrant Women: Crossing Borders and Changing Identities* (Oxford: Berg).

Bradiotti, R. (1994) *Nomadic Subjects* (New York: Columbia University Press).

Carstens, S. A. (2004) 'Constructing Transnational Identities?' Mass Media and the Malaysian Chinese Audience, *Ethnic and Racial Studies*. 26: 321–44.

Christiansen, C. C. (2004) 'News Media Consumption Among Immigrants in Europe,' *Ethnicities*, (4)2: 185–207.

Clifford, J. (1994) 'Diasporas', *Cultural Anthropology*, 9: 302–38.

Cohen, R. (1997) *Global Diasporas: an Introduction* (London: UCL Press).

Cunningham, S. and Sinclair, J. (2000) *Floating Lives; The Media and Asian Diasporas*. (Queensland, Australia: University of Queensland Press).

Dahan, M. and Sheffer, G. (2001) 'Ethnic Groups and Distance Shrinking Communication Technologies', *Nationalism and Ethnic Politics*, 7(1): 85–107.

De Santis, H. (2003) 'Mi Programa es su Programa: Tele/visions of a Spanish-language Diaspora in North America' in K. H. Karim (ed.) *The Media Of Diaspora* (London: Routledge).

Floya, A. (1998) 'Evaluating Diaspora: Beyond ethnicity?', *Sociology*, 32(3), 557–80.

Froehling Internautas, O. and Guerilleros (1999) 'The Zapatista Rebellion in Chiapas, Mexico and Its Extension Into Cyberspace' in M. Crang *et al.* (eds), *Virtual Geographies: Bodies, Space and Relations*. (London: Routledge)

Georgiou, M. (2005) 'Diasporic Media Across Europe: Multicultural Societies and the Universalism-Particularism Continuum', *Journal of Ethnic and Migration Studies*, 31(3): 481–98.

Gillespie, M. (2000) 'Transnational Communications and Diaspora Communities' in S. Cottle (ed.), *Ethnic Minorities and the Media* (Buckingham: Open University Press).

Gilroy, P. (1997) 'Diaspora and the Detours of Identity' in E. Woodward (ed.) *Identity and Difference* (London: Sage).

Hall, S. (1990) 'Cultural Identity and Diaspora' in J. Rutherford (ed.), *Identity; Community, Culture, Difference* (London, Lawrence and Wishart).

Hall, S. (1992) 'New Ethnicities' in J. Donald and A. Rattansi (eds), *Race, Culture and Difference* (London: Sage) pp. 252–60.

Helmirich, S. (1992) 'Kinship, Nation and Paul Gilroy's Concept of Diaspora', *Diaspora*, 2:2.

Juss, S. S. (1993) *Immigration, Nationality and Citizenship* (United Kingdom: Mansell).

Mardianou, M. (2005) 'Contested Communicative Spaces: Rethinking Identities, Boundaries and the Role of the Media Among Turkish Speakers in Greece,' *Journal of Ethnic and Migration Studies*, 31(3): 521–41.

Milikowski, M. (2000) 'Exploring a Model of De-Ethnicization: The Case of Turkish Television in the Netherlands', *European Journal of Communication*, 15(4): 443–68.

Morley, D. (2001) 'Belongings: Place, Space, and Identity in a Mediated World', *European Journal of Cultural Studies*, 4(4): 425–48.

Morley, D and K. Robins (1995) *Spaces of Identity: Global Media, Electronic Landscapes and Cultural Boundaries* (London: Routledge).

Naficy, H. (1993) *The Making of Exile Culture; Iranian Television in Los Angeles* (Minneapolis, MN: University of Minnesota Press).

Naficy, H. and Gabriel, T. (eds) (1993) *Otherness and the Media* (New York: Harwood).

Nandy, A. (1990) 'Dialogue and the Diasporas,' *Third Text*, 11: 99–108.

Robins, K. (2000) 'Introduction: Turkish (Television) Culture is Ordinary,' *European Journal of Cultural Studies*, 3(3): 291–5.

Robins, K. and A. Aksoy, (2001) 'From Spaces of Identity to Mental Spaces: Lessons from Turkish-Cypriot Cultural Experiences in Britain,' *Journal of Ethnic and Migration Studies* 27(4): 685–711.

Robins, K. and Aksoy, A. (2005) 'New Complexities of Transnational Media Cultures' in: O. Hemer and T. Tufte (eds), *Media and Global Change: Rethinking Communication for Development* (Buenos Aires and Sweden, CLACSO/Nordicom) pp. 41–58.

Roman-Velazquez, P. (1991) *The Making of Latin London* (Aldershot, UK: Ashgate, 1999).

Safran, W. (1991) 'Diasporas in Modern Societies: Myths of Homeland and Return,' *Diaspora*, (1) 1: 83–99.

Schlesinger, P. (2000) 'The Nation and Communicative Space' in: H. Tumber (ed.), *Media Power, Professionals and Politics*. (London: Routledge) pp. 99–115.

Schutte, O. (2000) 'Negotiating Latin Identities' in: J. J. E. Gracia and P. De Greiff (eds), *Hispanics/Latinos in the United States; Ethnicity, race and Rights* (New York: Routledge) pp. 61–76.

Sibley, D. (1995) *Geographies of Exclusion* (London: Routledge)

Sinclair, J. and Cunningham S. (2000) Go with the Flow; Diasporas and the Media', *Television and New Media*, 1(1): 11–31.

Tololyan, K. (1996) Rethinking Diaspora(s): Stateless Power in the Transnational Moment', *Diaspora*, 5: 3–36.

Tsagarousianou, R. (2001) 'A Space Where One Feels at Home': Media Consumption Practice Among London's South Asian and Greek Cypriot Communities', in R. King and N. Wood (eds), *Media and Migration; Constructions of Mobility and Difference* (London: Routledge).

Sreberny, A. (2000) 'Media and Diasporic Consciousness: an Exploration Among Iranians in London,' in: S. Cottle (ed.), *Ethnic Minorities and the Media* (Buckingham: Open University Press).

Vertovec, S. (1999) 'Conceiving and Researching Transnationalism,' *Ethnic and Racial Studies*, 22(2): 447–61.

Webner, P. (1999) 'Global Pathways Working Class Cosmopolitans and the Creation of Transnational Ethnic Worlds,' *Social Anthropology*, 7(1): 17–35.

Webner, P. (2004) 'Theorizing Complex Diasporas: Purity and Hybridity in South Asian Public Sphere in Britain,' *Journal of Ethnic and Migration Studies*, 30(5): 895–911.

12
All That Diaspora Allows: Film Between Queer and Diaspora

Gary Needham

Introduction

Through an extended analysis of the recent 'queer diasporic film' *Touch of Pink* (Canada/UK 2004) this chapter outlines the contribution that the categories of both 'queer' and 'diaspora' have to offer each other in ways that dislodge both terms from their limitations in accounting for, on the one hand questions of race and ethnicity, and on the other hand questions of non-normative sexuality. The subject of 'queer diaspora' as a lived experience, a critical discourse, and an object of theoretical analysis and reflection is a rich area of inquiry that, in its fusion of the terms queer and diaspora, productively names a double unfixing from both the already unfixed and anti-essentialist notions that queer and diaspora also names. The film *Touch of Pink* is one of a number of films recently directed by a diasporic queer filmmaker of colour that seem to offer useful insights into thinking about the fusion of these terms queer and diaspora through an articulation of the complexities and experiences of identity as they bristle against the diasporic queer's transnational sexuality, sense of belonging and relationship to 'home'.

While the subject of queer diaspora has been gaining momentum since the late 1990s and is, in many ways, emerging as its own distinct canon through the work of Gayatri Gopinath, Martin F. Manalansan, Anne-Marie Fortier and David L. Eng, my own contribution to the subject of queer diaspora is through a queer-inflected film studies as the academic subject area where I myself feel most at *home*. It is through film studies and its disciplinary specific approach to textual analysis that one can reveal how a film or video may offer useful ways of thinking about a particular filmmaker's stylistic choices and ability to explore the subject of queer diaspora through directorial agency and cinematic history. This is especially important when the filmmaker can and should be identified as a queer and/or diasporic individual like the director–writer of *Touch of Pink*, Ian Iqbal Rashid. While authorship and the *auteur* (the film director) have been contested categories of analysis in film studies (Caughie, 1980), I would strongly argue that it is still necessary to keep them at the fore as an organisational strategy for those directors and artists whose authorship responds explicitly from a place outside conventional and mainstream film practice, and not from within a hegemonic institutional filmmaking context such as Hollywood. As I have suggested elsewhere in relation to Asian cinema, this approach shifts the emphasis from the director who occupies the romanticised position of artist and instead, following Michel Foucault's contribution to authorship, considers the 'name of the author' as a discourse around which the director is a filter for lived experiences (Needham, 2006). Recognising the social, cultural and political experiences that give life to film and video texts through the director's agency is a crucial strategy for institutionally, culturally and socially marginalised directors and cinemas under which queer diasporic and transnational films and filmmakers would most certainly qualify.

Queer interventions

Queer Theory has been an important critical as well as political discourse that came to fruition in the early 1990s and offered a paradigmatic shift in ways of thinking about gender, sex and sexuality as well as reclaiming, appropriating and subverting official histories, cultures and ideas that have strategically excluded queers. Initially through the groundbreaking theoretical work of Judith Butler (Butler, 1990, 1993) and Eve Kosofsky Sedgwick (1991, 1993) as well as taking inspiration from artists and activists, queer theory's interrogation of homophobia, oppression, heteronormativity, and liberal-left and right-wing politics was called for an unfixing of identity from binary systems of categorisation that normatively align sex and gender. Queer theory was a breakthrough for both gay and lesbian scholars as well as feminists and its insights have extended beyond its initial mode of queer and feminist address to also include ways of reading popular culture (Doty, 1993; Doty and Creekmur, 1995). Queer theory has been canonised across academia but in many ways also progressively depoliticised and misunderstood, of which the most well known is probably the mainstreaming of Butler's gender performativity.

What a queer studies approach to diaspora explores is the specific articulations of dealing with the conflicts and tensions implied and experienced in both diasporic living and queer subjectivity and the ways in which a diasporic identity is often normalised through categories of *home* and *family*. The film studies approach entails an analysis of how a film and/or video text attends to a politics of film form and style, narrative and theme, as well as a taking in to consideration a film's place within a history, genre and canon defined through and against other films of its ilk. Therefore an integrated queer film studies can address both a politics of identity and a politics of style and narrative at the same time with the specific analytical insights and methodological rigour of both. What follows is an outline of how queer diaspora offers multiple challenges to the heteronormative assumptions of a diasporic epistemology and the homophobia of real diasporic contexts of living in addition to the frequent elision of discourses of diaspora, migration, transnationality, race and ethnicity in queer theories and studies. Therefore, out of necessity queer diaspora exists to challenge the assumptions and meanings of both the terms diaspora and queer and the contexts in which they have given rise to a range of homophobias and racisms. As Jasbir K. Paur suggests: 'the interfacing of "queerness" with "diaspora" critiques the very terms they seek to incorporate, and in which they are incorporated, forcing particular redefinitions of the original terms' (1998: 407).

The queer contribution to diaspora

Explanations of diaspora typically begin with the origin of the word itself through discussion of its Greek etymological (*diaspeirein*) meaning of dispersal across, dissemination and the scattering and sowing of seeds. For just a moment I want to hang on to this original meaning of diaspora for it actually embodies the very logic by which notions of reproduction and fertility become key to its understanding. To scatter, to increase and multiply, names the discourse of fertility and reproduction, of the seed and the seminal. For queers, these terms have a certain connotation that also corresponds to ways in which the family, the home, the community and the nation are places that come to be defined through their exclusion, destruction and rendering invisible of queers and queerness because, quite simply, queers don't reproduce or constitute normatively defined reproductive families. The link here of course is that so much of the discussion about diaspora and the understanding and organisation of diasporic communities, spaces and identities is in many ways anchored around the key terms of home and family, in addition to nation and belonging through which the family and the home are the nation's perceived social and ideological foundations (Gopinath, 1997). The family is the organisational structure through which the homeland is often maintained and imagined, yet it is the family as a normative concept of organisation and regulatory practice that is potentially hostile to those whose identity cannot be contained within the strictures of heterosexual and patriarchal structuring in addition to the more wide spread gendering of the private and public spheres. Therefore, those individuals who are both queer and diasporic, doubly marginalised as it were, bring to the fore certain complexities and tensions around queer subjectivity and the diasporic pressures of the familial and the homely as Karin Aguilar-San Juan recounts:

> For many years, I have been concerned with the way we, as Asian American lesbians and gay men, think about going home. Many of us simply cannot do so, at least not openly, because of the intolerance of parents, relatives, friends who bristle at our 'lifestyles' (1998: 25).

If one is both queer and diasporic it challenges the assumption that the family is always a place of safety and belonging where one is always welcome and can potentially return. The importance of gay communities and gay scenes, however they may be imagined, is in their ability to function as places of communal structuring, collective identity and solidarity, especially when one has no other place where they can experience a sense of belonging. In addition to Aguilar San Juan's concerns it is also worth drawing attention to the fact that a large number of gay, lesbian and transgender migrants are also seeking asylum because their sexual and/or gender identities at home and in the nation means that their lives are at risk from violent hostilities and abuses or worse, torture and death (Manalansan, 2006).

Lee Edelman's recent queer polemic on the role of the child in imagining a heteronormative nation-state, what he has termed *reproductive futurism*, offers a great deal of insight into how the logic of diaspora works according to the centrality occupied by the normative family and reproduction (Edelman, 2004). For Edelman, queerness is positioned and defined through its separation from reproductive acts as the side of those 'not fighting for the children' and therefore not fighting for the future (Edelman, 2004: 3). The potential of a queer politics is its very resistance to a logic of futurity. Therefore, the crucial definition of queerness as 'future-negating' (Edelman, 2004: 26) offers a radical way of working against the ideological role that reproduction occupies as a familial and heterosexual discourse both implicit and explicit in diasporic ontologies. How often do the media solicit an emotive response to debates about immigration and asylum through the image of the impoverished waif? Our immediate reaction to the media's exploitation of the image of the waif is perhaps to think of the child's future especially when confronted by the key semiotic trope: the close-up of a sad, teary-eyed and dirty face. The image of the child is where the future comes to be projected in a fantasy of *futurism* that Edelman argues is antithetical to those who don't count as the normative reproductive families.

> The consequences of such an identification both of and with the Child as the pre-eminent emblem of the motivating end, though one endlessly postponed, of every political vision *as a vision of futurity* must weigh on any delineation of a queer oppositional politics. For the only queerness that queer sexualities could ever hope to signify would spring from their determined opposition to this underlying structure of the political – their opposition, that is, to the governing fantasy of achieving Symbolic closure through the marriage of identity to futurity in order to realize the social subject (Edelman, 2004: 13–14).

Leaving the figure of the child aside and the fact there are gay and lesbian parents, it is useful to take on board Edelman's notion of *reproductive futurism* as a key strategy that can illuminate the role of the familial and the homely as heteronormative, in fact in a range of ideas about diaspora whose survival depends on the reproductive capacity to keep alive peoples, cultures, languages and traditions through motions towards the future. One is also reminded of the biblical dictum of reproductive futurity *par excellence*: be fruitful and multiply'. The securing of a community through is reproductive futurity, while absolutely essential in challenging the cultural, social and institutional racism of nations and states, is still problematic because queers and their queerness are the terms through which the heteronormativity of 'diaspora' is made visible and dangerous. Gayatri Gopinath argued (Gopinath, 1997): the 'suturing of "queer" to "diaspora" points to those desires, practices and subjectivities that are rendered impossible and unimaginable within conventional diasporic and nationalist imaginaries' (Gopinath 2005: 243). As queers themselves can never be afforded the 'positive social value' (Edelman 2004: 6) associated with reproducing the nation-state, in the ideological sense rather than the biological, it draws attention to the question of what place can queers be allowed in a orthodox heteronormativity dependent on reproduction and the connection to the words community, family, home and nation as they circulate in and around a diasporic ontology.

The diasporic contribution to queer

The opposite of queer is not gay or lesbian but the normal and the normative. While queer includes in its majority those who might also recognise themselves as gay or lesbian, the power of a queer identity is that it seeks to include a range of identities which run counter to the normalising tendencies of a normative, which includes in its majority those who would recognise themselves as straight or heterosexual. While gay and lesbian identities can themselves operate according to certain normative assumptions about gender and sex for example, those gay men and lesbians who play out certain social roles through a prism of heteronormative mimicry and without irony, are shaken up by the radical and dissident nature of a queer cultural praxis. Queer seeks to unfix the alignments that connect certain anatomies and bodies from cultural practices and behaviours at its very core the normative correlation between one's sex and one's gender. This is Butler's strategic move in *Gender Trouble* (1990), to interrogate the role that gender plays in determining normative assumptions about sex and sexuality and the way that bodies learn to be culturally heterosexual through the performative citations of appropriate codes of masculinity and femininity.

At its moment of inception in the early 1990s the queer shift seemed to be radical, political, utopian and inclusive in ways that gay and lesbian identities perhaps hadn't been for a long time. It brought together gay and lesbian, often together and separate, and included straight allies, transgender and transsexual peoples. It marked a radical departure from, and in fact is a direct response to, the 1980s and the AIDS crisis, which, in many ways reignited both the closet and the sexual shame of the previously oppressive decades before gay liberation and second wave feminism (Moore 2005). However, what has become a standard critique of queer identity and queer theory is the scant attention paid to questions of race and ethnicity (Muñoz 1999). Despite the radical sense of a paradigm shift in the cultures, politics and identities that would come under the rubric of queer, it seems that many of the age old problems with western gay culture were still being reproduced vis-à-vis race and ethnicity. The fact of the matter is that issues of racism, exclusion, and ethnic stereotyping were as present as ever in the shift from gay to queer. What is now being understood in the historicisation of the 1990s in relation to its queer moment is how North American, white, and gay male centric the entire discourse of queer has been. For example, Jose Munoz takes the groundbreaking 1990s New Queer Cinema, so emblematic of the queer moment, to task for its uncritical stance on whiteness (Muñoz, 1998). In more general terms this argument has been explored by Martin F. Manalansan who accounts for the problems inherent in the larger historical narrative of gay and lesbian identity, the place of the coming out narrative, the experience of the closet, and the degree zero of gay liberation at New York's Stonewall Inn in 1969. Manalansan reveals the way in which the US centric history of gay liberation is a hegemonic narrative that believes it speaks for a global gay identity and community. In his study of Filipino gay men living both in the Philippines and in New York, Manalansan reveals how the 'narratives of these diasporic Filipino gay men show how the closet is not a monolithic space and coming out is not a uniform process' (Manalansan, 1997).

Therefore, what an attention to diaspora means for discourses of queer, gay and lesbian, is a way of making visible the racial and ethnic silences and erasures by confronting the latent and manifest racisms which have structured its histories, communities and identities. In conclusion, it is worth including the following accounts of queer diasporic experience because they outline the difficulty of being on the gay scene or part of gay communities and cultures because of the racism and negative value of the non-white bodies.

I went to my first gay bar when I was 18 years old. In gay bars you can't dazzle people with insights into D. H. Lawrence or T. S. Eliot. You can't talk politics or art or assert the million and one cultural signifiers which testify to your Westernness. Apart from anything else, the music is too loud. Gay bars are places where you are what you look like, even if that is at odds with how you feel about yourself. In gay bars, I was/am Chinese. That is how I am/was judged. As it turned out, being Chinese in a gay bar was one of the worst things you could be (Ayres, 1999: 89).

What Anglo queen on the scene was going to associate us with our rich Asian culture of literature and art, and who was to know that some of us had risked our lives to escape totalitarian regimes of both the left and the right to be in this country? Were we not more likely to be associated with fast food, cheap imitation products, "rude" manners and loud talk? (Chuang, 1999: 35).

Queer/diaspora/film

There are a number of films and videos in recent years that have examined the relationship between queer identity and diasporic identity in ways that correspond to the theoretical explications discussed above. This body of films includes *Head On* (Australia 1998), *Lola and Billy the Kid* (Germany 1999), *Young Soul Rebels* (UK 1991), *My Beautiful Laundrette* (UK 1985), *From the Edge of the City* (Greece 1998), *Drôle de Felix* (France 2000) *The Wedding Banquet* (US/Taiwan 1993), *Under One Roof* (US 2002), *Chicken Tikka Masala* (UK 2005), as well as *Touch of Pink*.

What is striking about these films is how they are similarly engaged with the debates and ideas raised in the theoretical accounts of queer diaspora including both white people and people of colour. Therefore, we need to afford the same value and authority to films directed by queer diasporic artists and films about queer diaspora as legitimate theoretical texts on the subject. While the films do vary in terms of their political sensibilities and aesthetic qualities, as well as their imagined audience, they all share a similar set of concerns about queer diasporic experience. This queer diasporic experience usually positions the main protagonist of the film against the pressures of family, tradition and community (its reproductive futurity), as well as against a complicated and often unresolved queer identity. The best known of these queer diasporic films is probably *The Wedding Banquet*, directed by the transnational *auteur*, Ang Lee. (Pidduck, 2006) In *The Wedding Banquet* gay Asian–American Wai-Tung has been living contently in the US with his white American partner Simon that is until Wai-Tung's parents decide to visit from Taiwan. The parental visit throws the gay couple into a panic that results in a de-gaying of their living space, a trope also used in *Touch of Pink*, and a closeting of their sexual identities. Due to family pressure Wai-Tung marries his female friend Wei-Wei, simultaneously getting her the green card she needs and pleasing his father through marriage. However, Wei-Wei seduces Wai-Tung on their wedding night resulting in her pregnancy. When all this comes to light and the gay couple are outed the patriarchal father overcomes any anxiety around his son's sexual identity because he will have a grandchild and the family's future is guaranteed. Despite being a hugely enjoyable comedy, *The Wedding Banquet* is deeply conservative in the way that it reconfigures the queer Wai-Tung by affording him value through a momentary act of reproduction and subsequent reconfiguration within a family structure even if it actually allows the woman to come off worst of all. (Chiang, 1998; Feng, 2002). None the less the film does highlight the complexities of those whose lives are divided by familial loyalties and pressures on the one hand and non-normative sexual identities on the other. The film draws attention to the ways in which the hetero-patriarchal family enforces a closeting and demands its future at the same time. While *The Wedding Banquet* concludes with the most un-queer resolution of all the films mentioned above, it does bring to the fore how family, parents, ethnic and diasporic communities work against, intentionally and unintentionally, queer and non-normative sexual identities across a terrain of transnationality. Diasporic queers are moulded into structures that guarantee the family's reproductive futurity and radically oppose and quash the dissident aspects of their non-normative sexualities whose potential for social and political change, as 'future-negating' queers, is denied. Yet, the diasporic queers in these films are also confronted with problems of 'fitting in' to gay communities and scenes in ways that also highlight the previous discussion of both the exclusive white-centricity of queer and the latent and manifest racisms and exclusions of gay culture. Therefore, queer diasporic lives, especially those queers of colour, are somewhat defined by a liminality of being in between the pressures of diasporic logic and queer identity, resolving and challenging both through the terms by which their liminality originally comes to be figured.

Touch of Pink

Touch of Pink is about the relationship between Alim (Jimi Mistri), his partner Giles (Kristen Holden-Ried) and his widowed mother Nuru (Suleka Mathew). Alim is conflicted between his love for Giles and his need to stay in the closet in order to protect his mother, and by extension the family, from knowing his queer identity. In order to deal with the anxieties of his internalised racism and gay shame Alim invents a fantasy friend in the guise of 1940s Hollywood film star Cary Grant (Kyle MacLachlan). With an upcoming family wedding in Canada, the question of Alim's marital status also looms large and his mother decides to pay him a visit in London in order to see why he is still unwed. When Nuru finds out about Alim and Giles she returns to Canada and in the process lies to her friends and family about her son's sexual identity and white partner. Alim follows his mother to Toronto where Nuru discovers the bridegroom Khaled's (Raoul Bhaneja) own hidden sexuality identity and history of sexual shenanigans with Alim. Nuru accepts that it is better to be open and honest rather than deceitfully enter a marriage of convenience for the sake of family pretence and honour. In the end Nuru welcomes Alim and Giles into her home as sign of her blessing and acceptance.

Touch of Pink is the first feature length film by director-writer Ian Iqbal Rashid. Born in Dar-Es-Salaam and having lived in Tanzania, India, England and Canada, Rashid is not only transnational but also gay and Muslim. Open about his queer diasporic identity in interviews, Rashid stresses the importance of how his identity shapes his work and passion for cinema. Rashid has also directed the earlier short films *Surviving Sabu* (1998) and *Stag* (2001) both of which deal with themes and issues pertaining to a queer diasporic identity and history. *Touch of Pink* is produced with Canadian and British investment and was picked up for distribution by Sony Pictures Classics, the largest independent division of the Japanese owned Hollywood film studio. *Touch of Pink* also raises questions about the mobility of people and the circulation of cinema as a popular cultural form through its conditions of production, finance and location. Mobility is a central theme within the film as Alim and Nuru fly between Toronto and London as an unquestioned aspect of both their transnationality and class. Mobility is also reflected in the cultural production contexts of contemporary diasporic and transnational filmmaking where multiple sites of production and consumption are challenging the conventional boundaries of national cinemas and audiences.

Touch of Pink might not be the most obvious title for a film about a queer and diasporic gay man of South Asian descent living between Toronto and London but the title alludes to the clever interlocking of homosexuality, whiteness and cinema in its titular reference. *Touch of Pink* obviously refers to associations of homosexuality with the colour pink, culturally gendered feminine, but also the colour of white skin, as when Nuru touches the skin of Alim's white boyfriend Giles and comments on its pinkness. This does draw attention the connection between race and sexuality as gayness (through the pink association) also corresponds to whiteness. In addition to this, the title of the film refers to Hollywood's post-war decades of the 1950s and 1960s, explicitly to the film *That Touch of Mink* (US 1962), and the ouevre of its white star Doris Day. As one of the biggest film stars of the period, Doris Day's stardom and appeal were grounded in her associations with

McCarthy era conservative family values. (Clarke and Simmons 1980) The period to which these films belong and the star Doris Day herself, often paired with Rock Hudson, also gesture towards a very specific economy of gay *cinephilia* and camp reception that has structured white gay men's relationship to popular culture, cinema in particular. (Doty, 1993; Farmer, 2000). Farmer outlines the particular history and dynamic between gay men and the cinema through their mutual over invest-ment and passion for the cinema and film stardom as indicative of a non-normative and shared behaviour. Loving movies too much is there-fore, queerly perverse. The director of *Touch of Pink* is making an inter-esting intervention in terms of positioning his South Asian queer diasporic voice within a history of exclusively white gay *cinephilia* and reception. Rashid's approach is an intervention in using the queer-inflected language of cinephilia as a kind of camp intertextuality to examine how racism often structures the experiences of queer Asian diasporic men through exclusive bonds between race, sexuality and popular culture. What is also interesting here is how the character Alim's love of Hollywood classics is positioned at one point as the cause of his queer desires, corrupted as it were by a passion for and over-investment in the wrong kind of popular culture, namely Hollywood. As his mother Nuru tells him after the disclosure of his sexuality, 'those movies are evil ... they led you down the wrong path', even though it was she who nourished her gay son's *cinephilia* through their frequent trips to the cinema when he was child. However, this acknowledgment of cinema's supposed contamination of Alim is also one of the films post-colonial moments, a camp twist on Fanon's *Black Skin/White Mask* politics of identification, masking at it were Nuru's own disillusion-ment, coming from Mombassa to London with dreams of living out a lifestyle like the ones she identified with in Doris Day movies of the 1950s and 1960s. What Nuru really means is that it is not the love of movies that is contaminating or perverse but the mis-identification of the possibilities of Hollywood's mode of address and happy endings as something available to everyone. Although *Touch of Pink* concludes on a similarly utopian ending of a gay romantic union against the odds, which often signals some kind of attempt at narrative and ideological containment, the film's subversive edge is that it racially queers a love of Hollywood through *the diasporizing of gay cinephilia*.

The genre that *Touch of Pink* is most familiar with is the romantic comedy genre and the film sits quite comfortable alongside the recent Doris Day/Rock Hudson pastiche *Down with Love* (US 2003) and its banal pairing of Rene Zellweger and Ewan MacGregor. In fostering the romantic inclinations of its generic roots, *Touch of Pink* does skip over both the radical potential of depicting queer sex (and reclaiming it from the colonial fantasies evident in its flip side in gay pornography) and a brutal and frank presentation of racism and homophobia in favour of the odd, and rather unconvincing, kiss and mumbled disapproval of the 'homosexual lifestyle'. In short, *Touch of Pink* can be read as equally conservative as *The Wedding Banquet* in many ways, especially through not facing up to the reasons why individuals remain separate from their families and how families try to reconstitute their sexually dissident members. The family in *Touch of Pink* is stereotypical of the wider South Asian diasporic representations in film, with an emphasis on caricatured aunties, spectacular marriages, and petty family bitchiness, but underneath these amusing caricatures and narrative dilemmas are spectres of heteronormativity and reproductive futurism. Through Edelman's polemic, it is clear that such queers of diaspora simply have no future since they neither guarantee the future of the family nor the traditional happy endings of popular cinema. But in arguing for *Touch of Pink* as a progressive text, the film concludes through the formation of a non-normative family as Nuru welcomes her gay son and his white lover wholeheartedly into her small apartment. The ending of the film also hints at Nuru's possible future transgression by falling in love with a character who we must assume is the gardener, obviously of a lower social class, itself a reference to Douglas Sirk's melodramatic classic of social conflict and impossible love, *All That Heaven Allows* (US 1955), which this chapter's title alludes to.

Despite the film's genre positioning within the romantic comedy, *Touch of Pink* is indebted to the tradition of British-Asian filmmaking pioneered by directors like Gurinder Chadha and writers Meera Syal and Hanif Kureishi. *Touch of Pink* is easily placed alongside *Bhaji on the Beach* (UK 1993), *Bend It Like Beckham* (UK 2002) and *East Is East* (UK 1999) in sharing so many of the tactics of observation about the predicament of living a diasporic life marked by the pressures exerted and shaped by and through cultural hybridity. These British-Asian films, often informed by a Black British cultural studies, challenge the alignment between Britishness with whiteness and are equally critical of traditional Asian culture through inter-generational conflicts constructed as limiting, oppressive and patriarchal. These films celebrate cultural hybridity, defining new identities and new cultures, albeit for those who can be constituted within the limits of a heterosexual familial organisation. These landmark British films are forward thinking in terms of a politics of race and ethnicity, challenging the very idea of

British cinema itself, but they fall short in accounting for sexuality in ways that *Touch of Pink* and the earlier film *My Beautiful Laundrette* do attempt to mobilise. There is a telling scene in *Bend It Like Beckham* where footballer Jess chats to a male relative about her love of David Beckham both as a sporting icon and as an object of desire. Her friend acknowledges this too and much to her surprise finds out that he is also besotted by David Beckham. While this character has a reasonable place within the narrative vis-à-vis the family and football, his story is never told and his sexuality forgotten in favour of the plenitude of heterosexual closure that many popular films are institutionally bound to represent. For a queer diasporic spectator, this fleeting moment when one's sexuality is acknowledged to exist is so precious, and it is unfortunate that a critically and commercially successful film like *Bend It Like Beckham* and an intelligent director like Chadha can only gesture towards the possibility of making such identities matter.

The first ten minutes of *Touch of Pink* are indicative of many of the questions this chapter raises, including the conflict of a diasporic and queer identity and the director's strategy in diasporizing gay cinephilia. Film texts are organised according to, but also in opposition to, conventions of time and space, narrative and narration, and image and sound. These formal properties of film are also the means by which it can construct a particular form of cultural critique and analysis. These specificities of the filmic text are central to how such an examination of the queer diasporic debate can be mobilised through the medium. Therefore, in accounting for *Touch of Pink*'s contribution to a queer diaspora debate one must link the thematic aspects of the film to its formal and stylistic properties. The first ten minutes of the film seems to do this rather well.

Touch of Pink begins with a pastiche of the opening scene from *That Touch of Mink* with the faux Cary Grant who begins by addressing the audience directly. The music and font of the credits also recall the style of the Hollywood period and the setting or *mise en scène* is marked by a deliberate artifice. Throughout the film, attention is drawn to the artifice of Hollywood as a *mise en scène* of fantasy in the scenes depicting Alim's imaginary friend Cary Grant. These scenes of stylistic fantasy are deliberately artificial, like the Douglas Sirk film mentioned above, not only in paying homage to the period of Hollywood, but in the sense that such fantasies for diasporic audiences are absolutely fantasy in that one can only misidentify with them like Alim's mother who comes to London dreaming of Doris Day. These pastiche sequences are also framed differently; they employ different lighting techniques to mark them out and are presented in a different aspect ratio from the rest of the film, a nostalgia for a widescreen aspect ratio denied to independent productions because of budget restraint. This formal and stylistic opposition helps to organise the film along a division of Hollywood fantasy and diasporic reality between the text and its audience, allowing the director to re-imagine Hollywood history through his diasporizing of gay cinephilia and camp intertextuality. Furthermore, Rashid's creatively queer diasporic agency repositions the exclusively white vernacular of old Hollywood as an antidote to the more common resignification of the Bollywood tradition evident in several other films produced and directed by South Asian diasporic filmmakers like Gurinder Chadha. After this brief introduction we are then introduced to Alim standing in the middle of a film set, allowing us to understand what we have just seen as a daydream but also drawing attention to the constructed nature of the filmmaking process. Alim loses himself through Hollywood daydreams and his imaginary friend in addition to his occupation as set photographer. As Alim leaves work to meet his partner Giles outside a London underground station we cut immediately to Toronto and to Alim's mother Nuru and the extended family and friends making preparations for an upcoming wedding. This is where the medium specificity of film is able to put into play certain formal devices that juxtapose the conflicts and contradictions of a queer identity *vis-à-vis* the diasporic community. This editing pattern of cutting between two different spaces and narrative events is termed parallel editing and it is often used to generate suspense and tension because it allows the spectator to occupy a position of narrative knowledge greater than any character and thus foretell certain potential conflicts and misunderstandings. Parallel editing is being used here in order that we can experience the conflicts between Alim's queer life in London and his mother's diasporic life in Toronto with family and friends and how remote, culturally and geographically, they are from each other. If we look at the way each of these spaces is constructed and the meanings that they try to convey, we can begin to see how the debate is played out in terms that are entirely and only possible through film's medium specificity. The space of London in this sequence quickly moves to the gay club where Alim and Giles first met and where Giles's sister and family are waiting to celebrate the anniversary of their meeting. Alim registers his embarrassment through a displacement – 'it's too smoky' – that the celebration of their anniversary of their first meeting was in a gay club, suggestively called The Ramrod. While the film establishes the white parents as the epitome of liberal cool through their unflinching presence in a gay club, complete with obligatory drag queen and bare-chested dancer, the film's alignment with Alim allows the director to level a criticism at the London gay scene, as Alim's discomfort at not belonging is carried through to the club space which is represented as promiscuous and white. This queer space is also marked through its momentary hedonism of loud music and dancing, sexy bodies and cruising, that have often defined the contours of the gay club in its conventional media representations. These are also the conditions upon which Alim partially comes to be positioned outside the gay scene because of the visibility of his Asian-ness and the unresolved flux of his queer identity in conflict with the internalised diasporic feelings of belonging. In contradistinction to this queer space of excess in London, the parallel editing reveals the space of home and the family in Toronto to be marked by excess in a different way. Toronto and its inhabitants are established as upper middle-class in their brightly lit palatial home with Nuru's friend Dolly (Veena Sood) dragging her around the house dressed in a garish feathered robe and hair curlers. Dolly fusses over domestic minutiae while all the family's thoughts and conversations are directed towards the upcoming wedding, producing grandchildren and grandmothers, and the conspicuous single status of Alim. The discussions around marriage, and family and the occupations of everyone's fiancée are intense and obsessive in its focus but also stereotypical of South Asian diasporic film. The mise-en-scene crowded with friends and family orchestrated in a cacophony of competing voices that contrasts with the loud music of London's gay scene. This milieu here is utterly characterised by one's potential or actual ability to pair off and reproduce to the point that it almost becomes a motivation of existence. One should also think about how the stereotypical convention of South Asian diasporic film, focused as it were on weddings and heterosexual relations, might make a queer diasporic viewer feel in terms of identification and belonging. The domestic space of Toronto is also marked by an overinvestment in appearance; Dolly's excessive costuming, nouveau riche tastes in furniture, swan shaped topiary and pretence for setting the scene with classical music. Nuru's home is later revealed and is more modest and homely in anticipation of the acceptance of her queer son at the film's conclusion yet all her furniture is encased in clear plastic stressing the unnaturalness of the home. In playing off these two spaces against one another, *Touch of Pink* wrestles with the central idea driving the queer diaspora question that frames this chapter, namely, where does one belong?

Conclusion: queer futures/diasporic futures?

The lesson to be learned from this queer diasporic film *Touch of Pink*, and the lessons that the terms 'diaspora' and 'queer' can teach each other, is to make explicit relations between race and homosexuality as they correspond to family, home and belonging in diasporic contexts and in complicating the white exclusivity of metropolitan gay cultures. While it is fair to suggest that queer discourses are still in catch up where debates about race are concerned, diasporic discourses equally need to account for how the normative privileging of formations of home and community, are often exclusive in their definitions of identity that exclude queers. Furthermore, metropolitan gay scenes and queer communities, often predominately white, can themselves be zones of exclusion for diasporic queers of colour and in many cases openly discriminatory and racist.

What *Touch of Pink* ends up suggesting at its conclusion in the final scenes with Alim, his mother, Giles, and Nuru's potential love interest in apartment block gardener Karim, is that the formation of a new type of inclusive family is the way forward. A queer family, mixed by class, sexuality and race, not defined by its role in the logic of *reproductive futurism* nor a nostalgia for the potentially oppressive traditions of an homeland but in its ability to imagine a sense of belonging beyond patriarchal, racial and heternormatively defined roles that work to secure their own future. While *Touch of Pink* is a commercially orientated romantic comedy, we shouldn't overlook the insights of its queer diasporic director who suggests ways in which we might begin to think about potential futures, queer and diasporic, where the conflict between both, the tensions between race and sexuality, homophobia and racism, no longer shape our contemporary contexts and futures of being together.

References

Ayers, T. (1999) 'China Doll: the Experience of Being a Gay Chinese Australian' in Peter A. Jackson and Gerard Sullivan, (eds), *Multicultural Queer: Australian Narratives* (New York and London: Harrington Park Press).

Butler, J. (1990) *Gender Trouble* (London and New York: Routledge).

Butler, J. (1993) *Bodies That Matter: On the Discursive Limits of Sex* (London and New York: Routledge).

Caughie, J. (ed.) (1980) *Theories of Authorship* (London: British Film Institute).

Chiang, M. (1998) 'Coming Out into the Global System: Postmodern Patriarchies and Transnational Sexualities in *The Wedding Banquet*' in D. L. Eng and A. Y. Hom (eds), *Q&A: Queer in Asian America* (Philadelphia: Temple University Press).

Chuang, K. (1999) 'Using Chopsticks To Eat Steak' in P. A. Jackson and G. Sullivan (eds), *Multicultural Queer: Australian Narratives* (New York and London: Harrington Park Press).

Clarke, D. and J. Simmons (1980) *Move Over Misconceptions: Doris Day Reappraised (BFI Dossier 4)* (London: British Film Institute).

Doty, A. (1993) *Making Things Perfectly Queer* (Minneapolis: University of Minnesota Press).

Doty, A. and C. Creekmur (eds) (1995) *Out in Culture: Gay, Lesbian and Queer Essays on Popular Culture* (Durham: Duke University Press).

Edelman, L. (2004) *No Future: Queer Theory and the Death Drive* (Durham: Duke University Press).

Eng, D. L. (1997) 'Out here and Over There: Queerness and Diaspora in Asian American Studies', *Social Text*, autumn–winter, 52–3.

Eng, D. L., J. Halberstam and J. E. Muñoz (2005) 'Introduction: What's Queer About Queer Studies Now', *Social Text*, autumn–winter, 84–5.

Farmer, B. (2000) *Spectacular Passions: Cinema, Fantasy, Gay Male Spectatorship* (Durham: Duke University Press).

Feng, P. X. (2002) *Identities in Motion: Asian American Film and Video* (Durham: Duke University Press).

Fortier, A.-M. (2001) 'Coming Home: Queer Migrations and Multiple Evocations of Home', *European Journal of Cultural Studies* Vol.4, No.4, 405–24.

Fortier, A.-M., Anne-Marie (2002) 'Queer Diasporas' in D. Richardson and S. Seidman (eds), *Handbook of Gay and Lesbian Studies* (London: Sage Publications).

Fortier, A.-M. (2003) 'Making Home: Queer Migrations and Motions of Attachment' in S. Ahmed, C. Castañeda, A.-M. Fortier and M. Sheller (eds), *Uprootings/Regroundings: Questions of Home and Migration* (London: Berg Publishing).

Gopinath, G. (1997) 'Nostalgia, Desire, Diaspora: South Asian Sexualities in Motion' *Positions* 5.2.

Gopinath, G. (2005) 'Bollywood Spectacles: Queer Diasporic Critique in the Aftermath of 9/11', *Social Text*, autumn–winter, 84–5.

Juan, K. A.-S. (1997) 'Going Home: Enacting Justice in Queer Asian America' in D. L. Eng and A. Y. Hom (eds), *Q&A: Queer in Asian America* (Philadelphia: Temple University Press).

Manalansan IV, M. F. (1997) 'In the Shadows of Stonewall: Examining Gay Transnational Politics and the Diasporic Dilemma', *GLQ: Journal of Gay and Lesbian Studies*, Vol. 2 No. 4, 425–38.

Manalansan IV, M. F. (2006) 'Queer Intersections: Sexuality and Gender in Migration Studies', *International Migration Review*, Vol. 60, No. 153.

Moore, P. (2006) *Beyond Shame: Reclaiming the Abandoned History of Radical Gay Sexuality* (New York: Beacon Press).

Muñoz, J. (1998) 'Dead White: Notes on the Whiteness of New Queer Cinema', *GLQ: Journal of Gay and Lesbian Studies*, 4.1.

Muñoz, J. (1999) *Disidentifications: Queers of Color and the Performance of Politics* (Minneapolis: University of Minnesota Press).

Needham, G. (2006) 'Film Authorship and Taiwanese Cinema' in D. Eleftheriotis and G. Needham, (eds), *Asian Cinemas: A Reader and Guide* (Edinburgh: Edinburgh University Press).

Paur, J. K. (1998) 'Transnational Sexualities: South Asian (Trans)nation(alism)s and Queer Diasporas' in D. L. Eng and A. Y. Hom, (eds), *Q&A: Queer in Asian America* (Philadelphia: Temple University Press).

Pidduck, J. (2006) 'The Transnational Cinema of Ang Lee' in D. Eleftheriotis and G. Needham (eds), *Asian Cinemas: A Reader and Guide* (Edinburgh: Edinburgh University Press).

Sedgwick, E. K. (1991) *The Epistemology of the Closet* (Berkeley: University of California Press).

Sedgwick, E. K. (1993) *Tendencies* (Durham: Duke University Press).

Part IV

Voices Across Cultural and Political Diasporic Media Spaces

13
Equal Participation of Ethnic Minorities in the Media – the Case of the Netherlands

Susan Bink

Media and minorities in the Netherlands

The Netherlands has a population of 16 million people of which 10 per cent is of non-western origin. Most ethnic minority groups live in big cities like Amsterdam or Rotterdam where more than 50 per cent of the population are ethnic minority youngsters (0–14 years) (CBS, 2005). Despite this strong presence, different ethnic, cultural and religious groups fail to be equally or fairly represented in Dutch media. There are still relatively few media professionals from ethnic minority groups working in the media and there is a scarcity of stories, issues, debates and characters that adequately represent the views and cultures of minority ethnic communities.

When viewing the history of media and minority policies in the Netherlands, it can be concluded that the Dutch policy has developed from one of exclusion in the 1970s to one of inclusion as from the 1990s (d'Haenens and Koeman, 2006). In the 1980s, the Government attached importance to special programmes for ethnic minorities in their own language. These programmes were said to stimulate the integration of immigrants in the Dutch society. Later on, this vision changed and the foreign language programmes became a responsibility of local broadcasters only. In national broadcasting, the multicultural society was supposed to be a self-evident ingredient of the programmes on the public broadcasting channels. Therefore, cultural diversity has been given considerable encouragement in media policy. Through the Media Act and the Concession Act, the Dutch Government encourages a more varied media supply as well as greater cultural diversity in the media workplace. Still, ethnic minorities do not recognise themselves sufficiently in the Dutch media. Recent studies of the Visitation

Commission Public Broadcasting (2004) and the Netherlands Scientific Council for Government Policy (WRR) (2005) showed that the public broadcasting organisations do not adequately reach ethnic minorities and youngsters.

More balanced reporting

The aftermath of the September 11 events in the year 2001 clearly illustrates the impact of global and national media coverage on the position of ethnic minority groups in Dutch and other European multicultural societies. In the Netherlands, this became even clearer after the murder of Theo van Gogh on 2 November 2004 by a Muslim extremist. Theo van Gogh was a Dutch filmmaker and column writer who openly criticised Islam in his columns and who made a controversial anti-Islamic film. In the media, the word 'extremist' seems to have attached itself to the word 'Muslim', suggesting that all Muslims are capable of extreme acts.

Journalists have an essential task and responsibility by offering unbiased information and a platform for dialogue. However, journalists often have no time to do research on background information and to find interesting and trustworthy experts and spokespersons. Here NGOs and minority organisations can be of help by providing journalists with (directions to) alternative information and (online) databases with ethnic minority experts. For instance, Perslink is a Dutch database, developed by Mira Media[1] in cooperation with the public broadcasting organisation, the Dutch Association of Journalists (NVJ) and IRP, containing contact information of more than 7,000 organisations and 10,000 individuals. Men and women who – because of their profession and/or cultural background – have considerable knowledge of current topics in the multicultural society. As a consequence, ethnic minority spokespersons will have to learn themselves how to deal with journalists once they are invited for a programme or an interview. Therefore, Mira Media also developed a programme of media training for ethnic minority spokespersons and experts.

Ethnic minority media professionals

Many recommendations have been made concerning the introduction and implementation of diversity policies in the media. It proves relatively easy to write and endorse such policies. Yet, putting them into action seems to be rather difficult, as skilled ethnic minority media professionals are still relatively low in numbers. Thus, in order to change this situation in the long term more young people of ethnic minority origin need to be aware that a career in the media is a meaningful and viable option. Introduction of intercultural media education in school curricula, vocational orientation projects, including media career days in secondary schools in co-operation with the media industry and vocational training institutes are very important. Also NGOs and ethnic minority organisations can play an important role by involving youngsters in media projects in co-operation with ethnic community media and social activity centres.

Mira Media has a specific helpdesk for ethnic minority media professionals to support them in their careers. Information is given on vocational training, contents of jobs and individual intercultural coaching facilities. Mira Media also facilitates network meetings for ethnic minority media professionals and organises coaching courses for aspiring scriptwriters and documentary makers with an ethnic minority background.

Strategies for change

To make cultural diversity part of broadcast reality requires change. This change is needed in both the production and distribution of radio and television programmes and personnel policies. Personnel have to be re-trained. Diversity policies have to be introduced, implemented and monitored. Journalists should debate how to make their structures accessible to journalists from minority or excluded groups. Minority spokespersons will have to be empowered to put themselves in the picture. Media training centres need to review their curricula and most important of all, more young people from immigrant and of ethnic minority origins will have to choose a career in the media. This, in coherence with each other, will lead to a greater diversity both within the industry and in what is distributed through the media.

Note

1. Mira Media is an independent national media organisation dedicated to equal participation of ethnic minorities in the media. Mira Media's overall aim is to empower ethnic minority people and communities who face exclusion and disadvantage, and to promote a rich and diverse media culture that will meet the aspirations and needs of multicultural societies. Mira Media celebrates her 20th anniversary in 2006 and is nowadays the only organisation in the Netherlands striving for cultural diversity in the media.

References

CBS (Statistics Netherlands) (2006) *Demografie van de allochtonen in Nederland* [Demography of Ethnic Minorities in the Netherlands, 2005]. URL (consulted on 29 March): http://www.cbs.nl/nl-NL/menu/themas/dossiers/allochtonen/publicaties/artikelen/default.htm

d'Haenens, L. and J. Koeman, (2006) 'From Freedom of Obligation to Self-Sufficiency, 1979–2004: Developments in Dutch Integration and Media Policy'. In R. Geißler & H. Pöttker (eds), *Integration durch Massenmedien*. *Mass Media-Integration* (Bielefeld: transcript).

Visitatiecommissie Landelijke Publieke Omroep (Visitation Commission Public Broadcasting) (2004) *Omzien naar de omroep* [Looking back at broadcasting] (Hilversum: Public Broadcasting Organisation).

WRR (Netherlands Scientific Council for Government Policy) (2005). *Focus op functies: uitdagingen voor een toekomstbestendig mediabeleid* [Focus on Functions: Challenges for a Stable Future Media Policy] (The Hague: WRR).

14
Muslim Communities and the Media in France

Mohammed Colin

The state of press dealing with Muslim issues

Despite the large number of Muslims living in France, and unlike the situation in English-speaking countries and Spain, there is a notable absence of media in France dealing with Muslim issues. Apart from a magazine called *Le Musulman*, launched in the 1960s by Professor Muhammad Hamidullah, and aimed at Muslim intellectuals living in France, there was nothing else until the late 1990s. And *Le Musulman* stopped appearing in 1998. There are many reasons for this state of affairs. Unlike the USA and Great Britain, very few Muslim intellectuals migrated to France. Also, Muslim immigrants to France were more likely to see themselves as 'foreign workers' than belonging to a category called 'Muslims'. It was not until the third generation of these migrant families that Muslims started to make efforts to set up community newspapers. The end of the 1990s saw the emergence in France of magazines such as *Islam de France*, *La Médina*, *Hawwa*, *Saphir Le Médiateur*, and *Réflexions – Reflets de l'Islam*. But these publications disappeared again, soon after they had come out. Another contributing factor is that commercial advertisers are still not ready to invest in publications dealing with Muslim issues.

Nevertheless, there is a sizeable potential readership, with an estimated six million Muslims in France, mostly from North Africa, Turkey, sub-Saharan Africa and Comores. But the national media are often out of touch with the Muslim community in France. When issues dealing with Muslims and Islam are reported, even those with a French basis, it is often the security angle that is emphasised (e.g. terrorism, cultural infiltration, etc.), and rarely the social and cultural realities of Muslims. Even when national media do report on Muslim current affairs, such as the Eid festival marking the end of Ramadan, the festive and spiritual activities are systematically embedded in a context of other reports dealing with the tragic events of the Middle East and international terrorism. This kind of editing creates a confused amalgam, which, like the Kuleshov effect in cinema, ends up negating the peaceful content of the reports on the festivities.

In the end, viewers only retain an image of fear and chaos when Muslim issues and Islam are reported. The print media use analogous means to produce the same results. This practice by the mass media reveals an attitude that still situates Muslims and Islam outside of France and Europe.

A place in the media where Muslims in French society can express themselves

We are aware that there is an opening for a different form of expression of Muslim culture in France and Europe, to which the mass media are currently unable to give space. SaphirNews.com[1] is totally committed to support the expression of the experiences of individuals born and raised in France who belong to Muslim culture, in its widest sense.

This new space has also taught us to assume our identity as journalists. Journalism does not have a very positive image among Muslim organisations, while journalists are not very credible in the eyes of the Muslim public. We are by no means yet a press enterprise, and most of our writers are still unpaid. However, we feel closer to our journalist colleagues working for newspapers and radio than to Muslim organisations. Because of our close identification with our subject matter, some of these organisations have tended to treat our journalists more like press attaches, expecting us to perform this kind of role. It thus became important for us to strive to achieve a certain distance from these organisations, without cutting ourselves off from our sources. This entailed a continuous effort of clarification and education with out interlocutors. This has especially been necessary when dealing with highly sensitive subjects where the stakes are high, such as representation for Muslims in France, where Muslim organisations – and personalities – fight each other for leadership, or where the State oversteps its interference in matters of faith, in a political context that is supposed to be secular.

This situation led us to reflect on our editorial approach. No matter what the individual opinions of our writers may be, there was never a question of supporting any particular party. Our position had to be 'above the crowd'. We were content to organise the debate, inviting those of different leanings to take part. This attitude has helped instil a climate of trust with stakeholders in the Muslim community, without sterilising the debate itself.

Treatment of information

Our treatment of Muslim issues has led us to make a clear distinction between national and international arenas. We are also especially careful to separate issues of religion and faith from the social and cultural aspects. We have also made an editorial choice to avoid isolating information on Muslim issues. This has led us to favour a generalist approach, offering our readers news about current affairs in general.

As regards the technical aspects, we have set up a network of journalists with all the online facilities, such as intranet, groupware, and messaging, needed to facilitate communication and workflow. Despite our modest resources, this enables us to continue to expand, welcoming new collaborators and correspondents.

Many challenges

- SaphirNews.com now needs to establish a viable business model so that it can continue to develop.
- SaphirNews.com also has to overcome two editorial challenges. One is to be able to offer our target readership, as well as the various players in society, and the generalist media, editorial content that is rich, subtle, and sufficiently faithful to the complexity of life for Muslims in France.
- The other challenge is to preserve our pluralist approach by providing a forum where Muslims of France can express themselves, in all their diversity (this is our main challenge), alongside civil society as a whole, in order to allow a confrontation of opinions in a spirit of open debate and, together, to forge ideas which link to ongoing debates within society.

Note

1. SaphirNews.com is a general news and community information website specialising in Muslim issues. It reaches a wide audience of people, not necessarily Muslims themselves, who are esterested in Muslims and Islam. Nevertheless, SaphirNews.com is primarily aimed at French-speaking Muslims, and currently receives over 200,000 hits a month, without any form of publicity, and sends its daily newsletter to more than 12,000 subscribers.

The site first went online in November 2002, as SaphirNet.info. It is an independent media, run by a non-profit association, Saphir Médiation, founded in 1999. The association has already made two previous attempts to launch publications. The first was a quarterly magazine called *Saphir le médiateur* and the second a tabloid called *Réflexions*. Each of these ceased publication after a few issues, due to a lack of adequate funding. This led the association to turn towards the Internet, to launch a daily web publication.

15
Media and the Ethnic/Religious Minorities

Bashy Quraishy

Dealing with media forms a large part of ethnic/religious minority NGOs work in Europe. They use it to receive information, as well as to distribute their own information. But their relationship with the media is often ambivalent. Many minority NGOs complain that their campaigns and issues are underrepresented, and their views misinterpreted, by the media. But the media also often complain that NGOs are unprofessional, or even that they are manipulated by activists.

NGOs do try to overcome these problems by perfecting their skills in setting up press events (researching an issue, preparing policy documents, organising a press event, sending out press releases, running a press conference, giving interviews) and having organised training sessions to improve these skills. Some times they are successful but often they fail to convince the media. Experience shows that journalists in the print media are especially good at telling the 'right' story but even they do not turn up at every events NGOs plan. As for television and radio, if reporters do come, they usually tell the 'wrong' story – giving a twist of their own.

Over the years, NGOs have found that despite investing considerable resources in improving their media skills, it has been nearly impossible to overcome the problems. But this has often been because they have focused on only one part of the media cycle and did not have a holistic approach.

Media response

Whenever media critics request journalists to consider some objections, their criticism is rejected out of hand with the following arguments.

- Media are just doing their job of informing the public.
- Media criticism is a hidden form of censorship which does not fit with democratic principles.
- Ethnic minorities cannot expect special treatment from journalists.
- Freedom of expression must be upheld at all costs.
- If media does not cover anti-immigrant feelings in the society and give people a chance to vent their anger through media, it can result in hostility towards minorities.
- If activists and minorities feel misrepresented, they can use their right of reply, complain to the editor, write to Press Ethic Committee or take legal action.

Seen from the media's perspective, all the above mentioned points are valid and make sense but they also reflect the mind set of the journalistic community. This refusal to listen is often based on self-assumptions of neutrality and objectivity and it smacks of professional arrogance.

Journalists often ignore that freedom of speech was never meant for the journalists alone but for the citizens who have difficulty to express their views in public against the powers that be. There has never been and never will be any form of absolute freedom of expression. It is always linked with ethical responsibility and common sense.

Power and responsibility lies with the media

The media have both a powerful influence on people's attitudes and perceptions and a weighty responsibility to contribute to this process of change. It can help in social integration of ethnic minorities. Unfortunately a great deal of media attention is given to the seemingly insurmountable differences that divide people, religions and cultures. This leaves them unable to highlight the efforts to overcome such differences. We believe that media have the means, will power, goodwill and technology to build bridges between the majority and the ethnic minorities living in EU.

Media can help people to understand that diversity can be a powerful source of social development. An important beginning would be to eliminate stereotyping based on religion, culture, gender, race, class, nationality and ethnicity from media programming. Having said that, it is imperative that ethnic and religious minorities do take practical steps to enhance their own visibility in the media debates as well as to raise awareness of media's importance, among their own communities. Journalists depend very much on the available information and time constraints do not leave them sufficient room for manoeuvre. Experienced based knowledge coming from minorities can be very helpful. This can be done in many ways.

Suggestions for better visibility

- Divert their attention towards journalism as a profession. Convince parents and youth that journalism is an important and valid profession.
- Show visibility by participating in media discussions on a professional level, not only on ethnic issues but also issues of common interests in the society.
- Arrange courses for members to empower them with knowledge, give them tools to formulate their views and most important of all, encourage them to speak up.
- Establish better contacts with those journalists who are willing to listen and invite media to hold discussions, seminars, conferences with NGO's on topics relevant to both minorities and the media.
- Send the journalists a list of names of contact persons from different ethnic groups who can give their opinion if need be.
- Impart information to the media. Many journalists are not used to inter-cultural, inter-ethnic and inter-religious thinking.
- Start a 'Study Group' to document, analyse and look at the media misrepresentations. Provide such data to journalists so that they can study it and hopefully use it.
- Do not forget to compliment if you see a good TV programme, a well-researched article or an informative radio programme. Criticism has to be made within the bounds of reason, politeness and factual accuracy.
- NGOs and ethnic minorities now have the possibility of supporting the present network of alternative media on the internet, establishing their own topic-oriented websites and E-mail chain letters.
- Many European countries have grassroots TV-Channels where local programmes can be made both in ethnic languages and host country's national language. Such TV programmes are public funded.

It must be stressed in no uncertain terms that our suggestions are in no way an attempt to curtail freedom of expression, self censure or to degrade the important work many journalist perform, often in difficult situations.

Ours is an appeal for a normal coverage where an individual act is presented as such. Minorities are as diverse, complex and opinionated as the majority. So condemn the guilty and praise the innocent, not as a cultural, religious or ethnic entity but as any other co-citizen.

This will in turn tremendously help the sense of belonging and ease the process of integration in the society. That is all minorities are asking for.

16
Ethnic Media in USA: Giant Hidden in Plain Sight

Sandip Roy and Sandy Close

The old American idea of the multicultural melting pot appears to be under great strain nowadays. The melting pot presupposed that there is a dominant stew into which we could add new ingredients – Italian oregano, Polish sausage and Chinese cabbage. Now, one in four Californians is foreign born, and projections are that by 2050 the USA will join California in having more nonwhites than whites, that dominant stew is gone. The question is more how are the Thaitowns and Little Saigons and Little Kabuls adjusting to each other in the New America?

Here are some facts

- By autumn 2019, the majority of young adults turning 18 and eligible to vote in California will be Latino.
- Between 1990 and 2000, the foreign-born population grew by 200 per cent or more in North Carolina, Georgia and Nevada. The foreign-born population grew between 100 per cent and 199 per cent in 16 other US states.
- Hispanics and Asians grew fourfold and over fivefold in California between 1970 and 1998. The population of whites increased 11 per cent over the same period.
- Joining California as majority-minority states, where no one group is the majority anymore, are New Mexico, Hawaii, and Texas.

These new Californians, and Texans and New Yorkers are privy to a bustling, thriving world of ethnic media that most other Americans have little access to. Often relegated to second place, as a sort of stepchild of American journalism, ethnic media has now become the indispensable new portal for reaching these new communities.

So how do you reach these new Americans? What is the person next to you on the bus reading? That's where ethnic media comes in. In 2005 New America Media (formerly New California Media) asked the polling firm of Bendixen Associates to find out where ethnic communities were getting their news and information. Here is what we found:

- 29 million adult Americans, 13 per cent of all US adults, prefer ethnic media to their mainstream counterparts for their news and information
- 51 million Americans, or one in four adults, regularly access ethnic media
- 87 per cent of all Hispanic adults are reached by ethnic media in the United States

It's no wonder then that the Annual Report of American Journalism stated in 2006 that 'In our first two years of (the State of News Media) report, we found that only online, ethnic and alternative media were seeing general audience growth ...'.

For New America Media the process began early in the 1990s. NAM was born out of the alternative wire service, Pacific News Service (PNS) where editors fluent in Chinese, Arabic, Spanish, Farsi, Vietnamese or embedded in black and Native American communities, began sharing stories from ethnic news outlets that put PNS ahead of the news curve. They knew about these stories because these issues were ones that impacted their communities – the historic spike in Hispanic voter registration that followed passage of a proposition affecting illegal immigrants in California to early plans for one million African American men to rally in Washington DC to the nationwide mobilization of Chinese immigrants on behalf of a then-unnamed China nuclear spy.

In the fall of 1996, PNS gathered representatives from more than a dozen ethnic news organizations – print, radio and TV – for a Chinese lunch. During lunch, as each media rep described their audience reach, it suddenly dawned on everyone that their combined reach outnumbered that of mainstream media in the San Francisco Bay Area. The idea of New America Media was born in that moment.

NAM has since helped to catalyze a remarkable exchange not only within the ethnic news sector but between ethnic news organizations and their mainstream counterparts. Sharing news content seemed an obvious place to start – 'what's it like to be Vietnamese in a Spanish-speaking city?' one Hispanic publisher from San Jose had asked his

Vietnamese counterpart. 'I'll write about it,' his neighbor replied, and PNS ran the piece on our syndicate. But knowing how to spot stories of significance for wider audiences, and how to 'transcreate' them to bridge the language and culture divides, took years to develop. It required language and cultural fluency, news savvy and a reciprocal relationship between ourselves and the ethnic media source. Now ASNE (American Society of Newspaper Editors) has embarked on an ethnic-mainstream partnership which pairs ethic media reporters with mainstream media colleagues covering topics as diverse as Vietnamese nail salons in Florida to black mortuaries in the aftermath of Hurricane Katrina.

Hurricane Katrina highlighted the key value of our ethnic media partnerships in covering a fast breaking story that mesmerized audiences around the world. When the Nguoi Viet, one of the country's largest circulation Vietnamese language dailies sent two reporters and a photographer to New Orleans to cover the fate of that city's sizable Vietnamese community, we translated and reported on their coverage. As a result, we discovered the remarkable story of how low-powered Vietnamese radio helped large numbers of beleaguered Vietnamese speaking residents avoid the Astrodome and go instead to a shopping mall where community volunteers relocated them.

In fact, what makes the model of collaboration work is that ethnic and mainstream media are two distinctive genres of journalism who leverage each other's strengths. Ethnic media are trusted story tellers in their communities: their intimate knowledge of their audiences – both here and in their home countries – is their greatest asset for mainstream journalists. In the absence of leaders whose voices carry outside their cultures, ethnic media become trusted public spokespeople almost by default. Black media have long set the template with names like Advocate, Sentinel, Voice, Crusader that many ethnic media embrace. When immigration officers started doing sweeps in California's Inland Empire, the paper that got flooded with calls was Spanish-language daily La Opinion. That was where immigrants turned to ask whether it was safe to go shopping or whether they could send their kids to school. When the INS special registration interviews started detaining hundreds of Iranians, it was Iranian media that got the alarm out. A call in radio station in Los Angeles announced the news, mobilized the community and got thousands of people out on to the streets to protest, all within 24 hours.

Mainstream media, for their part, fill a huge void in ethnic media by their expertise in reporting on policy and politics at the local, state and national levels – from investigating police reports to holding state and national leaders accountable. The synergy is there, if we choose to act on it. But there's more to the exchange than sharing stories or even editorial teams. NAM's ethnic media partners – from Univision and Telemundo to the country's 12 major in-language ethnic dailies with huge national circulations – now coordinate simultaneous publication of New America Media's multilingual polls, in a concerted campaign to insert the voices of their communities into the national dialogue.

Multilingual polling, which NAM launched in 2002, has been a key tool in getting the facts and figures that make sure ethnic communities are not ignored when the issues of the day are discussed. It is imperative to know what the Chinese Americans think of George Bush not just what they think of Taiwan politics. But most polls, and there is a new one everyday, will never include the person sitting in a bus in San Francisco reading the Sing Tao Daily. These people are not part of the American discourse. They are simply never asked often because the polls are only in English.

NAM's multilingual polls on issues like Iraq, presidential elections, tsunami, Katrina, healthcare have yielded often surprising results. On 27 March 2006, NAM released the first ever multilingual poll of legal immigrants on immigration reform which documented that, this population of 26 million backed pathways to citizenship by significant majorities in every major ethnic and racial group. This ran counter to popular theories that legal immigrants supported crackdowns on undocumented immigrants because they thought they were cutting ahead in line.

NAM's multilingual polls offer insights from people with direct experience on issues or regions of the world most Americans know little about. The polls, like accessing ethnic media coverage, are not just about building more inclusive discourse in our public life. They offer insight and information that all Americans need to understand who we are becoming and how we fit in the world. At a grassroots level, they also give ethnic media a key way to expand their coverage of each other's communities, thereby building inter-group understanding.

NAM also tries to build ethnic media's own strengths. The New America Media journalism awards, now its seventh year, honors the best reporting in ethnic media taking into consideration in its choice of categories, the particular strengths of ethnic media. NAM has a radio show called UpFront on public radio in San Francisco that features a news round-up from the ethnic media. New America Media works with government agencies and community based organizations on media campaigns that need to reach ethnic communities through ethnic media – for example to make ethnic communities award of the right to an interpreter when they go to the doctor or recruiting teachers from ethnic communities. As part of that campaign, instead of just running ads in ethnic media, the media took part in an essay contest called 'The teacher who changed my life' which provoked so much enthusiastic response, the winning essays became a book.

The impact of using ethnic media to reach out to ethnic communities can be illustrated by one example. Polls before the 2003 elections showed most ethnic Californians had the vaguest idea of Proposition 54 that would bar collecting of racial data. Those who had just heard about it or read the proposition for the first time thought it seemed to be a good idea. 46 per cent of Latinos and 41 per cent of African Americans were generally supportive of the proposition.

However, the '"No" to 54' campaign poured money into advertising in Hispanic and African-American media and that was a significant factor in turning the numbers around and the defeat of the proposition: '70 per cent of Latinos said 'no'.

Given these results, what is most surprising is that it has taken so long for the mainstream, whether media or civic, to discover ethnic media. It is truly the giant hidden in plain sight. Most of us come from towns where we are lucky if we have two major English language dailies. Orange County in California has some 30 Vietnamese publications. Los Angeles alone has over 15 Thai dailies, 15 Filipino publications not to mention Greek, Armenian, and a 24-hour Afghan radio station.

The New America Media National Directory for Ethnic Media lists over 50 ethnic groups from Afghan to Vietnamese. With some 25 entries from Arizona to 4 pages of entries from New York, the 2000 odd entries still represent just the tip of the iceberg. But in uncovering this iceberg we are moving beyond the 20th century paradigm of gathering, interpreting and disseminating news and information up and down competing vertical axes linking the public realm with private lives. We are developing what USC Annenberg journalism professor Felix Gutierrez calls a 'parallel' or 'alternative media universe' that runs on a horizontal axis along the spine of private society. What drives the exchange of news is not so much competition as collaboration as ethnic and mainstream journalists alike knit together the fabric of a global society.

17
Ambiguous Voices: Western Media and Refugees

Aime Claude Ndongozi

Introduction

Since the Second World War the increase in armed conflicts and violations of human rights across the world has forced more and more people out of their homelands to seek safety elsewhere. In 2000, the UNHCR estimated that one in every 300 people across the world was a refugee[1] (UNHCR, 2000). The most recent figures indicate that the overall world refugee population has decreased ever since to just under 10 million people at the beginning of 2005. However, estimates of internally displaced persons (IDPs) have reached an all time peak with the potential for more refugees across borders (UNHCR, 2006). Mass displacements of people and refugee crises seem to remain constant features in world affairs from decade to decade. This has fuelled emotionally charged social and political debates about refugee protection issues, especially in refugee receiving countries of the West. The media in these countries have been at the heart of these debates, often playing an ambiguous role, oscillating between sympathy and hostility towards refugees (Hayter, 2002; Harris, 2000). This chapter attempts to explore the root causes of this ambiguity. It takes a look at how Western media reporting about refugees interacts with the demands of the domestic news markets and end up fulfilling a self-serving role. There is a debate to be had here and the aim of this paper is more about raising the issues than providing the answers.

Sympathy for the hungry on dusty paths

It's almost impossible to imagine what our present World geared towards more and more globalisation of capital and information would be like, without the immense contribution of western international media. No one will deny the invaluable role of these media in drawing international public attention to humanitarian emergencies resulting from armed conflicts and ensuing human rights violations. Back in the last decade of the 20th century, we recall that western media reports provided dramatic images of desperate people fleeing from places such as Bosnia and Herzegovina, Chechnya, Iraq, Kosovo and Rwanda with a call for international solidarity (Nohrstedt *et al.* 2000; Moeller, 2002). While perhaps disagreeing in their analysis of the root causes of these conflicts and the best way to resolve them, most western media were consensual in their sympathy towards innocent civilian victims. Refugees were portrayed as innocent victims of state and non-state brutality for whom the media demanded compassion and western intervention and assistance. It is due to this media coverage that governments, international organisations and the public became increasingly aware of the plight of refugees and displaced people (UNHCR, 2000). Some argue that the resulting humanitarian solidarity was shown with double standards depending on cultural and historical ties, as well as regional geopolitical interests. Nonetheless, the international humanitarian solidarity borne from the action of the media contributed in saving the lives of thousands of vulnerable people otherwise condemned to death in conflict zones (Robinson 2000; Shapiro, 2002).

But where did this media sympathy towards refugees come from? Can Western media, owned by Western capitalist conglomerates be capable of mere sympathy towards hungry and suffering people from afar? A deeper analysis of what we have called sympathy so far is needed here.

It has been argued that due to their transience and lack of belonging to a nation-state, refugees become invisible as political actors. They are seen as victims who need protection and sympathetic international solidarity (Girardet, 1996; Minear *et al.*, 1996; de Waal, 1997). In particular, women and children are used to evoke sympathy in Western news consumers. Often viewed as innocents, without political attachments and involvement, they embody a sense of pure humanity because being a refugee has made them into the pure victim (Malkki, 1995: 8–17; Fair, 1996). Indeed, hungry refugees wandering with dying children along dusty paths in war-torn countries make good material for sensational reporting. In order to appeal to western audiences with little knowledge of the complex conflicts they cover, journalists often seek to shock rather than inform. The aim is to feed domestic audiences with sensational information and be the first to do so. In this news market, disasters and complex emergencies become big news to cover. Viewed from such an angle, western media sympathy takes on a different significance. It appears motivated by the need to meet a demand for sensational, shocking and emotionally charged news from markets ever hungry to hear about and watch the pain and suffering of others. Refugee images are therefore displayed on front covers and on television screens not because of genuine human altruism and sympathy but because they are good for business. News consumers are ready for it (Benthall, 1993; Minear *et al.*, 1996; de Waal, 1997). This view appears corroborated by the fact that the attention of media flags quickly when the scenes of massive human disaster decrease in intensity or the public becomes overfed and starts to expect something new, more sensational. In this context, the media have been criticised for playing a self-serving role, feeding their western audiences described by French as 'insatiable markets in images of horror' (French, 2004).

From sympathy to hostility

Refugees may have been presented with sympathy to western audiences when they were photographed or filmed in their conflict-torn homelands or overcrowded refugee camps. Ironically, the end of the honeymoon comes when the victims decide to flee for safety to those countries whose media appeared sympathetic. When refugees knock on the 'rich man's gates', they seem to deserve much less sympathy from international media. In fact, the true face of international media towards refugees loses its masks when some refugees manage to flee towards those countries in the West, whose media normally champion civil liberties, the rule of law and democracy (Dummet, 2002). Far from sympathetic portrayal of refugees, there emerges an intolerant, at times racist and xenophobic representation. Refugees are no longer presented as potential victims of state and non-state persecution whose primary aim in leaving their homelands is to seek safety. In the process of trying to reach Western shores, and once they do, they are depicted as economic migrants disguised as bogus asylum seekers, scrounging on rich countries' resources (Moorland 2001; Statham, 2002).

This mask-free portrayal of refugees could be traced back into the early 1980s when greater number of refugees moved from conflicts zones to seek asylum in Western Europe and North America. The benefits of granting asylum were then seen as outweighing its costs.

Public opinions were radicalised as immigration and asylum became a political issue, often played to different degrees, as an electoral card, by both right and left wing political parties. In this context, some sections of the media informed and echoed politics in the same time, steering resentment, racist and xenophobic attitude in the public, spreading myths about refugees as bogus economic migrants and scroungers. After the 9/11/2001 terrorist attack on the World Trade Centre, refugees have been presented as a security concern, potentially threatening peace and the western way of life (UNCHR, 2006). Consequently, more and more restrictive legislation and punitive measures have been adopted across Europe and rest of the Western World to keep asylum seekers out (UNHCR, 2000). Throughout this process, less and less balanced voices have been raised in the media, calling into question the so-called sympathy towards refugees when they were suffering in war-torn regions.

In the case of Britain, a report from Mori (2002) has shown that the British public feels that media representation of refugees in this country is too negative. Confusion is often deliberately entertained between refugees and 'illegal immigrant'. This phrase often carelessly and wrongly used has been found to be 'racist, offensive and misleading'. The Mori report concluded that 'reports in the media of refugees "flooding" into the UK, and Britain being an "Asylum haven" may have contributed to the public's over-estimation of Britain's contribution in receiving refugees' (Mori, 2002: 12). In its 2001 report, Amnesty International argued that 'very negative media coverage ... pandered to racial prejudice and created a hostile environment for many asylum seekers' (Amnesty International, 2001). This negative representation has been denounced by the United Nations High Commissioner for Refugees (UNHCR) criticising the British media for the hysterical coverage of asylum seekers and urging for moderation from the government (UNHCR, 2003). The British case is not alone in Europe as the work of Council of Europe's European Commission against Racism and Intolerance (ECRI) in its Second Report on the United Kingdom proves (16 June 2000).

Conclusion

Western media hostility towards refugees in countries of asylum sheds some light on the true face of western media ethics in dealing with the most vulnerable people. It can be argued that the sympathy-hostility ambiguity hides western media's selfish interests in meeting the demands of their news markets. To this end, they are able to put on a mask of sympathy or clearly declare themselves hostile to refugees depending on their news markets expectations. As long as they remain far from western shores, refugees are portrayed as victims of conflicts and violations of human rights who need solidarity and protection. This position can be sold to Western news markets. However, when refugees dare to enter western countries for safety, compassion gives way to hostility and misleading reporting, raising and echoing public fears and xenophobic sentiments. Amid this grim context however, fortunately, there are some brave voices who still rise, from time to time with accurate reporting and raising awareness on the real plight of refugees. These voices represent the future. They carry hope for a world, upholding human dignity.

Note

1. According to Article 1 of the 1951 United Nations Convention Relating to the Status of Refugees and its 1967 Protocol, a refugee is defined as someone who: 'owing to a well-founded fear of being persecuted for reasons of race, religion, nationality, membership of a particular social group or political opinion, is outside of the country of his nationality and is unable or, owing to such fear, is unwilling to avail himself of the protection of that country'. It is this definition used in this chapter to include those in the process of application for refugee status under the 1951 Convention (called asylum seekers) and those already granted refugee status by governments. For an overview of definitions, see United Nations High Commissioner for Refugees, 1993.

References

Amnesty International, *Annual Report 2001*. Http://web.amnesty.org/web/ar2001.nsf/webeurocountries/UNITED+KINGDOM?OpenDocument (May).

Benthall, J. (1993) *Disasters, Relief, and the Media* (London: I.B. Tauris).

Council of Europe, *Second Report on the United Kingdom* (2000). http://press.coe.int/press2/press.asap?B=62,0,0,105,0&M=http://press.coe.int/dossiers/105/E/-uk.htm (June).

de Waal, A. (1997) *Famine Crimes: Politics and the Disaster Relief Industry in Africa* (Oxford: James Currey).

Dummet, M. (2002) *On Immigration and Refugees* (London: Routledge).

Fair, J. E. (1996) 'The Body Politic, the Bodies of Women, and the Politics of Famine in U.S. Television Coverage of Famine in the Horn of Africa', *Journalism and Mass Communication Monographs*, no. 158.

French, H. (2004) *A Continent for the Taking: The Tragedy and Hope of Africa* (New York: Knopf).

Girardet, E. R. (1996) 'Reporting Humanitarianism: Are the New Electronic Media Making a Difference?' In Robert Rothberg and Thomas Weiss (eds), *From Massacres to Genocide* (Washington, DC: Brookings Institute), 45–67.

Harris, N. (2002). *Thinking the Unthinkable: The Immigration Myth Exposed.* (London–New York: I. B. Tauris).

Hayter, T. (2000) *Open Borders: The Case Against Immigration Controls.* (London: Pluto Press).

Malkki, L. (1995), 'National Geographic: The Rooting of Peoples and the Territorializing Of National Identity Among Scholars and Refugees', *Cultural Anthropology*, 7(1), 24–44.

Minear, L., C. Scott and T. Weiss (1996) *The News Media, Civil War, and Humanitarian Action* (Boulder: Lynne Rienner).

Moeller, S. D. (2002) 'Locating Accountability: The Media and Peacekeeping', *Journal of International Affairs*, 55(2), 369–90.

Moorland, C. (2001) *Asylum: The Truth Behind the Headlines* (Oxford: Oxfam). http://www.oxfam.org.uk/policy/papers/asylumscot01/asylum.htm

Mori Social Research (2003) *Attitudes Towards Refugees and Asylum Seekers: A survey of Public Opinion. Research study conducted for Refugee Week.* (London: Mori).

Nohrstedt, S. A., S. Kaitatzi-Whitlock, R. Ottosen, R. and K. Riegert, (2000) 'From Persian Gulf to Kosovo–War journalism and propaganda', *European Journal of Communication*, 15(3), 383–404.

Robinson, P. (2000) 'Research Note: the News Media and Intervention. Triggering the Use of Air Power During Humanitarian Crises', *European Journal of Communication*, 15(3), 405–14.

Shapiro, S. (2002) 'Conflict Media Strategies and the Politics of Counter-Terrorism', *Politics*, 22(2), 76–8.

Statham, P. (2002) 'The Contentious Politics of Asylum in Britain and Europe: a Research Outline' Centre for European Political Communications, European Political Communications Working Paper Series (March). http://www.leeds.ac.uk/ics/euro/paper1.pdf

United Nations High Commissioner for Refugees (1993) *The State of the World's Refugees: The Challenge of Protection* (Oxford: Oxford University Press).

UNHCR (2000) The State of the Word refugees. Fifty Yeas of Humanitarian Action (Oxford: Oxford University Press).

UNHCR (2003) *UK: UN Concern Over Coverage of Asylum Seekers* (February). http://www.unhcr.ch

UNHCR (2006) *The State of the Word Refugees 2006. Human Displacement in the New Millennium.* (Oxford: Oxford University Press).

18

Mediam'Rad – Ethnic Media in Europe

Reynald Blion

Ethnic media – media created by and for immigrant communities

The term ethnic media is used for all media that:

- have an editorial approach that is principally oriented towards the ethnic diversity to be found within European societies,
- address one or more of the constituent groups that make up this diversity,
- are mainly produced and disseminated in one or several of the States of the European Union,
- are produced by journalists and staff that are representative of the ethnic diversity of European societies,
- are directed by, or belong to persons who are representative of this diversity.

These media may be television, radio, print media, or Internet.

In France and in French, the term 'media of diversity' has been preferred to other usages, such as 'community media' or 'ethnic media', which have been adopted in the English-speaking world. The term 'media of diversity' seems to correspond better to the way these media see themselves and the contributions they make within their respective worlds, i.e. giving a voice to the diversity of the components of contemporary European societies.

Ethnic media in Europe: a very heterogeneous world

One of the main characteristics of ethnic media is their extreme diversity. In France there are about hundred newspapers and magazines, of which around fifty appear regularly. In Paris and its surrounding region, a quarter of local radio stations are so-called ethnic stations. However, there are far fewer ethnic television stations and even fewer have their own policy of production and broadcasting.

The frequency of publication of ethnic print media is also extremely variable. Many appear quarterly, some monthly, but very few appear fortnightly. Those published weekly are usually magazines and newsletters sent out via Internet.

The kinds of organisations that run ethnic media are also very diverse. While local radio stations are aften run by non-profit associations, ethnic media may also be privately owned (i.e. commercial). This is especially the case for national radio networks and many print media.

Nevertheless, there are major differences between European countries in the way these media are organised. In the United Kingdom, ethnic media groups exist (e.g. the *Ethnic Media Group*), publishing several different titles, but they are virtually non-existent in other countries in continental Europe.

However, ethnic media in Europe do have one characteristic in common, with a few – too rare – exceptions, namely, their vulnerability. These media encounter genuine difficulties in accessing both financial and human resources, which handicaps their capacities to develop, and limits their range of influence.

Ethnic media in Europe, original priorities and content

On the basis of initial observations prior to the launch of *Mediam'Rad*,[1] it emerges that the priority subjects dealt with by ethnic media include immigration, foreigners' rights, culture, integration, housing, education, health and citizenship. A second set of priority subjects deals with the countries or regions of origin of the different communities to which these media are mainly addressed. These two groups of preferred subject-matter set ethnic media apart from the mass media, which may be explained by the nature of their respective target audiences. Ethnic media, by definition, are targeted mainly at one or more immigrant communities, which have a need for specific kinds of information, not usually found in the mass media – which of course are aimed at the general public.

In addition to these preliminary observations, *Mediam'Rad* is currently carrying out an analysis to compare content in ethnic media and mass media. This analysis is focusing particularly on treatment of the G8 summit of July 2005. It is hoped that the results will lead to a better understanding of the various, respective editorial priorities and positions, as well as the manner in which international and intercultural relations are treated.

As well as developing their priority themes, ethnic media also help to promote the contributions of immigrants and their initiatives, whether to the economy, politics, society, literature, art or sport. Women's magazines, such as *Amina* and *Divas* for example, regularly feature women from the black community living in France, Europe, or elsewhere in the world. The mass media, in contrast, rarely do this, following the example set by mainstream women's magazines such as *Elle* and *Marie-Claire*. One of the primary contributions of ethnic media is therefore to show and to participate in the expression of the diversity of the components of European society today.

One question that crops up regularly concerns the impact of ethnic media on the integration of the communities to which they are addressed. In other words, do these media help to reinforce the notion of separate communities, or at least the social isolation of the various immigrant groups? Our preliminary observations, and regular discussions with those promoting these media, suggest the contrary, i.e. that there is a genuine willingness to open to the social and political environment in which they operate.

Ethnic media in Europe: from media to mediators

As far as editorial priorities are concerned, and thus the subjects they deal with, ethnic media produce and disseminate information which is complementary to that found in the mass media. This puts ethnic media in the role of relay, or mediator between the various groups that make up European societies.

One of the major challenges for the *Mediam'Rad* programme, being led by Panos Paris, is to reinforce this role of ethnic media as relay and mediator, by encouraging the development of alliances, partnerships and collaboration between these media, as well as with the mass media.

In this way, *Mediam'Rad* hopes to help ethnic media to reach a wider public, and, at the same time, to promote a better understanding of the concerns, issues and dynamics of the various immigrant communities that have settled in Europe. For the mass media, the interest of this collaboration lies in gaining access to more diverse sources of information on international and inter-cultural issues, and ways of treating them.

For all these reasons, *Mediam'Rad* considers that it is of great value for all players in the media to arrive at a better understanding of, and working relationship with the ethnic media. This should strengthen their capacities of production and dissemination, increase their access to resources, and assure their sustainability, as a complement to output by the mass media.

Institut Panos Paris

Institut Panos Paris, European programme leader of *Mediam'Rad*, is a non-governmental organisation set up in 1986 under a French law of 1901, specialising in support for media pluralism. Its objectives are: to strengthen media in the South (Central Africa and North Africa) and their capacities to produce and disseminate pluralist information; to support the production of information on various priority themes (e.g. peace and immigration, etc); to encourage journalists and opinion leaders to speak out, and to favour public debate; to encourage and nurture critical reflection on issues surrounding information, in a world that is being transformed by new information and communication technologies.

Note

1. *Mediam'Rad* is a European programme led by Institut Panos Paris. Its objectives are to help promote ethnic media, to publicise the information they produce and disseminate, and to foster an appreciation of their particular and varied contributions to both international and intercultural relations. *Mediam'Rad* was launched in January 2005, following initial research and reflection by Panos Paris since May 2000. Today, the programme is jointly run with two other organisations, *Cospe* (Italy), and *Miramedia* (Netherlands).

Index

.

Lightning Source UK Ltd.
Milton Keynes UK
UKOW06n1907061015

259964UK00006B/59/P